John Kennedy, Hugh M. Mackenzie

The Book of Daniel from the Christian Standpoint

With essay on alleged historical difficulties

John Kennedy, Hugh M. Mackenzie

The Book of Daniel from the Christian Standpoint
With essay on alleged historical difficulties

ISBN/EAN: 9783337238599

Printed in Europe, USA, Canada, Australia, Japan

Cover: Foto ©Lupo / pixelio.de

More available books at **www.hansebooks.com**

THE BOOK OF DANIEL.

" Can Time undo what once was true?"
F. T. PALGRAVE.

PORTRAIT OF CYRUS.

(Circ. B.C. 538.)

The oldest known relic of Persian sculpture. It stands at *Meshed Murghab* (the ancient Pasargadae). The features are European, the ornamentation Egyptian and Assyrian.

Frontispiece.

THE BOOK OF DANIEL

FROM THE CHRISTIAN STANDPOINT.

WITH ESSAY ON ALLEGED HISTORICAL DIFFICULTIES,
BY THE EDITOR OF THE "BABYLONIAN AND
ORIENTAL RECORD."

BY

JOHN KENNEDY, M.A., D.D.,

Honorary Professor, New College, London;
*Author of "The Self Revelation of Jesus Christ"; "The Resurrection of
Jesus Christ an Historical Fact;" "The Unity of Isaiah," &c.*

WITH ILLUSTRATIONS.

EYRE AND SPOTTISWOODE,
Her Majesty's Printers:
LONDON—GREAT NEW STREET, FLEET STREET, E.C.
EDINBURGH, GLASGOW, MELBOURNE, SYDNEY, & NEW YORK.

1898.

All rights reserved.

The Bible Student's Library.

1.—FOURTH EDITION.
THE FOUNDATIONS OF THE BIBLE: Studies in Old Testament Criticism. By Canon GIRDLESTONE, M.A.

2.—SECOND EDITION.
THE LAW IN THE PROPHETS. By the Rev. STANLEY LEATHES, D.D.

3.
PRINCIPLES OF BIBLICAL CRITICISM. By the Rev. J. J. LIAS, M.A., *Chancellor of Llandaff Cathedral.*

4.—511 pages.
SANCTUARY AND SACRIFICE: A Reply to Wellhausen. By the Rev. W. L. BAXTER, M.A., D.D.

5.
HEZEKIAH AND HIS AGE. By the Rev. R. SINKER, D.D., *Librarian of Trinity College, Cambridge.*

6.
ABRAHAM AND HIS AGE. By the Rev. H. G. TOMKINS.

7.
THE BOOK OF DANIEL. By the Rev. JOHN KENNEDY, M.A., D.D.

For particulars of the above see advertisement at the end of the Volume. Other Volumes in preparation.

PREFACE.

THE distinctive aim of this volume is indicated in its title, and is explained and defended in the pages which follow. The assault on the historical character of the book is based mainly, in most cases entirely, on certain alleged difficulties connected with the historic names which occupy a prominent place in its pages. And the defence of the book is so occupied with the discussion of these difficulties that both defenders and assailants often write as if the whole question of the claims of the book was involved in the issue. Would it not be a more logical course to examine the question first of all on general grounds, including such evidence, external and internal, as may contribute either to proof or disproof? Adopting this course the writer considers himself entitled as a Christian, and appealing to Christians, to begin with the personal testimony of our Divine Lord. He is all the bolder in taking this course that he remembers that the questioning of the character of the book originated in the Rationalism of an age not very remote from our own, and that the assaults of the older assailants were meant to discredit, not the Book of

Daniel alone, but the entire fabric and authority of Old Testament prophecy. Next to the personal testimony of Christ, corroborated in sundry ways, the most strengthening assurance is to be found in a calm study of the book itself, chapter by chapter, and the writer invites the reader to follow him in his attempt to bring to light the results of such a study.

By taking this ground, it is not meant that the charges of historical inaccuracy should be left unanswered. They are a great stumbling-block in the way of many. And in this volume there will be found an able and honest endeavour to meet them by a writer whose studies in Tablet Literature entitle him to speak with some authority. At the same time I decline to admit that the credit of the book is at stake if we cannot clear up every point in matters of general history which the work makes no pretension to record or explain. The grounds on which our faith in the book rests primarily and fundamentally, remain even in that case unshaken. While the difficulties of the alternatives to which we are shut up, if the book is not historical, are insuperable.

I offer no apology for the prominence which I have given to the recently published opinions of Dr. Farrar and Dr. Driver. From the former I differ absolutely. As to the latter, notwithstanding all that he says about "difficulties," and the late period to which he ascribes the writing of the book, I hold and argue, as will be seen, (pp. 157, 158) that on his own grounds he should take his position distinctly among the defenders of the historicity of the book. With the admission that Daniel was a prophet, and that the book is a "prophetic book"—in some respects the greatest of prophetic books—any other position is so illogical that I do not understand how it can be maintained.

In addition to my indebtedness to the author of the supplemental chapter on historical difficulties, I have to thank a learned nephew for his valuable paper on the connection of Babylon with other nations. I cannot omit thanking the Rev. Canon Girdlestone for the great kindness with which he has read my entire manuscript, and has favoured me with not a few valuable suggestions. The full and careful Index which has been prepared at my instance will greatly aid the reader in the study of the book.

J. K.

Hampstead, May 1898.

CONTENTS.

	PAGE
PREFACE	v–vii
INTRODUCTION	1

CHAPTER I.

CHRIST'S DIRECT PERSONAL TESTIMONY	5
INDIRECT WITNESS OF CHRIST AND OTHER CORROBORATIONS	15

CHAPTER II.

IMPLICIT EVIDENCE IN THE GOSPELS	18–28
1. THE MESSAGES OF THE ANGEL GABRIEL	18
2. THE KINGDOM OF HEAVEN	22
3. THE MESSIAH	23

CHAPTER III.

PRE-CHRISTIAN AND CHRISTIAN REFERENCES TO DANIEL	29–43
1. THE BOOK OF EZEKIEL	29
2. THE BOOKS OF NEHEMIAH AND ZECHARIAH	33
3. THE FIRST BOOK OF MACCABEES	35
4. THE SECOND BOOK OF ESDRAS, AND OTHER BOOKS	41
5. THE NEW TESTAMENT	41

CHAPTER IV.

DANIEL NOT A POST-CANONICAL BOOK	44–56
APOCRYPHAL CONTRASTS	54

S 7431.

CHAPTER V.

THE HISTORICAL PORTION STUDIED CHAPTER BY CHAPTER	PAGE 57–83
1. DANIEL AND HIS FRIENDS	57
2. NEBUCHADNEZZAR'S DREAM	59
3. THE IMAGE OF GOLD	64
4. THE KING'S MADNESS	71
5. BELSHAZZAR'S FEAST	75
6. THE LIONS' DEN	82

CHAPTER VI.

THE VISIONS IN DANIEL VII.–XII.	84–91
THE ASSERTED HISTORY OF THE VISIONS	85
A PRELIMINARY QUESTION	87
CONTRAST WITH THE OLDER PROPHETS	87
INTERPRETERS NOT AGREED	89

CHAPTER VII.

THE THEOLOGY OF DANIEL	92–96

CHAPTER VIII.

THE DOCTRINE OF THE MESSIAH IN DANIEL	97–110

CHAPTER IX.

THE OBJECT AND MORAL OF THE BOOK	111–133
CHRIST IN HISTORY	119
COMFORT UNDER PERSECUTION	125
A MORE LASTING SERVICE	127

CHAPTER X.

ON COUNTER THEORIES	133–164
1. DR. FARRAR'S DEFENCE OF FICTION	134
2. DR. DRIVER'S VIEW OF THE BOOK	146
CONCLUSION	165

CHAPTER XI.

SUPPLEMENTAL.—ON ALLEGED HISTORICAL DIFFICULTIES (by the Editor of the *Babylonian and Oriental Record*, the Rev. HUGH M. MACKENZIE) 172–191
    A. JEHOIAKIM AND "KING" NEBUCHADNEZZAR . . . 172
    B. BELSHAZZAR 174
    C. DARIUS 185
    D. SUMMARY BY THE AUTHOR 191

APPENDIX I.

OUR LORD'S INTIMATE KNOWLEDGE OF OLD TESTAMENT SCRIPTURE . 194

APPENDIX II.

NOTES ON THE CONNECTION OF BABYLON WITH OTHER NATIONS, EASTERN AND WESTERN, ILLUSTRATIVE OF SOME PASSAGES IN THE BOOK OF DANIEL; by JAMES KENNEDY, Esq., late Bengal Civil Service 206

LIST OF ILLUSTRATIONS.

PORTRAIT OF CYRUS - - - - - - - *Frontispiece.*

CAMEO PORTRAIT OF NEBUCHADNEZZAR - - - *facing page* 59

MUSIC AND WORSHIP IN ASSYRIAN TIMES - - ,, ,, 69

INDIA-HOUSE INSCRIPTION - - - - - ,, ,, 74

A CAGED LION ABOUT TO BE LET OUT TO BE HUNTED ,, ,, 82

BRICK OF NEBUCHADNEZZAR - - - - - ,, ,, 173

CLAY CYLINDER OF NABONIDUS - - - - ,, ,, 176

THE BOOK OF DANIEL.

INTRODUCTION.

THE Book of Daniel was written partly in Hebrew and partly in Chaldee or Aramaic: the first chapter to the fourth verse of the second in Hebrew: from ch. 2. 4 to the end of ch. 7 in Chaldee: the remainder in Hebrew. The first six chapters are mainly historical, and Daniel is spoken of in the third person: the remainder is mainly prophetic, and the visions which it records profess to be prefaced by Daniel in the first person. As to Daniel himself, he is represented to have lived to a great old age, having been taken to Babylon in the fourth year of Jehoiakim (B.C. 606), when he was somewhere between fourteen and eighteen years of age, and he was still alive in the third year of the reign of Cyrus (ch. 10. 1), about B.C. 534.

The book, however, is not a history of the life of Daniel, not even of the events of which he might say, *magna pars fui*. For example, we are told nothing of what he was, or what befell him during the years that intervened between the contents of the first chapter and the king's dream recorded in the second; nothing of his political administrations either during the reign of Nebuchadnezzar (2. 48, 49) or that of Darius (6. 1–3), beyond the fact that his enemies and rivals could find no ground on which their jealousy could fasten to injure him, except his fidelity to his God; and no account of the last days of his life.

Nor does it profess to be a history of the period which is embraced in the life-time of Daniel—either Jewish, Babylonian, or Persian. For example, it contains no record of the wars of Nebuchadnezzar with Palestine, Egypt, Tyre, and other places; and it contains no record of the conquests of Cyrus, not even of the battles which ended in the taking of Babylon—a fact which we shall see has an important bearing on an objection which has been persistently made against the book. The contents of the book are limited to facts of a strictly religious character which revealed and declared the will of Jehovah, the God of Israel, in the face of the idolatries of the conquering powers to which the people of Israel were subjected—with visions that were prophetic of a future in which both Israel and the world were interested.

The main question which confronts us when we open this book is whether it is truly and strictly historical, or whether it is something else which it is not easy to define. If historical, the question of authorship may be regarded as subordinate. And yet the two questions can scarcely be separated. As to the first part of the book, though written in the third person, if the writer was not himself Daniel his information must have been derived directly or indirectly from Daniel. And as to the second part, from the seventh chapter onward, Daniel is represented as speaking in the first person, and the writer, *if the story is true*, must either be Daniel or someone who copied from Daniel—a distinction without a difference. If the book is not historical, I have said it is not easy to define what it is, that is, to define how those would describe it who say that it is not historical. We are familiar with the ideas of parable and allegory, and in these days with the idea of the historical novel. "Daniel" can scarcely be any of these. Dean Farrar says, "Its worth and dignity can only be rationally vindicated or rightly understood by supposing it to have been the work of an unknown moralist in the Maccabean age." And he even ventures to suggest the name of a possible or probable author. "That the stories of Daniel (he says) offered peculiar opportunities for this treatment [*i.e.* by 'artistic guise'] is shown by the Apocryphal additions to the book." "Stories, which may be regarded as moral legends, possibly based on a groundwork of real tradition." Only *possibly*, be it observed. The nearest approach to an admission of a real Daniel being in these words : "That Daniel was a real person, that he lived in the days of the exile, and that his life was distinguished by the splendour of his faithfulness, I hold to be entirely *possible.*"*

Dr. Driver has no doubt on this point. "Daniel, it cannot be doubted (he says), was a historical person, one of the Jewish exiles in Babylon, who, with his three companions, was noted for his staunch adherence to the principles of his religion, who attained a position of influence at the Court of Babylon, who interpreted Nebuchadnezzar's dreams, and foretold as a seer something of the future fate of the Chaldean and Persian empires." But the book, he says, could not have been written earlier than B.C. 300. And "grounds exist which make it probable that the book, as we have it, is of the age of Antiochus Epiphanes."†

In studying the questions with which we are thus confronted, Christians have a right to consider them from the Christian stand-point, and in doing so they only assume what on other grounds they have already attained—the conviction

---

* *On the Book of Daniel*, pp. 84, 85, 37.
† *Introduction to the O.T.* Fifth Ed., pp. 479, 477.

that Christianity is Divine, that Jesus Christ was and is all that He avowed Himself to be; and it cannot be required of them to re-assert the grounds of their conviction in discussing every question which is more or less dependent on it. They are bound, moreover, to give the Christian argument a first place, though not necessarily an exclusive place, in their discussion of the question. If, in the study of grounds that are independent of, or foreign to, the witness of Christ, they find evidence which is corroborative of the Christian argument, they may accept it thankfully, not as the basis of their faith, but as an aid to it. If such study should lead to results that seem irreconcileable with explicit words which are found in the Gospels, the considerate enquirer will not rush at once to the conclusion that the *seeming* is *real* and that the apparent contradiction admits of no true and honest explanation; and he will not shrink from the honest study of the difficulty. It has often been found that objections to Biblical testimony which have been urged with a great show of reason and scholarship, have proved in the end only the means of furthering the faith which, it was alleged, they must destroy.

Meantime the Christian enquirer is entitled to begin his inquiry where he has already attained to certainty, and to make that certainty his starting point. In doing so he is not acting illogically. The Theist is not illogical when, already believing in God, he assumes God in further argument. Nor is the Christian illogical when, already believing in Christ, he assumes Christ in further argument. The reader of this volume will soon find, however, that its author does not shrink from battle with outsiders on the open field. But it is painful to have to battle with *Christians* who either deliberately pass by the teaching of their Master, or who expend their strength, not in expounding it, but in the endeavour to neutralise it.

CHAPTER I.

CHRIST'S DIRECT PERSONAL TESTIMONY.

IN one of the last days of our Lord's earthly ministry He took the occasion of certain questions put to Him by His disciples to utter a remarkable prophetic discourse which is recorded in the first three Gospels (Matt. **24**. 1-42, Mark **13**. 1-37, Luke **21**. 5-36). These three records supplement and elucidate each other. But at one point there is a remarkable variation. In the Third Gospel we read "when ye shall see Jerusalem compassed with armies, then know that the desolation thereof is nigh. Then let them which be in Judea flee to the mountains, and let them which are in the midst of her (R.V.) depart out of her," and so on. These words are clear, and refer to the environment of Jerusalem with hostile armies and a consequent "desolation." History tells us how remarkably our Lord's prophecy was fulfilled, and how the Christians of Jerusalem remembered His warning and took advantage of an apparently causeless withdrawal of the Roman troops for a space—leaving the city and finding safety in the mountain region beyond the Jordan. St. Matthew and St. Mark make no mention of armies compassing Jerusalem. But what they do say (Matt. **24**. 16-18, Mark **13**. 14-16) clearly implies the investment of the city which St. Luke tells us our Lord foretold.

While St. Luke mentions one point which the others omit, they mention one which he omits—that our Lord found in the desolation which was about to befall Jerusalem the fulfilment of an ancient prophecy. And in neither case is the omission any presumption against the genuineness of the omitted portion. What is attested by St. Luke is not doubtful, although it is not mentioned by St. Matthew and St. Mark; and what is attested by St. Matthew and St. Mark is not doubtful, although it is omitted by St. Luke.

In two of the Gospels, according to the Authorised Version, we find these words ascribed to Christ: "When ye shall see the abomination of desolation, spoken of by Daniel the Prophet, stand in the Holy place [or where it ought not] (whoso readeth let him understand), then let them which be in Judea flee to the mountains" (Matt. 24. 15). The Revised Version of Mark 13 is somewhat different: "But when ye see the abomination of desolation standing where it ought not (let him that readeth understand), then let them that are in Judea flee unto the mountains." It is not to be assumed that the revised reading is certainly the true reading; critics as competent as the Revisers object strenuously to not a few of the changes which the Revisers propose. But the difference is not in this case of consequence, for the words "whoso readeth let him understand" remain in both. Christ referred those who heard Him to a book which was in their hands and in His, as containing a prophecy of the abomination of desolation standing where it ought not. And it is not questioned, it is fully admitted, that this was the very Book of Daniel which has come down to us. Christ put His seal on a prophecy which it contained, and which His hearers regarded as Daniel's, being in his book, to which He referred them as such. The testimony thus borne, both to the prophecy and to Daniel, through whom it came, could scarcely have been more explicit, even if Christ had not named Daniel in connection with it, as we find in St. Matthew that He did.

We turn now to the parallel passage in St. Matthew. The Revisers throw no doubt on the authorised reading here, according to which Christ named Daniel as the author of the prophecy which He quoted. The absence of the name in St. Mark cannot on any principle be construed into doubt or difficulty as to the truth of the statement of St. Matthew that Christ did name Daniel. On the contrary, as we have seen, the statement in St. Mark asserts implicitly what St. Matthew asserts explicitly.

How can this testimony of Christ to Daniel and his book be denied or evaded? An attempt has been made by such an artifice as the following: "There is nothing to prove that He Himself uttered either the words 'let him that readeth understand,' or even 'spoken by the Prophet Daniel.' Both of these may belong to the explanatory narrative of the Evangelist, and the latter does not occur in St. Mark." (Farrar on *Daniel*, p. 101.) This is worse than slipshod criticism. It is criticism which sets aside the authority of the Gospels, and leaves the words which they ascribe to Christ at the mercy of every reader who dislikes them and who chooses idly to say "I don't know that Christ spoke them." "Nothing to prove that Christ spoke the words" that are recorded in these Gospels! What proof would you have? Both Evangelists ascribe to Christ the words "whoso readeth let him understand"; they are to be found in every known manuscript and version. Yet we are to suppose that both the Evangelists deemed it necessary at this particular point of the narrative to throw in these words, though not spoken by Christ, 'whoso readeth let him understand.' Why should they? What occasion was there for their doing so? They throw no additional light on Christ's prediction of coming disaster. To call this an "explanatory narrative" is utterly misleading. There is not a single explanatory word in either the twenty-fourth of Matthew or the thirteenth of Mark. The Evangelists held the words of

Christ too sacred to be tampered with by comment of theirs.

There is nothing more remarkable in the Evangelists than the way in which the personality of the writers is hidden or forgotten. What St. Paul says of his Christian life, "not I but Christ that dwelleth in me," may be applied to those who were honoured to record the earthly life of the Master. And it seems to me a desecration of the Gospels to suggest the very possibility that emphatic words, having a distinct purpose, which two of the Evangelists say Christ spoke in very solemn circumstances, were not Christ's words, but theirs,—they at the same time not giving the slightest hint by which this might be discovered.

This mode of exegesis has consequences so very serious that I must quote another example of it to show how unsatisfactory it is. What Dr. Salmon says is true: "It is hard to refute a theorist who feels himself at liberty to reject as an interpolation every passage inconsistent with his theory." "An antagonist who does this," he says, "is one who runs away from every blow."*

The example to which I refer is in Dr. Farrar's comment on our Lord's reference to Jonah. "The allusion to Jonah being three days and three nights in the whale's belly occurs in Matt. 12. 40 alone, and not in the parallel passage in Luke 11. 30, 32. The reference, moreover, involves several serious difficulties, which make it doubtful whether it may not represent a comment or marginal note by the Evangelist or some other Christian teacher. For not even by the Jewish mode of reckoning was our Lord three days and three nights in the heart of the earth, but only two nights and one day. This is but a slight peculiarity of language. Had it stood

---

* Professor Salmon, *Introduction to N.T.*, p. 237.

alone it might have passed without notice ; but when taken in connection with St. Luke's *omission* of so remarkable a reference it has led many critics to suppose some misapprehension on the part of the disciples." *

I refer to this matter, not to argue the question whether our Lord's reference to Jonah can be reconciled with the theory that Jonah is an allegory and not history—although I might with advantage quote Dr. Farrar himself, who says, " whatever explanation may be offered of the perplexities presented by some parts of Scripture, the fallacious extension of allegory must be rejected as a mere subterfuge " (p. 71) ; and these other words of his : "an allegorical method may, within subordinate limits, be adopted for purposes of illustration, as it was by St. Paul, but it cannot be used to set aside plain history " (p. 57).

Whether the use of this "method" to explain the book of Jonah does or does not "set aside plain history " is not the present question.† There are those who hold that it does not, *but they do not seek to support their position by questioning the accuracy of St. Matthew's report of our Lord's words.* Against the suggestion of a possible misreport of these words by the Evangelist, or a possible addition to them by the profane hand of some unknown "Christian teacher," I cannot protest too strongly. It were easy to show that the less full report of them by Luke *implies* what is reported by St. Matthew ; and as to the time of Christ's entombment He said Himself on one occasion that He should be killed, and " *after three days* rise again " (Mark **8**. 31).

But returning to the words in which Christ named Daniel, even if we grant, the critic argues, that Christ spoke the

---

* *The Supremacy of the Bible*, p. 240. Substantially the same in Dr. Farrar's book on the *Minor Prophets*.

† See *On the Book of Jonah—A Monograph*. By the Author.

words that are ascribed to Him, they may have been only a passing reference of no force in questions of this sort. He says, " If He (Christ) directly refers to it as a book known to His hearers, His reference lies wholly outside all questions of genuineness and authenticity, as does St. Jude's quotation from the Book of Enoch, or St. Paul's (possible) allusions to the assumption of Elijah, or Christ's own passing reference to the Book of Jonah."* These illustrations may be disposed of very briefly. As to the Book of Jonah, it was not a passing reference to it that Christ made. He made a distinct affirmation, and used the *facts* which He affirmed as a prophetic sign of His coming death and resurrection.† As to the (possible) assumption of Elijah, I do not understand the references, 1 Cor. 2. 9; Eph. 5. 11. As to Jude's supposed quotation from the Book of Enoch, whatever may be its true history, and whatever may be the true explanation of its use by Jude, it has but a very remote bearing on the question of the authority which we may or may not give to the Gospel report of the words of Christ. Why not appeal to Christ's own manner of teaching, of which we have abundant illustrations in the Gospels? It will be found that very much of that teaching comes under the head of "passing references"; that is, it was *occasional*—arising out of and suggested by occasion or circumstances. Take the case of His appeals to Moses; His declaration "Before Abraham was I am"; His interpretation of the great truth taught by the voice from the Burning Bush; His allusion to the serpent in the wilderness, in which

---

* *On Daniel,* p. 102.

† Even those who regard the book as symbolical rather than historical, do not question the fact that Christ's reference was to a *book* then regarded as *canonical.* Dr. Farrar himself says, " It is fully admitted that, whether exactly in its present form or not, the Book of Daniel formed part of the Canon in the days of Christ," p. 102.

He found a type or symbol of Himself as a Saviour. His citation of Daniel was no more a passing reference than these. It was an emphatic and solemn appeal to an ancient prediction which was about to have a more complete and awful accomplishment than any which it had, even in the days of that most cruel enemy of the nation, Antiochus Epiphanes—an accomplishment, the prospect of which filled the heart of the Saviour with sorrow, and drew from Him the pathetic wail, "O Jerusalem, Jerusalem, how often would I have gathered thy children together as a hen doth gather her brood under her wings, but ye would not. And now your house is left unto you desolate." A passing reference indeed! which we dare not construe into an argument in favour of the Book of Daniel, or in proof that Daniel had any connection with it, or was in any true sense the subject of its story! How much of the history of Christ and of His teaching might be swept away by such criticism as this it would be difficult to say—rather, it would be difficult to say how much might not.*

When all other means have failed to minimise or set aside what seems to be Christ's testimony to Daniel and his book, the critic seeks help by an appeal to the so-called Kenotic theory, that is, to a certain construction that is put upon the great mystery asserted by the Apostle in Phil. 2. 6-8, or certain deductions drawn from it. His argument runs thus: (1) Doubt whether Christ really spoke the words ascribed to Him, either in whole or in part, although they rest on the authority of two of the Evangelists. (2) Even if they were spoken, and are correctly reported, they are of no logical consequence in such questions as are raised by

---

* See Appendix I. on our Lord's references to Old Testament Scripture.

modern criticism. And now (3) the possible limitation of Christ's knowledge in His state of voluntary humiliation stands in the way, to say the least, of positive inferences from such words as those that are reported by St. Matthew and St. Mark. With all appearance of reverence towards Christ's authority in this way of putting the matter, it cannot be concealed that this ending of the argument is worse than the beginning. For what does it amount to but this: Christ may not have known, perhaps could not have known, whether Daniel was a prophet or not, and, in asserting that he was, He was only following a national tradition, a tradition which, according to the critics, was mistaken, and in following which Christ was led into mistake. In fewer words, Christ was either ignorant of the truth in regard to the matter, or, knowing the truth, He chose to leave His followers in ignorance. Devout expounders of the Kenotic theory do not hesitate to maintain that Christ's teaching was infallible, and that He was "incapable of misleading." (Gore.) This is enough in reply to any argument drawn from the supposed or real limitation of Christ's knowledge. No distinction can be drawn here between the author of the prophecy quoted by Christ and the prophecy itself. If the prophecy was genuine it could *be no other's* than Daniel's, for it was there in the book in which Christ told his hearers to *read* it, and nowhere else, and that book ascribed it to Daniel.

Turning from Christ's testimony to the book to the book itself, we can place our finger on the very words to which our Lord referred, and in which He saw the prediction of a great catastrophe which was drawing terribly near. In the eleventh chapter we read, "They shall pollute the sanctuary of strength, and shall take away the daily sacrifice, and they shall place the abomination that maketh desolate," *v.* 31.

In the twelfth chapter we read, "from the time that the daily sacrifice shall be taken away, and the abomination that maketh desolate set up, there shall be a thousand two hundred and ninety days," *v.* 11; and in an earlier chapter, in a prophecy of the Messiah who should "be cut off," there is a reference to the overspreading of abominations which should make desolate (**9. 27.**)

In these passages quoted or referred to by our Lord, it will be observed that the prophetic words were originally spoken, not *by* Daniel, but *to* Daniel by a heavenly Messenger. And the distinction is indicated in the form of our Lord's reference, being literally, as recognised in the margin of the Revised Version, "the abomination of desolation which was spoken of *through* Daniel the prophet." The words of Gabriel *to* Daniel come to us *through* Daniel, in the book which bears his name; and they are words which, from their very nature, could have been reported to the world by none but the "man greatly beloved," who was honoured to hear them. Apart from the distinction between *by* and *through*, which may or may not be implied in the form of the passage which we have in the parallel text in Mark, the *usus loquendi* would justify the words of our Lord taken in their most literal form. A prophecy vouchsafed by the Spirit of God to Isaiah or Jeremiah would, being recorded by the prophets, be to us a prophecy of Isaiah or Jeremiah.

But was Daniel a prophet according to the book which bears his name? He appears there rather as a statesman who had more to do with the affairs of Babylon and Persia than with the affairs of his own nation. We read of no call to the prophetic office, such as was given to those others whose books we have in the Old Testament, but we find him actually exercising the two great functions which distinguished the prophetic office : (1) receiving and communicating intimations of the Divine will, and (2) foretelling future events.

Of the first of these functions we have a first illustration in his interpretation of the dreams of Nebuchadnezzar. These dreams were of God, according to the book, and Daniel's knowledge of them and of their meaning was of God. It was not the fruit of "any wisdom that he had more than any living," but was "revealed" to him by God Himself (2. 29, 30). It was the same in the matter of the mysterious writing on the wall which alarmed Belshazzar and his lords. Daniel himself had dreams and visions, to which he could appeal with all the confidence of one who could say, "Thus saith the Lord" (7. 1 and 8. 1).

As to prediction, there are no predictions in the prophetic volume more remarkable, none more distinctive as predictions, none more significant of great things to come, than those which we find in the Book of Daniel. The very first of them, which was embodied in the dream which Nebuchadnezzar had of a "great image," foreshadowed, in terms of singular fitness, the kingdom of Christ; and later visions granted to Daniel himself foretold much of the world's history as it bears on the history of the Jewish nation, until the coming of the Messiah, and indicated the very period of that coming in prophetic form.

So real, or realistic, are these predictions, that unbelief can find no means of evading their witness to the supernatural in the ancient prophets and the supernatural in Christianity, except by assuming that they are not predictions at all, but histories written after the events to which they refer. Of this later on. The point at present is this—that Christ, with a certain book in His hand, which He asked those who heard Him to *read*, called Daniel a prophet; and opening the book for ourselves we find the very prophecy which Christ quoted. (King David, though not a prophet professionally, is called a prophet by the Apostle Peter, Acts 2. 30.) Daniel, being a great statesman in a foreign land through a long life, is called a prophet by Christ, and his book is occupied far less by the story of his statesmanship than by prophecies in which Christ Himself is a main figure.

In our Lord's prophetic discourse on the last day of His earthly ministry there are other words which point to the Book of Daniel; for example, these in Matt. 24. 21.: "There shall be great tribulation, such as was not since the beginning of the world." Now Daniel had said, "There shall be a time of trouble such as never was since there was a nation even to that same time," ch. 12. 1. Again our Lord said, "There shall appear the sign of the Son of Man in Heaven, and then shall the tribes of the earth mourn, and they shall see the Son of Man coming in the clouds of Heaven with power and great glory." In Daniel we read (7. 13), "I saw in the night visions, and behold, one like the Son of Man came with the clouds of Heaven, and came to the Ancient of Days, and they brought Him near before Him, and there was given Him dominion and glory."

These cannot be accidental correspondences. The words of our Lord in the Gospels cannot be less than echoes of words in Daniel with which He was familiar, and He cannot have used them perfunctorily or unconsciously. But this is especially true of words which are ascribed to Him more or less fully in the three Gospels. No more solemn occasion ever occurred in the life of our Lord than when the High Priest adjured Him to say whether He was the Christ, the Son of God. In reply He said, "Thou hast said: nevertheless I say unto you, Hereafter shall ye see the Son of Man sitting on the right hand of Power and coming in the clouds of Heaven" (Matt. 26. 64). In using these words He was appropriating to Himself the words of a prophetic vision of Daniel as plainly as if He had added, "as saith Daniel the prophet." The Jewish doctors who heard Him could not fail to recall words with which they were familiar: "I saw in the night visions, and behold, one like the Son of Man came with the clouds of Heaven, and came to the Ancient of Days, and they brought Him near before Him. And there was given unto Him dominion, and glory, and a kingdom, that all people and nations and languages should serve Him: His dominion is an everlasting dominion, which shall not pass away, and His kingdom that which shall not be destroyed" (Dan. 7. 13, 14). The Rabbinical Doctors, we are told, are unanimous in the opinion that "The Son of Man" (or a son of man), the person in human form, borne upon the clouds of Heaven, is the Messiah; and it is certain that their predecessors in the ancient Sanhedrim received from Christ's words the impression that He claimed to be the subject of the prophecy, and that in doing so he meant to claim, at the very least, an affinity with God, which, in their estimate of it, amounted to blasphemy.

Our Lord's quotation of the words of the vision of Daniel suggests questions of deep interest, to which my present object allows me to refer but very briefly, questions as to the origin and the meaning of the designation "The Son of Man." As to its origin we need not ask whether it was self-originated on the part of Christ, or whether He derived it from the prophecy of Daniel. That it was spontaneous in the sense that He was conscious of its rightfulness, conscious that He was what He called Himself, is evident from the frequency and constancy of His use of the term. At the same time He must have been conscious that in this, as in other things, He was fulfilling, or was the fulfilment of, ancient prophecy. As to the meaning or significance of the term, it was more than a mere averment of His humanity—He was not only *a* son of man but *the* Son of Man, evidently in a sense in which no one else ever was. It was at once a title of humiliation and of dignity. To be *a* son of man was on His part a humiliation: to be *the* Son of Man was a high distinction. "Though in its original connexion (says Dr. J. Pye-Smith) it is combined with lofty characters of majesty and honour, the expression in itself is such that nothing can be conceived more simple and unassuming. It was therefore admirably calculated to answer the purposes of our Lord's habitual testimony concerning Himself during that period in which His wisdom saw it right to suspend the universal declaration of His Messiahship."*

Enough at present to remark on Christ's reference to the vision of Daniel as an implicit testimony to the prophet and his book. His mind was full of the thought and full of the imagery of the book. In both He saw Himself as clearly as He did in the book of the Prophet Isaiah, when He unrolled that prophet's book in the synagogue of Nazareth and read the words, "The Spirit of the LORD is upon me."

---

* *Scripture Testimony*, i., 465.

CHAPTER II.

IMPLICIT EVIDENCE IN THE GOSPELS.

1. The Messages of the Angel Gabriel.

WE find a very remarkable parallel between an important passage in one of Daniel's visions, and the angelic message to the father of John the Baptist and to the mother of our Lord. We have in both (1) the angel Gabriel named as the messenger of God. Nowhere else in Scripture, Old Testament or New, do we find him mentioned, or any part or action ascribed to him personally. (2) In both we find him claiming to speak in the name of God, and with special authority from God. To Zacharias he said, "I am Gabriel that stand in the presence of God, and am sent to speak unto thee and to show thee these glad tidings" (Luke 1. 19). Of his visit to Mary it is said, "the angel Gabriel *was sent from God* unto a city of Galilee, named Nazareth," and having told the message which he had "from God," he confirmed it by saying, "for with God nothing shall be impossible" (Luke 1. 26, 37). His commission from God to Daniel was equally explicit. Daniel says, "While I was speaking in prayer, even the man Gabriel, whom I had seen in the vision at the beginning (8. 16), being caused to fly swiftly, informed me and talked with me and said, O Daniel, I am now come forth to give thee skill and understanding" (9. 21, 22). (3) In both cases the angel Gabriel had a special message to deliver respecting the reign of the long-expected Messiah. The message to Daniel revealed the time when "Messiah the

Prince" should come, to fulfil promise and prophecy and to bring in everlasting righteousness. Of the child of whom Mary was to be the mother, whose name was to be JESUS, because He should save His people from their sins, Gabriel said, "He shall be great, and shall be called the Son of the Highest, and the Lord God shall give Him the throne of His father David, and He shall reign over the house of Jacob for ever, and of His kingdom there shall be no end" (Luke 1. 31-3). A paraphrase this, of the appellation "Messiah the Prince," and an echo of much other Old Testament prophecy.

How shall we account for this very significant parallel or correspondence between the mission of Gabriel to Daniel, and his mission six hundred years later to the father of John the Baptist and to the mother of our Lord,—a mission that had to do largely with the same theme, the reign of Messiah the Prince? To call it chance is nothing short of absurd. We have some insight into its importance in the Apostolic statement that angels desire to look into the things that were foretold by the prophets (1 Pet. 1. 12). If we do not know all that these two missions of Gabriel signified, we can at least understand the bearing of the record on the question which we are considering—the claim of Daniel to a place among the prophets of God, and the claim of the book to be considered as a genuine book *of history*. The Gospel story of the Nativity does not name Daniel and does not quote his utterances. But his words, as written in the book which bears his name, have to be accounted for. They cannot have been borrowed from the Gospel narrative, for they were written hundreds of years before Christ was born,—six hundred, as we believe—the most reckless criticism admitting that they were written at least one hundred and sixty years before He was born. It is easier to believe that they were written 600 B.C. than that they were written 160 B.C., for to believe the former is to believe that they were written by an inspired man of God; and to believe the latter is to believe that they were written by some one who had no authority, but who by some chance imagined them, and by that chance fell somehow—no one can say how—into line with wonderful things which were to happen and to be written generations after. On this theory he imagined or invented the name Gabriel, a name not found in the whole prophetic literature of the nation, but which chanced to be the name of the great angel who, "standing in the presence of God," was sent long after to Nazareth to announce the greatest event in the history of the world. And similarly he imagined or invented all that is put into the mouth of this hitherto unknown Gabriel in his (invented) "talk" with Daniel. But it would be waste labour to pursue further this later supposition, even if we dignify it with the title of an hypothesis.

But if the writer of Daniel cannot have borrowed from the Gospels, may not the writer of the Gospels have borrowed from Daniel? This question cannot be answered without knowing what it means, or what possibly underlies it. If the Gospel be not a genuine and trustworthy history, you may make what suppositions you please as to the materials and their sources out of which its author fabricated it. But in this case you have to account not only for "the angel Gabriel," who may have been found in Daniel, but for the whole story, including all that the angel said to Zacharias with all that followed, and all that he said to Mary and all that Mary said to him,—for none of all which was there anything in Daniel to aid him even by way of suggestion. The author of the history of the Nativity could have borrowed nothing from Daniel but the name of the angel, and how that name had occurred to the writer of Daniel on the hypothesis that the story of the vision in Daniel is not genuine, must remain a mystery. But on other grounds, apart from this *reductio ad absurdum*, we accept the history of the Nativity as genuine and trustworthy, and then we ask how we are to explain the correspondence which we have traced between the *contents* of the vision which Gabriel conveyed to Daniel, and the *contents* of the message in which he described to Mary the reign of the child of whom she was to be the mother.

To talk of the borrowing of the one from the other is quite aside from the mark, unless we profess to know, more than it is possible for us to know, how the angels of heaven become acquainted with the progress of God's church on earth and even with the records of that progress. The correspondence in the matter before us explains itself, if you accept both the vision and the history of the Nativity as genuine. The angel of the vision was the angel of the Nativity. What he was commissioned to reveal in the vision, was the progress towards the completion of the great scheme of redemption which holy men of God had announced from the beginning of the world. What he was commissioned to do when he was sent down to Nazareth in Galilee was practically the same, only now the hour was at hand, not six hundred years distant as before; and he had the high honour of announcing not redemption merely, but the Redeemer, and that His birth was at hand. These were two chapters in the same glorious story, the fountain of which is to be found in the love of God "before the foundation of the world" (1 Pet. 1. 20). On the hypothesis that both the vision in Daniel and the history of the Nativity are genuine, the correspondence is perfectly natural and intelligible. They throw light the one upon the other. On no other hypothesis can the correspondence be explained. And thus the mission of Gabriel to the Virgin Mary confirms our faith in the reported mission of the same angel to Daniel "in the first year of Darius the son of Ahasuerus."

2. The Kingdom of Heaven.

Very closely connected with this earliest incidental, but most significant, Christian history confirmation of the Book of Daniel, we find another in what we may call the formula which was used both by Christ and His forerunner in the opening of their ministry—"The Kingdom of Heaven is at hand."

There were many prophecies which foreshadowed the coming of a great King who should be a son of David, and whose reign should be more glorious and permanent than any which had gone before. But in Daniel we find not only the substance of such prophecies, but the very designation of the expected kingdom, which was used both by Christ and by His forerunner, and we find it nowhere else. "In the days of those kings *shall the God of heaven set up a kingdom* which shall never be destroyed: . . . . and it shall break in pieces and consume all these kingdoms, and it shall stand for ever" (2. 44). The proclamation made by Christ, and by His herald John, connects itself with these words as closely and literally as if they had been written yesterday and not centuries before. The nation had passed through great crises; kingdoms had risen high and fallen low, kingdoms for the most part enemies to the people who considered themselves the chosen of God, kingdoms in whose hands this chosen people seemed helpless, and who made their land the battlefield of their own selfish ends. But the life of Israel was indestructible; and Israel, which was often unfaithful to its God and to its own high calling, never wholly lost sight of the oracle which foretold the rise of a kingdom in its midst which should "break in pieces" all opposing powers and should stand for ever. Israel would owe this kingdom not to any of the ambitious powers which contended for the mastery of the world, but to "the God of heaven." For long periods before the birth of Christ the Jewish people had become feverishly impatient for the coming of this kingdom, and out of the low depths into which they had fallen under the imperial domination of Rome, one and another rebel against Rome, patriots, after their fashion, raised their standards with the cry, "To your tents, O Israel." But in vain. The power of Rome was absolute and crushing. At last, on the banks of the Jordan the cry was heard, "The Kingdom of Heaven is at hand." It was raised by one who was as unsoldierly as can be imagined. And he was speedily followed by the King Himself, who said, "The time is fulfilled, and the Kingdom of God is at hand; repent ye and believe the Gospel,"—the time foretold by Daniel was fulfilled,—and from that hour the Gospel, "the good news of the Kingdom of God" was proclaimed throughout the land.

3. "The Messiah."

We have another link between Daniel and the Gospels—or a sign of connection—in both the untranslated designation *Messiah*, and in the essential idea of the term, "*The Anointed.*" There is evidence that before the birth of Christ "the Messiah" had become the recognised designation of the long-expected Head of the Kingdom of God. In the very beginning of the public life of Jesus of Nazareth, before He had asserted Himself in any way, we find Andrew announcing to his brother Simon, "We have found the Messiah"—an announcement the very form of which indicates familiar acquaintance with the title, and implies that His appearing was in their circle the subject of thought and the object of expectation. This designation was familiar even to the people of Samaria (John 4. 25).

We turn to the Book of Daniel not so much for the word, as for the idea which it embodied. In the Authorised Version we find these words: "Know that from the going forth of the commandment to restore and to build Jerusalem unto the Messiah the Prince," and so on. And in the next verse, after threescore and two weeks shall Messiah be cut off, but not for Himself (**9. 26**). The Revised Version (omitting "but not for himself") translates "Messiah the Prince" into "The Anointed the Prince," and says in the margin, "Or the Messiah the Prince," or "An Anointed One the Prince."

By this term, as we have said, the people of Israel had designated their coming Prince long before He came, and it was only in Daniel that they found Him so designated. The Messianic promise of a deliverer dates, we believe, "from the very cradle of our race," and the great person in whom that promise should be fulfilled was indicated variously in successive ages, notably in 2 Samuel, ch. 7. But for the first and only time He receives the definite appellation of the Messiah, or the Anointed Prince, in one of the visions with which Daniel the prophet was honoured. In the word itself there is nothing occult or mysterious; being interpreted, it is "The Christ" (John **1. 41**). Other and inferior servants of God—prophets, priests and kings—were anointed, and are described as anointed. Even the heathen Cyrus is so described (Isa. **45. 1**). But at last it came to be appropriated to Him who was to be a Priest upon His throne, that in all things He might have the preeminence. No unusual process this in the matter of names. What more common than the name Joshua, even to this day, which, being interpreted, is Jesus, Jehovah, Saviour. In the Greek form of *Jesus* it was not uncommon in Israel before the birth of the Son of Mary, of which we have an example in the well-known author of the Book of Ecclesiasticus. But now it belongs only to the Son of Mary, and our reverence for Him will not allow us to call any other by His Name. Even so with "The Christ," "The Messiah," "The Anointed One," it was well that before the voice of prophecy was silent it should gather up all the sacred associations that clustered round the idea of Divine anointing—regal, prophetic, and priestly—and designate the Saviour of the world as the Messiah. And this title was placed imperishably on the roll of the book in which it was found in the days of the Jesus of Nazareth, the book of the Prophet Daniel.

True it is, sadly true, that the popular expectation of the Messiah in the time of Christ was far from being a truthful embodiment of the prophetic reality. This needs neither proof nor illustration. But Jesus was not a Messiah after the type of popular expectation; and we ask with wonder how He was able to separate Himself so absolutely from His age and nation. There is no solution of this problem except in the fact that He was, and knew Himself to be, the Messiah of the Prophet Daniel. Even within the brief limits of the prophetic dream of the King of Babylon we find one of the two main characteristics of His Kingdom and of what He should be Himself. The stone cut out of the mountain without hands foreshadowed the fact that the new Kingdom was not to be of human origin and built up by human hands. To this our Lord gave prominence in His teaching: "My Kingdom is not of this world." And the prediction that the Messiah should be cut off foreshadowed His death by violence. As to this, from the very thought of which His disciples shrank to the last, He said to them reproachfully, "O foolish men, and slow of heart to believe all that the prophets have spoken! Behoved it not the Christ (the Messiah) to suffer these things and to enter into His glory?"

At the time of our Lord's coming we find in the Gospels that there were some devout ones who were looking for the consolation of Israel, the long-promised redemption, such as Simeon, the aged Anna, and Joseph of Arimathea. Of Anna it is said that she spoke of the child Jesus to all them that were looking for the redemption of Jerusalem, words that suggest that they may have been many; and of Simeon it is said that he took the child Jesus in his arms and blessed God and said, "Lord, now lettest Thou Thy servant depart in peace according to Thy word: for mine eyes have seen Thy salvation, which Thou hast prepared before the face of all people: a light to lighten the Gentiles and the glory of Thy people Israel."

Nor can we overlook the remarkable incident of the visit of the Magi to Bethlehem, as some evidence that the expectation of a Messiah at this period was not confined to Judea. Who the Magi were, what measure of Divine enlightenment they possessed, whence they came, and what the star was whose guidance they followed, does not concern us; nor need we determine how far the expectation of a Messiah had spread in the Gentile world, or how it originated, whether in the prophecies which the Jewish dispersion carried with them wherever they went, or whether the old prophecy of Balaam touching a star that should come out of Jacob, and a sceptre that should rise out of Israel (Num. 24. 17), had anything to do with it. That Judea itself was its birthplace is more than probable, and its spread thence is sufficient explanation of its existence elsewhere. But all this may be left undetermined without affecting the fact which concerns our argument, which is this: that we have evidence which cannot easily be explained away; that at the time of our Lord's birth there were devout souls which had attained the conviction that the hour of Israel's redemption had arrived, and that this conviction had been reached—we know not how—by men whom we must regard at least as thoughtful men and students of the times, who, in the strength of it, travelled far to find, and believed at last that they had found, the object of their hope and search in a new-born babe in the town of Bethlehem.*

The faith of Simeon and of those others of whom we read in the Gospel of St. Luke, who at this time were looking for the coming of the long-promised Saviour, connects itself naturally with the prophecy of Daniel. Many as were the prophecies which went before, and glorious as they were, the honour was reserved for Daniel to indicate the time of their fulfilment, and this he did in terms which, we shall see later on, are not capable of any reckoning which does not bring us, some believe to the very year, certainly approximately, to the time of the birth at Bethlehem and to the time of the great Oblation of the Cross.

We have noted the fact that it was revealed to Simeon that he should not see death until he had seen the Lord's Christ. But this does not affect or weaken our argument. Simeon was already waiting for the consolation of Israel, as were Anna and those others who are not named, and who, it may be presumed, spoke often one to another concerning their great hope that the Lord was about to come to His Temple (Mal. 3. 1). The revelation to Simeon was personal, not originating the hope, but assuring him that, aged as he was, he should not die till he should see the hope fulfilled.

The evidence which we have thus briefly traced in support of the claim of the Book of Daniel to be considered a trustworthy record, is all the more important that it is for the most part incidental and implicit. The book was not written on a plan that would anticipate and answer all possible objections to its contents. It is all unconscious of any question which friend or foe might ask about it, telling its story without

---

* See Edersheim's *Life and Times of Jesus the Messiah*, i., p. 2, etc.

any explanation that might add to the credibility of its most marvellous incidents. Then as to the Gospels, it is needless to say that they contain no discussion on the claim of the book to be received as true. No one doubted its genuineness and truth. It was in the hands of Christ and of His nation, as were the Books of Isaiah and Jeremiah and others, and the incidental references to it are all the more conclusive just because they are incidental. Even Christ's naming of Daniel the prophet was incidental, and the other incidents in which we trace references to the book are more incidental still, for they are not formally connected in any way with the *name* of Daniel. But he must be a bold man, if he is not a blind man, who can see nothing but chance or accident in the correspondences with the book which we have traced in the Gospel history, in the mission of Gabriel, in activity, in the formula "The Kingdom of Heaven," in the designations "Son of Man" and "Messiah," and in the solemn appropriation to Himself by Christ of an important and mysterious passage in one of the visions of Daniel when He stood arraigned before the Jewish Sanhedrim.

CHAPTER III.

PRE-CHRISTIAN AND CHRISTIAN REFERENCES TO DANIEL.

1. The Book of Ezekiel.

WE may now enquire with advantage whether any light can be thrown on the subject by contemporary or later references in the literature of the Jews. And we are almost startled by the explicitness of a reference to Daniel by a contemporary of his own, a captive like himself, though not in Babylon. In the Book of Ezekiel (**14.** 14) we read, "Though these three men, Noah, Daniel, and Job, were in it (Jerusalem), they should deliver but their own souls by their righteousness, saith the Lord GOD," and in a few sentences further on the statement is repeated with still greater emphasis (*v.* 20). Some have not hesitated to suppose that possibly Ezekiel referred to some other Daniel unknown to history. But apart from the groundlessness of any such supposition, it would deprive the solemn words of God of all force and meaning. The Daniel, named with Noah and Job, of whom it is said that he could deliver only his own soul, must have been some great and good man like these others, of whom it might be supposed a possibility that he might deliver "son or daughter" as well as himself, not some obscure person of whom the readers of the book knew nothing. This is so obvious that it should need no argument. But apart from this there is another passage in Ezekiel in which there is a small *touch* which at once identifies the Daniel to whom his brother prophet refers. It is in words addressed ironically to proud Tyre : "Behold, thou art wiser than Daniel ; *there is no secret that they can hide from thee*" (**28.** 3).

We cannot mistake the reference of these words to the Daniel who had discovered the great *secret* of the vanished dream of the King of Babylon, but who devoutly disowned the possession of any capacity of his own to effect the discovery; saying, "There is a God in heaven that revealeth secrets . . . . as for me, this *secret* is not revealed to me for any wisdom that I have more than any living" (ch. 2. 28, 30). The King's words were a just comment on the whole matter: "Of a truth it is that your God is a God of gods and a Lord of kings, and a revealer of secrets, seeing thou couldst reveal this *secret*" (v. 47). The words of Ezekiel addressed to Tyre are an unmistakeable echo of the story of the King's dream and its interpretation, told in the second chapter of the Book of Daniel. Not only is there no other Daniel, there is no other prophet, no king, no saint, of Old Testament story, of whom the words of Ezekiel would have been a characteristic description.

The wisdom of Daniel, not of himself, but of God, and the great mystery of his discovery and interpretation of the dream of Nebuchadnezzar, had soon acquired what we may call world-wide fame. There was nothing so likely to excite the wonderment and to fill the imagination of the age. The achievement of a great victory was an every-day event in comparison. The pretensions of the Magians were notorious, not only in Babylon, but in all the regions that were traversed by the Babylonian army. But now something new had happened, and that in a department of mystery which the Magians claimed as their own, and in which they were utterly baffled, and for their failure were threatened with death. The mystery was solved and the lives of the Magians were saved by a young Jewish captive, who thereby rose at once to honour and power. A story this to be carried on the wings of the wind, not only to the banks of the Chebar, which were not many days distant from Babylon, and to other parts watered by the Euphrates in which Jewish exiles were to be found, but to Palestine and Tyre and Egypt, where men feared and hated the very name of Babylon. Daniel it is reckoned had been fourteen years in Babylon when Ezekiel addressed to the elders of Israel who had visited him the words which we find in his fourteenth chapter, and still longer when he delivered the prophecy concerning Tyre. So that there is not the shadow of improbability in the occurrence of the name of Daniel in the writing of one who was his contemporary.

Nor does any improbability arise from the use which is made of his name. It may seem strange that he should be associated as he is with such ancients as Noah and Job, but the purpose for which his name is used not only redeems it from the appearance of strangeness or arbitrariness, but gives emphasis to the fitness of the prophet's allusion. The prophet is instructed to enforce on the elders "who sat before him," and who, though sharing in exile the calamities which had befallen or were befalling their land because of its idolatry, had carried their idols in their hearts (14. 3) to the banks of the Chebar,—the old prophetic lesson that nothing but repentance would avert the doom which was hanging over the nation and the holy city. Even repentance was now too late. A terrible succession of judgments was decreed and could not be averted. It had been promised to Abraham that if ten righteous persons could be found in Sodom, that wicked city should be spared. There might be more than ten righteous persons in Jerusalem, but let no hope be founded on their presence and prayers. Even these three men, Noah, Daniel, and Job, if in Jerusalem, should deliver only themselves by their righteousness. Noah was privileged to deliver his family when the flood swept away an ungodly race; Job was privileged to obtain by his intercession, the forgiveness of friends who had offended by not speaking that which was right of God. There was one man living even then not less righteous than Noah and Job, who received at a later period an angelic assurance that he was "greatly beloved," that is, it may be assumed, greatly beloved of God. Even now it was known by all Israel, and wherever the affairs of Israel were known, that Daniel's prayer to the God of Israel had received a most wonderful answer, the consequence of which was the saving of his own life and the lives of three friends who were in peril with him. But even Daniel, of whom it might be said, as of one of the fathers of the nation, that he had power with God and prevailed, could not prevail now to do more than deliver himself by his righteousness. The association of his name with those others so famed in Bible story added great force to the prophetic warning. It would be amusing if it were not painful to observe how some critics stumble over the words of Ezekiel. They would have it that the conjunction of the three names mentioned is incongruous; but if it is, the prophet is at fault! It cannot be denied that he wrote the words, and that his words are a witness to the existence and the fame of Daniel.

What shall we say then? These passages in Ezekiel are phenomena to be accounted for. How shall we account for them? There is no doubtful unsolved question about Ezekiel. He is no myth. His existence is as certain a historical fact as is that of the invader of his country, the King of Babylon. Nor is there any question about the authorship and integrity of the book which bears his name. Now in that book, as we have seen, we find Daniel mentioned with repeated emphasis (**14.** 14–20), in connection with Noah and Job, as one who might be supposed to find favour with God to avert Divine judgment; and in another passage (**28.** 3) we find him named in a connection which indicates that he was distinguished even in far-off lands for his wisdom, with an incidental and unexplained reference to *secrets*, in the uncovering of which his wisdom had been shown. Suppose for a moment that the Book of Daniel did not exist, and that we knew nothing of the man to whom Ezekiel refers. How we should search all contemporary records to find if possible a key to the words of Ezekiel! And, failing in our search, how we should set our imagination to work if perchance we might fashion for ourselves a man who should realise in himself greatness, goodness, wisdom, and mystic power; a man who must be represented as living in Ezekiel's own days, or as having lived, like Noah and Job, in an earlier age. Baffled in our historic search and in the endeavour of our imagination to create a Daniel, a book is put into our hands which bears the name of Daniel, which professes to tell us of a Jewish exile who was the contemporary of Ezekiel, and who in early life received power from God to discover and explain what baffled the whole college of Chaldean Magians. We have now the key to the words which were written on the banks of the Chebar, and which would otherwise have remained for ever unexplained. We have no hesitation in founding on the passages which we have quoted an argument in proof that Daniel is as little a myth as Ezekiel, and that as early as the days of Ezekiel he was known to have discharged the most special prophetic function, the supernatural revealing of the Divine will. Nor is there any mystery or difficulty in the matter of the widespread fame which the reference of Ezekiel to Daniel implies.

2.—The Books of Nehemiah and Zechariah.

The references in these books are brief but not unimportant. The prayer of Daniel recorded in his ninth chapter, and the prayer of Nehemiah recorded in the first chapter of the book which bears his name, are based on ancient threatenings and promises, with which both these God-fearing Israelites were familiar. And it cannot be held as certain that the one borrowed from or was suggested by the other; but, to say the least, there is such a likeness between them, not only in tone and spirit, but also in some of their most striking expressions, that the probability is that the later was familiar with the language of the earlier. The words of Nehemiah (1. 7) are strikingly like the words of Daniel (9. 7), and if either is an echo of the other, there can be no doubt which was the earlier voice, and that the story of Daniel's prayer was in the hands of Nehemiah in some written form.

The Book of Zechariah has important bearings on the question of the Book of Daniel, mainly by furnishing us with a defence, if defence be needed, of the peculiar forms in which prophetic revelations are said to have been given in visions to Daniel. If objection be taken to the latter, the like objection must be taken to the former, and likewise very largely to the apocalypse of St. John. But of this later on. There is one passage in Zechariah which seems to have a specific reference to a marked characteristic of Daniel's visions. In ch. 1. 18, 19, we read: "I lifted up mine eyes and saw four horns. And I said unto the angel, What are these? These be the four horns which have scattered Judah, Israel, and Jerusalem. And the LORD shewed me four carpenters (R. V., smiths). Then said I, What be these? And he spake, saying, These are the horns which did scatter Judah, so that no man did lift up his head, but these are come to fray them, to cast out the horns of the Gentiles which have lifted up their horns over the land of Judah to scatter it." Whether we have here any reference to the four empires foretold in Daniel, both in the dream of Nebuchadnezzar (2. 37–40) and in the later vision of ch. 7, is too uncertain for us to rest on it any positive conclusion. But it is noteworthy that we have here what has so prominent a place in the visions of Daniel, *horns* as the symbol of great secular powers which Providence employed both to destroy and to save.

3.—The First Book of Maccabees.

"The Law and the Prophets were until John," our Lord said. Between the close of the volume which was known as "the Law and the Prophets" and the appearing of the second Elijah, John the Baptist, the voice of prophecy was silent. But there were teachers during that period of some of whom at least semi-historical traditions have survived; and books were written—Josephus speaks of them as many—which laid no claim to Inspiration or Divine authority, and if they did, it would be belied by their contents. Some of them are known to us under the general title of "apocrypha," and their value is great, inasmuch as they throw side-lights on a period which, so far as the internal condition of Judaism is concerned, would be an almost entire blank. Such of them as are in biographic or historic form are for the most part fables or romances.

But there is one of them which is entirely free from the legendary element, and in this respect it stands alone. This is the First Book of the Maccabees, which is universally acknowledged to be an honest and reliable record of one of the most critical and heroic periods of the whole history of the Jewish nation. It is the story of a great insurrection against the resolve of one of the Greek rulers who inherited a portion of the empire of Alexander of Macedon, absolutely to root out the faith which had separated the Jewish nation from all the world beside from the very beginning of its existence.

In the first chapter of this book, which tells the story of the resolve of the sons of the God-fearing Mattathias that it should not be so, we find a passage which has important bearings on the question of the Book of Daniel. After reciting what had been done by "overseers" whom Antiochus Epiphanes had appointed to go from city to city to enforce his wicked ordinances, we read thus: "And on the fifteenth day of Chislev, in the hundred and forty and fifth year [B.C. 168], they builded an abomination of desolation upon the altar, and in the cities of Judah on every side they builded idol altars. And at the doors of the houses in the streets they burnt incense. And they rent in pieces the books of the Law which they had found, and set them on fire. And wheresoever was found with any a Book of the Covenant, and if any consented to the Law, the king's sentence delivered him to death. And on the five and twentieth day of the month they sacrificed on the idol altar, which was upon the altar of God."[*]

The first point that arrests our attention here is, that "they builded an abomination of desolation on the altar" of the Temple. Whence this singular phrase? Nowhere, nor its equivalent, but in Daniel. It is said of Manasseh that "he built (idol) altars in the house of the LORD,"—"that he built altars for all the host of heaven in the two courts of the house of the LORD," 2 Kings **21**. 4, 5. And these doings are described as "abominations" (*v.* 11). But extreme as his apostacy was, and cruel as were the ways he enforced it, there is nothing in the record of his history to suggest the phrase "the abomination of desolation," or "the abomination that maketh desolate." This we find only in Daniel, chaps. **9**. 27; **11**. 31; **12**. 11. Looking at this matter from a purely literary point of view, a literary critic might at once pronounce that the writer of Maccabees found the expression in the Book of Daniel. But we have here more than a verbal likeness. There is a sub-

---

[*] Translation in the Cambridge Edition for Schools and Colleges.

stantial likeness between the circumstances to which our Lord applied the expression (Matt. 24. 15) and the circumstances to which the writer of the Maccabees applied it. The investment of Jerusalem by the Romans, and the ruin and dishonour done to the Temple of God at the time, was clearly indicated in the prophecy of Daniel (9. 27). The assault of Antiochus on Jerusalem and the cities of Judah was still more directly aimed at the religion of the Jewish nation and at the dishonour of their Temple, than was the action of the Romans,—the motive of Rome being primarily secular, the motive of Antiochus being primarily religious. What perception the writer of the "Maccabees" may or may not have had of the prophetic anticipation of events that were still distant by more than two hundred years, he could not fail to see the events of his own time foreshadowed (Dan. 11. 31) in the very language which foreshadowed the events of which our Lord warned His disciples many years before they occurred. The sameness of the language is not accidental. The events were in a sense the same. And thus the earlier was a providential anticipation of the later.

In this we assume that the author of the Book of the Maccabees had the Book of Daniel in his hands, and, if he had, so had the people in whose times he wrote. But this is no mere assumption. One ground for it has already been argued, in the use of the very peculiar Daniel-phrase, "the abomination that maketh desolate." But the evidence goes beyond this. The writer goes on to say that the agents of Antiochus "rent in pieces the books of the Law which they found and set them on fire. And wheresoever was found with any a Book of the Covenant, and if any consented to the Law, the king's sentence delivered him to death." It would be quite arbitrary to limit the phrase "books of the Law" and "Book of the Covenant" to the Pentateuch or to such portions of the Pentateuch as specify the "covenant" of God with Israel. It would not satisfy the malignity of Antiochus or accomplish his purpose to rend in pieces the books of Moses, and leave, in the possession of the people, the great series of historic and prophetic books in which they believed that God had revealed Himself to their fathers through many ages. His purpose was no less "thorough" than that of Diocletian, who in the third century after Christ aimed at extirpating Christianity from the root by the destruction of the Christian Scriptures. The evidence is beyond dispute that in the age of the Maccabees the Hebrew Scriptures (not the Pentateuch alone) were known in their entirety and in the classified divisions with which the New Testament has made us familiar; the earlier form of these divisions being "The Law, the Prophets, and the other books" (or writings). This expression is found in the prologue with which the translator of the Book of Ecclesiasticus prefaces the work of his grandfather Jesus Ben Sirach. The translator tells us how his grandfather devoted himself much to the reading of the "Law and the Prophets and the books of the Fathers." The expression occurs three times, in one instance the third division being described as "the remaining books," the description in every instance suggesting that the classification was old and familiar. Ben Sirach's book was written in Hebrew (possibly in Aramaic), and although its date cannot be fixed with certainty, it cannot have been much short of a hundred years before the days of Judas Maccabeus. And all doubt that the historic Scriptures which his studies embraced were known in the days of this patriot, is removed by the address in which Mattathias, the father of Judas, roused his sons to patriotism and self-sacrifice.

"Call to remembrance (he said) the deeds of our fathers which they did in their generations, and receive great glory and an everlasting name." He reminds them of men who had gone before, and whose names were as household words: Abraham, Joseph, Phinehas, Joshua, Caleb, David, and Elijah. He completes the roll thus: "Ananias [=Hananiah], Azarias, and Misael, by believing were saved out of the flame. Daniel for his innocency was delivered from the mouth of lions."* "And then consider ye (says this venerable man to his sons) throughout all ages, that none that put their trust in Him shall be overcome." His appeal is to the experiences of all ages. He does not quote book, chapter, and verse, but he quotes facts which we find recorded in books which were in the hands of the people of his time, both in Hebrew and in Greek. And among these facts are the deliverance of Daniel from the mouth of lions, and of his three friends from the burning fiery furnace. The possibility of these later facts being known by tradition need not be denied. But it cannot be to tradition that Mattathias owed his knowledge of the long series of great historical events from the days of Abraham, in which he and his age found a legacy of illustrious examples of faith in God. His words are evidence that the most wonderful stories in the Book of Daniel are not fictions of the Maccabean age, but true histories of great Divine deliverances such as were wrought in former ages for God's chosen people, from the days of Abraham onward to the times in which he spoke. For his knowledge of them he was indebted to books that were written by holy men of old.

---

* There is no process by which the evidential importance of the reference of Mattathias to Daniel as recorded in the First Book of Maccabees can be neutralised. He did more than mention the name of Daniel; he referred to the most extraordinary incidents in the life of the prophet and of his three friends—the fiery furnace, and the lions' den. The omission of the name of Daniel elsewhere, as in the Book of Ecclesiasticus (ch. 49. 11-13) really proves nothing. In the same passage we might have expected to find the name of Ezra, the great spiritual reformer and restorer of the nation, whose work could not have been unknown or unappreciated by Ben-Sirach; but it is not there. In fact there is no reason why we should expect a complete list of contemporary worthies in the passage referred to.

We feel that in this argument we are standing on solid ground from which we cannot be moved. The Maccabee patriots were all unconscious that there was in their midst or within their reach, a contemporary who could claim prophetic authority or capacity to speak in the name of God. When Judas and his brothers went up to Sion after a victory they had gained, they made great lamentation over the ruins of the holy places, and consulted what to do with the altar of burnt offerings which had been profaned, and they thought best to pull it down lest it should be a reproach to them because the heathen had defiled it ; wherefore they pulled it down, and laid up the stones in the mountain of the Temple in a convenient place, "*until there should come a prophet to show what should be done with them*" (**4.** 39-46). Then on the death of Judas, we read that "There was a great affliction in Israel, the like whereof was *not since the time that a prophet was not seen among them*" (**9.** 27). And when his brother was selected to succeed him, we read that "the Jews and priests were well pleased that Simon should be their governor and high-priest for ever, *until there should arise a faithful prophet*" (**14.** 41). It is evident from these passages that in the time of the Maccabees there was no one known who assumed the rôle of a prophet, and they produce the impression (especially **9.** 27) that the nation had long been without the presence and counsel of a prophet.

But Daniel was known to them as one of the martyr-men of their nation, who through trust in God had been delivered from great peril. And in the record of his life the father of the Maccabean heroes could find unfailing assurance that the people of God could be reduced to no circumstances too desperate for God to be their refuge and their strength.

4.—The 2nd Book of Esdras, and other books.

It would be interesting to trace such references to Daniel as are found in other books that are included in the Apocrypha; but they could add little, if anything, to the clear and positive evidence which we have adduced from the First Book of the Maccabees. With the exception of Ecclesiasticus and the Wisdom of Solomon * they are full of legendary matter, and their age is uncertain. But they serve a good purpose, though it be a negative one, in this respect, that they show that, in neither myth nor legend nor history—so far as traditional history is found in them—is there the remotest suggestion that Daniel and his book were other than what they seemed to be. In the ages with which these books are in any wise connected the doubt had not yet dawned that the history of Daniel was not genuine. In one of them there is mention of a vision of Daniel and something like an attempt to enlarge or expound the vision; it is in 2 Esdras, ch. **12**. The author had a vision, and " this is the interpretation thereof: The eagle whom thou sawest come up from the sea is the kingdom which was seen in vision of thy brother Daniel," *v.* 11. This whole chapter and the preceding and following are interesting studies as human attempts at an Apocalypse after the manner of Daniel, perhaps honest attempts to further develop the visions of the prophet; but when they were written it is impossible to say.

5.—The New Testament.

While, for the reason which I have stated, I do not seek confirmation of the genuineness of the Book of Daniel in the books of the Apocrypha generally, for a very different reason I do not now appeal to the books of the New Testament.

---

* These two, for the most part, may be regarded as a collection of paraphrases upon passages of Holy Scripture, or of reflections upon them.

When we open these we are not in a region of fog and doubt, but of light and certainty. But so far as the plan and purpose of this book are concerned, any appeal to them would only prove that their writers, servants of Christ, were not greater than their Lord : He believed in the Book of Daniel, so did they ; if He was mistaken, so were they—but only then. Apart from indications of acquaintance with the Book of Daniel which may be traced in occasional thought and phrase, there is one New Testament book which stands in a singularly close and significant relation to it—the Revelation of St. John—and we shall make use of it in a later chapter in repelling certain objections that are taken to the visions that are ascribed to Daniel. Meantime, we are in a position to maintain that, accept the Revelation to and by John as genuine, and you supply us with a strong argument, at this stage of our study, for the genuineness of the Revelation to and by Daniel. " John " is sometimes said to be *based* on " Daniel," but the expression implies too much ; for we must hold, first of all, that if the two be genuine they come from one Divine source ; that is, Daniel and John were each of them in immediate communication with the Spirit of prophecy—the Spirit of God —just as were any two of the ancient prophets, such as Isaiah and Jeremiah. But, secondly, the Divine Spirit, in His wisdom and grace, adapts His ministrations to His servants and to their circumstances according to His will. And we know of no reason why He should not employ the method of one to aid and guide another. There was an analogy, not superficial, in the circumstances in which Daniel was called to foretell the things that should be hereafter, culminating in the first coming of Christ, and those in which John was called to foretell things that should be hereafter, culminating in His second coming. Let the mind and heart of John be filled with the visions of Daniel, and much exercised by them, and he would be thus prepared to receive visions of a like character from the same Divine Spirit and by a like agency—that of ministering angels. The result would be what we have in the general likeness of the two books—a result not attained by one author copying from and imitating the other, but by the action of common causes in which the Divine and the human were combined.

If we are right in this, it follows that we have proof that the Apocalypse of Daniel was anterior to the Apocalypse of St. John, and that in a sense the latter could not have been what it is but for the former. At the same time the fact should not be overlooked that by far the larger portion of the Christian Apocalypse is what we may call original; that is, that it has no type or counterpart in that of Daniel, so that John could not have worked out his Apocalypse out of that of Daniel.

CHAPTER IV.

DANIEL NOT A POST-CANONICAL BOOK.

THE position which we ascribed to the Book of Daniel, on the faith of Christ's testimony, is confirmed by all that *we know* of the history of the canon of the Old Testament. I say *by all that we know*,—for criticism has a great deal to say, many questions to ask, many difficulties to suggest, many problems to solve, which do not lead to results of which we can say *we know*. Leaving to others to traverse the whole region of criticism, I venture to state only what seems essential to my argument, distinguishing between admitted facts and our deductions from them.

The first fact which we are entitled to assume is, that from the time of Malachi to the time of John the Baptist, no *prophet* appeared in Israel. It would be reasoning in a circle to quote in evidence at this point the words of Christ, "All the prophets and the law prophesied until John" (Matt. 11. 13). For what we want at present is not Christ's own dicta, which we have already considered, but collateral evidence. And of this there is no lack. Let us turn to Malachi. It foretold the coming of the Lord to His Temple, and the coming of Elijah to prepare His way; and meanwhile the nation was to remember the Law of Moses, the servant of God, and the institutions which were founded in Horeb. The prophet knows, or feels somehow, that he is standing on the edge of a period which separates a great past from a greater future. His prophecy is based on the fact that it is so. He was in succession to an order of men who had appeared at intervals through many generations, and on the occasion of many crises in the history of his nation. Nearly a hundred years had passed since his immediate predecessors, Haggai and Zechariah, had ministered. *He* was the last of his order. We do not argue that he was expressly or divinely told that he was. But what he was told by God we are told by him, not indeed expressly, but by implication, that no prophet was to be expected until the herald of the Great King should announce His coming. We know, what he could not have known without further prophetic revelation, that for some hundreds of years to come the nation was still to occupy its ancestral home, and to pass through crises, some of them more painful than were those which subjected them to Assyria and Babylon. Only whatever might be the time, long or short, "the Law and the Prophets must *prophesy*" (Matt. 11. 13), must fulfil the prophetic function, must be the guides and teachers of the nation, in the place of the living voice of inspired men.

The intimation thus given by Malachi is verified in "the silence of four centuries,"[*]—silence, that is, so far as fresh prophetic revelation is concerned. But these four centuries are not, as we have seen, a blank historically. If they were we might suppose that prophets had appeared and been forgotten. But history tells us much both of Judaism and of the outward condition of the Jews, and contains the expression of regret, already quoted from 1 Maccabees, that the nation had no prophet to say what should be done in a case of ritual difficulty. The tone or form of the lamentation indicates that "ages" had passed without a prophet (from two to three hundred years, as we know, from Malachi to the Maccabees), and intimates the hope of the coming of a "faithful prophet" at some future time.

---

[*] In *Four Centuries of Silence*, by the Rev. R. A. Redford, M.A., the reader will find a useful history of the period "from Malachi to Christ."

THE BOOK OF DANIEL.

What we thus know corresponds with, and justifies, the statement which Josephus makes with reference to the Jewish Scriptures. He is not recording a personal opinion, but the universal belief of the Jewish people, when, after describing and classifying the books which were "justly accredited as divine," he says, "From the time of Artaxerxes, moreover, until our present period, all occurrences have been written down; but they are not regarded as entitled to the like credit with those which precede them, because there was no certain succession of prophets. Fact has shown what confidence we place in our writings. For although so many ages have passed away, no one has dared to add to them, nor to take away from them, to make alterations." *

The learned author of the Introduction to the Book of Daniel in the *Pulpit Commentary*, the Rev. J. E. H. Thomson, concluding his discussion of the subject, says, "It seems, then, that somewhere about the end of the Persian rule, that is to say, about the time the Talmudists place the Great Synagogue, the Canon was fixed. The principles on which they selected the Books which were to form the Canon seem to have been those laid down by Josephus—that the Book must be reputed to have been composed before the death of Artaxerxes Longimanus, and to have been the work of prophets. If this is granted—and, in the light of the evidence, it is impossible reasonably to resist it—the Book of Daniel must certainly date so much before the end of the Persian period, that its claim to belong to the Babylonian period could not be challenged at the time. At all events, the date assumed by the critical school, namely, B.C. 165, is definitely to be put aside as clearly false," p. xxxvi.

---

* On the testimony of Josephus and the books included in his list, see "The Foundations of the Bible," by Canon Girdlestone, p. 3, *et seq.*

That Daniel was in the Canon whose sacredness and unalterableness Josephus thus describes is not questioned. And if it were, there is an incidental reference to it in his *Antiquities* (book x., sec. x. 4) enough to silence doubt. Reciting the history of the dream of Nebuchadnezzar, and Daniel's interpretation of it, he stumbles as an unbelieving Jew might be expected to stumble, when he comes to "the stone cut out without hands." What can this mean? With worldly wisdom he evades the question, and says, "since I have only undertaken to describe things past or present, but not things that are future; yet if any one be so very desirous of knowing truth as not to waive such points of curiosity, and cannot curb his inclination for understanding the uncertainties of futurity, and whether they will happen or not, *let him be diligent in reading the Book of Daniel, which he will find among the sacred writings*."

The Jews to this day count no books as sacred but those which were reverenced in the time of Josephus. A few of the books which we know as Apocrypha appear to have been originally written in Hebrew; but they have not been preserved in that language, nor do they appear ever to have been set by those who used it on a level with the ancient sacred books.

"The agreement of the Canon of Melito with that of Josephus proves that late in the second century the Christians of Palestine were in substantial agreement with the Jews as to the Old Testament Canon. This is only what might have been expected, since it is plain from the New Testament that our Lord and His Apostles had no difference with the Jews on this subject of the Canon. In every part of the New Testament the authority of the sacred books of the nation is assumed as undisputed; and in all controversy with the Jews it continued so" (Salmon).

"As regards the Book of Daniel," says Edersheim, "it is an important fact that its right to canonicity was never called in question in the ancient Synagogue. The fact that it was distinguished as 'visions' from the other prophecies, has, of course, no bearing on the question, any more than the circumstance that later Rabbinism, which, naturally enough, could not find its way through the Messianic prophecies of the book, declared that even Daniel was mistaken, and could not make anything of the prophecies concerning the latter days. On the other hand, Daniel was elevated to almost the same pinnacle as Moses; while it was said that, as compared with heathen sages, if they were all placed in one scale, and Daniel in the other, he would outweigh them all. We can readily understand that in times of national sorrow or excitement these prophecies would be eagerly resorted to as pointing to a glorious future." *

We may now regard it as an established fact that the order of prophets ceased at or near the close of the reign of Artaxerxes Longimanus, that is, near to B.C. 424—the time, in short, of the Malachi whose book is the last in our Old Testament.

The bearing of this on the question of the Book of Daniel may be shown in a sentence. There being no prophet, so far as we know, after the days of Malachi, there could have been no prophetic book, no book containing new or fresh Divine revelations, no book stamped with the seal and authority of a prophet. But the Book of Daniel professes to be prophetic. It contains prophecies, or professed prophecies, marked and specific, declared by Daniel to have been received and recorded by himself (8. 1, 15 ; 9. 2, 22 ; 10. 1, 2, 7). The conclusion is unavoidable that it is one of those books which *preceded* the period at which the Jews believed that Divine prophecy

---

* *Life and Times of Jesus the Messiah*, vol. ii., pp. 687-8.

ceased, or, if not, that it is a fabrication of a period in which the Jews believed that no prophet was found among them. Accept this latter alternative, and you have to explain how the Jews could have been deceived or tricked into the acceptance of so gross and wicked an invention, and so deceived as to give it a place among the books which they considered Divine, and which they guarded with an almost superstitious care.

Our argument may be based very briefly on the twofold admission of the most adverse critics : (1) The Book of Daniel was in the Jewish Canon in the time of Christ, that is, it was one of the books which the Jews regarded as inspired and authoritative ; (2) In the age of the Maccabees, both before and after, there was no prophet, no one who could claim to be inspired, either to write the book, or, when written, to stamp it with his authority. When or how, if written in that age, did it find its way into the Canon ? Edersheim, a most competent witness in this matter, says : "Few students of Jewish history would be disposed to assert that a book which dated from 165 B.C. could have found a place in the Jewish Canon, and that it should have passed the repeated revision of different Rabbinic "colleges"—and that at times of considerable theological activity—without the suspicion being ever raised that its authorship dated from so late a period as a century and a half before Christ."

To the question how a book dating from B.C. 165 could be introduced into the Jewish Canon, no answer can be given that does not involve fraud on the part of the writer and incredible credulity or carelessness, if not intentional complicity with the writer, on the part of the nation.

What is known of the history of the Septuagint translation confirms, so far as it goes, the conclusion which we reach on other grounds. "This version contains all the canonical books of the Old Testament in what is virtually the form in which we possess them. We have fairly reliable information of the time at which the translation was undertaken, viz., in the time of Ptolemy Philadelphus, who reigned from B.C. 284 to 247, although the date of its completion is not so certain. Since it is natural to suppose that the books were regarded as canonical before they were translated, we may conclude that a Canon of some compass existed before the translation was undertaken, and that the whole Canon existed before it was concluded. Seeing, however, that the date of completion of the translation is uncertain, and seeing also that in the Septuagint collection there are included other books besides the canonical books of the Hebrew Bible, we must look for other evidence of the independent existence and high authority of the Canon."*

To this careful and cautious statement by Prof. Robertson, of Glasgow, may be added a point which bears on the question of the age of the Book of Daniel. It is true that we cannot fix definitely on the date of its translation into Greek, but (*a*) it is certain that the translation was made from a Hebrew original, and (*b*) it is almost as certain that the additions to it which appear in the Apocrypha (Bel and the Dragon, etc.) had no Hebrew original. Apart from contrasts to which I will appeal immediately, have we not a right to infer that the Hebrew Daniel belonged to an earlier age than these additions, and that its beginning, not in Greek, but in Hebrew, must be traced to an earlier age.

The use which some critics make of the fact that the Book of Daniel was not placed alongside Isaiah and the other older prophets in the Jewish Canon, but among the books which

---

* *Guild Text Books*—" The Old Testament," p. 11.

have come to be called Hagiographa, is founded on an entire mistake. Christian critics, at least, should be deterred from the reckless assertion either that the Jews deliberately refused to Daniel a place in their Canon, or that they *shunted* him—to use a modern phrase—into an inferior or subordinate position, by the fact that their Lord quoted an express prophecy from his book, and the additional fact that He distinctly recognised the division of the Canon in which the book was placed by the name which it then bore. The quotation need not be repeated or recalled.

His recognition of the "Hagiographa" stands side by side with His recognition of the other portions of the Canon; thus —"All things must be fulfilled which were written in the Law of Moses, and in the Prophets, and in the Psalms, concerning Me," Luke 24. 44. Each of these three terms was an abbreviated description of the books which it included. The third division came to be called "The Psalms" because the Book of Psalms was the first portion of it; but it included not fewer than eleven of the books which we have in our Hebrew Bible— Psalms, Proverbs, Job, Song of Songs, Ruth, Lamentations, Ecclesiastes, Esther, Daniel, Ezra, Nehemiah, and Chronicles. The classification which separated these books from the Law and the Prophets was not based on any conception of their inferiority, but, as a glance at their titles and subjects sufficiently indicates, on the fact that their variety did not admit of a more specified designation. The earliest reference which we have to the three-fold division of the Hebrew Bible is in the Prologue to the book known as the Wisdom of Jesus Ben Sirach, otherwise known as Ecclesiasticus. The grandson who translates the book into Greek says that his grandfather, who must have written about B.C. 200, was familiar with "the Law and the Prophets and *the other books* which follow them," or, as he again describes them, "The other books of the

Fathers," or, "The rest of the books." The third portion of the sacred books, thus described in general terms, constituted an entirety, or a recognised whole, as much as the first and second. These facts are so well known that critics are without excuse who persist in talking of the Hagiographa as an inferior portion of the Hebrew Bible, less inspired than the rest, if inspired at all.

Why Daniel was not placed among the so-called prophets involves neither mystery nor difficulty. He was not a prophet in the professional sense, but a great statesman, to whom the word of the Lord came in very different circumstances and in a very different form from that which we associate with the names of those who ministered to the nation of Israel. But those who deduce from this the inference that his prophecies, if indeed they are his, should be placed in a category below that in which we place those of Isaiah, should not overlook the fact that the testimony of Christ to the prophecies of Daniel is as explicit as His testimony to the prophecies of Isaiah. In Matt. **13.** 14 and **15.** 7 we find Him naming Isaiah expressly, while in Matt. **24.** 15 He names Daniel with equal explicitness.

Some critics in their zeal to dethrone Daniel from the undisputed position which he held in the time of our Lord, are not content with drawing a false inference from the fact that his book was placed in the third division of the Old Testament Scriptures, although that division contained, as we have just seen, many other books whose canonicity is not questioned, but boldly aver that it belongs to a class of Jewish writings known by the name of *Haggadah*. The most charitable construction that can be put on this proceeding is that these critics know not what they say or whereof they affirm; their zeal outstrips their knowledge; or if they have knowledge, we must put a worse construction on their proceeding. Any reader who thinks it worth his while to seek acquaintance with the character of two classes of Jewish Rabbinical books known as *Halakhah* and *Haggadah*, representing two branches of Jewish Theology, will find what he wants in Edersheim on the *Life and Times of Jesus the Messiah*, vol. i. Enough for the present purpose to say that they are all post-Christian, some of them as late as the second and third centuries. Of the Haggadah Edersheim says, " By the side of what is pure and noble, what a terrible mass of utter incongruities and conflicting statements and too often debasing superstitions, the outcome of ignorance and narrow Nationalism ; of legendary colouring of Biblical narratives and scenes, profane, coarse, and degrading to them ; the Almighty Himself and His Angels taking part in the conversations of Rabbis and the discussions of Academies ; nay, forming a kind of Heavenly Sanhedrim, which occasionally requires the aid of an earthly Rabbi. The miraculous merges into the ridiculous, and even the revolting. Miraculous cures, miraculous supplies, miraculous help, and all for the glory of great Rabbis, who by a look or word can kill and restore to life." It is with such writings as these—of which Edersheim says that modern criticism should own the terrible contrast existing side by side ; Hebrewism and Judaism, the Old Testament and traditionalism that it is suggested that the Book of Daniel should be classified. I am reminded again and again of words which I have already quoted elsewhere, the words of the late learned Dr. Cairns : " The dulness of criticism (of the Rationalist School) is seen in the non-appreciation of the grandeur of Daniel, which every fool of the Maccabean Age is supposed capable of having written, or, according to some, a joint-stock company or fortuitous concourse of fools and fanatics, whose fabrications run into such sublime shapes as we find in the Book of

Daniel. Surely the time will come in all lands when some sort of elementary feeling for the sacred and the great will be so diffused as to nip such absurdities in the bud, and serve as a foundation for positive scriptural criticism and exposition to build upon."

Apocryphal Contrasts.

We find another collateral support of the genuineness and integrity of the Book of Daniel in the contrasts between it and the additions to it which are found in the books of the Apocrypha. The Song of the Three Holy Children is prefaced in the English translation by the statement that its place in the book is between $v.$ 23 and $v.$ 24 of the third chapter, and that "it is not in the Hebrew." The first part of the Song is mostly a prayer for deliverance, and the second is a call to the whole creation to join in blessing the Lord God. In this second part—well known in the English Prayer Book as the *Benedicite*—we have nearly forty verses in which everything under heaven is described with a minuteness, which would tax the knowledge and memory of the most observant student of nature sitting at his desk with his pen in hand. In the Song "the three are presented as having praised, glorified, and blessed God in the furnace," repeating "as out of one mouth," this great catalogue of all things in the universe around them. How different from the simple, unadorned statement of fact which we find in the book. The song ascribed to the three men in the fiery furnace is sometimes compared with the words ascribed to Jonah in the second chapter of his book; but the contrast is greater than the likeness. Nothing could be more natural than the thoughts of Jonah, whether they were put into words during his mysterious entombment or after his deliverance. But the song known as the *Benedicite* is plainly an elaborate composition, by some one whose imagination failed to realise what was fitting and natural to men in the position of the three Hebrews in the fiery furnace, while he laboured to summon all creation to unite in the praise of the Creator.

The History of Susanna, "set apart (as the preface to the English translation says) from the beginning of Daniel because it is not in the Hebrew—as neither the narrative of Bel and the Dragon—is the story of a wicked intrigue against the honour of a virtuous woman, and how it was baffled at the last moment by Daniel, by a process as simple as that which is ascribed to Solomon in the case of two women who disputed the possession of a living child. It is a romance worthy of a place in the "Thousand and One Arabian Nights."

Bel and the Dragon professes to tell how Daniel detected the fraudulency of the priests of Bel, who pretended that food which was placed daily before the image of Bel was consumed by the god during each night that followed. The plan which he adopted was just such as we can imagine a modern "detective" adopting for the discovery of crime. The book is entirely fabulous.

These books, it will be observed, do not claim to have been written originally in either of the languages in which the Book of Daniel was written. And there is no means of determining when, where, and by whom they were written. And I refer to them only to mark the contrast between them and the Book of Daniel. The Apocryphal Gospels are often referred to, to point the contrast which they present to the four historic Gospels to which we owe our knowledge of Jesus Christ. And well they may, for if Jesus Christ had been the invention of the age or ages to which we owe the Apocryphal Gospels, He would have been very different from the Jesus Christ that we know. The contrast between the Apocryphal additions to the Book of Daniel is by no means so great and violent as that which we find in the case of the Gospels, because the parts ascribed to him involve no dishonour to him, and are not irreconcileably opposed to his known character. But they give us the impression, not of a great man who in critical circumstances and for great purposes was honoured with Divine revelations, but of a clever man, a Magian perchance, who moved about among his fellows, exciting wonderment by His clever pronouncements in matters which were very simple, after all, but which baffled the skill of other men.

Placing these Apocryphal additions and the Book side by side with each other, we conclude that they belong to different ages, and to entirely different conditions of thought. Those who conceived and wrote the additions were both intellectually and spiritually incapable of appreciating the book and its contents; and had the book originated in their time and grown out of the imaginings of that time, it could not have been what it is, it would have betrayed the age and parentage of its origin.

The Book of Daniel may be contrasted not only with the Apocryphal additions which are connected with his name, but with other Apocryphal books. If it were right to classify them together, the legitimate conclusion would be to exclude it from the Bible as these are excluded; no acknowledgment of mere superiority would justify its separation from them. We do it injustice when we speak of it as the beginning or beginner of the class of writings to which they belong, and which are often described by a term which in this case well fulfils one design which is ironically ascribed to language, that of concealing thought, the term Apocalyptic.

CHAPTER V.

THE HISTORICAL PORTION STUDIED CHAPTER BY CHAPTER.

THE conclusion to which we are brought by the evidence which we have attempted to set forth in the preceding chapters is that the Book of Daniel is what Jews and Christians have hitherto believed that it is—a true record of events which occurred in a pre-Christian period of the history of the Kingdom of God in the world. This conclusion, we believe, will not be shaken, but confirmed, by a careful study of the contents of the book, chapter by chapter. Let us open the book, then, and read it, to see whether its statements can be accepted literally, or whether, for one reason or another, the literal is inadmissible and must give place to an interpretation which necessitates the hypothesis of conscious fiction or invention on the part of the unknown author or authors, associating with it, peradventure, the claim that fiction was used only for the holy purpose of religious instruction. In doing so we shall reserve matters which are supposed to involve historical difficulties for consideration in a supplemental chapter by a friend who has made modern Tablet literature a careful study.

1. Daniel and his Friends (Dan. 1).

The first chapter of the book tells us of the deportation from Jerusalem by the King of Babylon, in the third year of Jehoiakim, of three youths connected with the royal family of Judah. They are selected partly, perhaps, because of their royal blood, to be educated in the learning of the Chaldees, a position which involved danger to their Jewish faith, but to which they continued steadfastly true.

There is nothing in this chapter that can be called crucial. True, it reads like history, nothing suggestive of its being anything else; only let it be admitted that a skilful writer of fiction might, without evil intention, affect a historical air after the manner of Robinson Crusoe. But in estimating his achievement in this beginning of his story, and still more in the development of it in the chapters which follow, it must be remembered that the negative theory ascribes the creation of the fiction to the age which is somewhat vaguely called the age of the Maccabees, some two hundred and fifty or three hundred years after the time in which the story is dated; and it is not to be forgotten that between the age to which Daniel belonged—that of the great Babylonian conquerors, and after them their Persian conquerors—and the age of the Maccabees, when both Babylon and Persia had given place to the inheritors of the divided empire of Alexander, the nation had undergone a vast social revolution. Accordingly, the question we have to face is whether in circumstances so greatly changed, and in the absence, which the hypothesis requires, of all knowledge of the social life of Babylon, with its distinctive classes of Magians and Chaldeans, except such as might have survived through vague tradition, it was possible for a writer of fiction to re-create such a picture of those then olden times as we have in the beginning of this book.

Assuming the picture to be historical, as it professes to be, it has all the appearance of being true to its age, true to the character of devout godly Jewish youths, and true to the circumstances into which, as the captives of Babylon, they were thrown, including their training for important positions

CAMEO PORTRAIT OF NEBUCHADNEZZAR.

A votive offering engraved on a black stone, dedicated to Merodach.

in the service of those whose captives they were. The historical hypothesis is without difficulty ; not so that which ascribes the book to the creative imagination of some hundreds of years after prophets had ceased out of the land.

The last verse of the first chapter connects the end of the life of Daniel very significantly with its beginning. It is as if the historian or biographer should say: Such is the beginning of the life in Babylon of a captive who lived to see the end of the captivity of his people, and who, though a captive and a stranger in a strange land, and from the first "undefiled" by its idolatries, rose to high dignities and powers, to the great benefit both of his own people and of the people whose servants they were. The verse thus understood is a key to the whole record which follows, which, as already remarked, is not a history either of Babylon or of Judah or of Persia, but of important events in relation to them all, in which Daniel was the interpreter and minister of the Divine will.

2. Nebuchadnezzar's Dream (Dan. 2).

The second chapter records one of the most important events in the life of Daniel. The God of Daniel revealed to the King of Babylon, in a dream, a future so great and so different from all the king's own conceptions of things that even when interpreted the king's idea of it must still have been imperfect and shadowy. We are told how the Magians failed to discover the dream which had vanished from the king's mind, and how they were threatened with death.

This chapter may be regarded as one of the decisive chapters of the book. The difficulty of accounting for its contents, if they are not historical, is ten times greater than that on which I have remarked in relation to the first chapter.

The *creation* of the story which it contains by anyone living three hundred years after the days of Nebuchadnezzar, may well be called a literary impossibility. There is not a single touch in it, or reference, or shade of expression, that betrays the age of the Maccabees or any later age; whereas the whole is in keeping with the age of the despotic monarchs of Babylon, and of great professors of, or pretenders to, superhuman knowledge and authority, known as Magians and Chaldeans. The Magians were at once the masters and the slaves of the king, ruling him by the force of superstition, but absolutely at his mercy when they failed to do his pleasure. The requirement that they should recover for him his forgotten dream may seem very unreasonable, but the requirements of tyrants are not measured by reason but by passion. And in this instance the passion of the tyrant was heated by the dread that there was some terrible secret hidden in his lost dream. And if he could not extort it from the Magians, or from the powers which they professed to have at their command, he could at least wreak his vengeance upon them.

The part ascribed to Daniel and his companions is worthy of the God-trusting and God-fearing men who are introduced to us in the first chapter. He and they took refuge in the God whose they were and whom they served—the God of their fathers—and *He* revealed to Daniel, in a "vision of the night," what the king had forgotten. It was a matter of deep concern, affecting many generations, and ended in a prediction in which the ancient promise to Abraham should at length find a glorious fulfilment.

The mode in which the prediction was given, both to the king and to Daniel, was one of the "divers manners" in which, according to the author of the Epistle to the Hebrews, God was pleased to speak to the Fathers. We have other instances of it in the history of Abraham and of Abraham's great-grandson

Joseph, and even in the history of circumstances connected with the birth and childhood of our Lord (Matt. **1.** 20; **2.** 13, 19). In the case before us the mind of a heathen monarch, while he slept, was made the medium through which God was pleased to make known what was to happen in days to come, the issues of which would reach to the end of time. But the certainty and reality of the revelation vouchsafed to the King of Babylon was not left to depend on his word or memory. Both the fact and the meaning of it come to us through one whom our Lord calls a prophet, and who is represented as declaring that he owed both the fact and the meaning to God Himself.

Is this history or is it fiction? As history there is nothing in it to cause stumbling to the Christian; for with the Christian it is not an open question whether God foreknows "things that should come to pass hereafter," nor is it an open question whether, foreknowing, God may reveal the future to others. Nor ought either of these to be open questions, matters of doubt, even with Theists; for the true Theist cannot limit either the knowledge of God or His right and power to communicate of that knowledge "according to the good pleasure of His will." That there have been and that there are pretenders to the gift of prophecy is certain, and we are bound to try the spirits whether they be of God. But we are not at liberty to assume that a Scripture claiming to be prophetic is *ipso facto* to be condemned, or at least to be treated as we would treat a suspicious character.

Reserving for a later page some important considerations relating to this matter, what we have to note at present is the *fact* that the dream, re-discovered and interpreted by Daniel, is an avowed prophecy, and the further *fact* that even if you defer its origin to the age of the Maccabees, or any other, two or three hundred years after the days of Daniel, it is still prophetic. It culminates in one of the most remarkable predictions of the Old Testament, that of the stone cut out without hands, which smote the image which the king had seen in his dream, and which became a great mountain and filled the whole earth (*vv.* 34, 35). Interpreting the stone that was cut out of the mountain without hands, Daniel says, "In the days of these kings [described in *vv.* 31–43] shall the God of Heaven set up a kingdom that shall never be destroyed; and the kingdom shall not be left to other people, but it shall break in pieces and consume all these kingdoms, and it shall stand for ever" (*vv.* 44, 45). That this is a prophecy of the kingdom of the Messiah cannot be doubted by any Christian. Not only is there no other interpretation of it possible, or possessed of the shadow of reasonableness, but it supplied, as we have seen, Christ and His herald with the very terms in which they announced their common mission, "The Kingdom of Heaven is at hand."

Here, then, we have a real prophecy, specially honoured by Christ and His forerunner, who linked to it their own glorious mission. How shall we account for it? Was it of man or of God? Was the conception which it embodied of the reign of the long-expected world's Ruler and Saviour, the fruit of the profound meditations of some godly thinker hundreds of years after the days of Daniel? If so, that thinker must have been a prophet; and, as a prophet, filled with godly jealousy for the honour of God and of truth. He could not hide the truth concerning it, and invent the strange story of a dream by a heathen monarch who had been in his grave some hundreds of years, and of an interpretation by a Jewish captive, of whose very existence the non-historical hypothesis stands in doubt: inventing at the same time conversations between the imaginary dreamer and the imaginary interpreter, to cloak the fiction with an air of truthfulness. Can all this be thought credible? It is not after the manner of true prophets. There is nothing more notable in the story, as it lies before us in the book, than the godly concern of the man to whom the interpretation of the dream is ascribed that the king and all others should clearly understand that he owed his knowledge of it entirely and absolutely to God. By his training and professional position he might have posed as one of a class who claimed to be possessed of superhuman powers, before whose eyes hidden things in heaven and earth were revealed. But he would not let it be thought for a moment that he was gifted with any such powers. His Magianism was nought, and could render him no more service than it did those other members of his class whose lives were now in dire peril. He took pains, before he made known to the king the great discovery which he had made, to impress on his mind that this discovery was of God, and the king so understood it. With whatever superstition, as well as favour, the king might regard the person of the interpreter, his confession is clear : " Of a truth it is that your God is a God of gods, and a Lord of kings, and a revealer of secrets, seeing that thou couldst reveal this secret."

In the concern thus shown for the honour of God we have surely the very heart of the writer of the narrative, the heart of one who would tremble either to speak or write falsely for God, even for the honour of God. And we ask again whether it is credible that this story is an imaginary invention, or anything else than the truthful history of a revelation which God was pleased to give of things that should come to pass hereafter.

This one great prophecy respecting the Kingdom of Heaven carries with it the entire weight and burden of the prophecies which precede it in the dream, and of the circumstances of their interpretation, as will be further shown when we consider Dr. Driver's admission of the genuineness or reality of this prophecy.* The whole must stand or fall together. Fiction and prediction cannot be commingled here. There is a very general consensus of opinion as to the significance of at least the greater part of the image which Nebuchadnezzar saw in his dream. But prophecies may be genuine, even should good wise men fail to agree as to their meaning, a notable example of which we have in the case of prophecies relating to the second coming of our Lord in the book of the Revelation; but of this more will have to be said later on. Meantime we claim this second chapter of the Book of Daniel as historical, and, we may add, Divine.

3. The Image of Gold (Dan. 3).

The reader must not fall into the mistake of supposing, that the events recorded in the third chapter took place in immediate succession to the events recorded in the second. If they did, wonder would be felt at once how the man who had been so impressed by the discovery and interpretation of his dream by Daniel, that is, by Daniel's God, should act the part that is ascribed to him here. But the events of the two chapters are separated by many years, possibly twenty, for it was in the nineteenth year of the reign of Nebuchadnezzar that the siege of Jerusalem was completed (2 Kings 25. 8), and they were years of incessant war, and of an almost unbroken series of victories.

But it was no part of the function assumed by the author of the Book of Daniel to record the history of these victories.

---

* Dr. Driver in his Introduction, p. 459, after describing the various interpretations given of the four kings or kingdoms spoken of in the dream, says, "In any case the stone cut out without hands represents the kingdom of God, before which all earthly powers are ultimately to fall"; and on p. 479 he says that Daniel "interpreted Nebuchadnezzar's dreams, and foretold, as a seer, something of the future fate of the Chaldean and Persian empires." The significance of these admissions will be pointed out later on.

Let the men of Babylon do that in their own way and in their own spirit, glorifying Nebo, Bel, and Merodach, and the conqueror who, in the name and for the honour of his gods, had trodden under foot, as Sennacherib claimed to have done (Isa. **36.** 19 ; **37.** 12), the gods of all the nations that opposed his progress. Nor did the author of the book concern himself even to tell the story of the life of Daniel and of his three faithful companions during the many years that followed their great triumph, or, rather, the triumph of their God, in the matter of the king's dream. What a field there was here for myth, or legend, or tradition ; in short, for such fiction as originated the stories of Susanna and Bel and the Dragon. The absence of everything of the sort is a tribute to the historic *bona fides* of the book, and a proof of the high and exclusive aim of the author not to glorify a man, not even to gratify a legitimate curiosity respecting him, but to set forth great events of Divine providence which concerned not only the time then being, but all the times that were to be.

Nebuchadnezzar is now at home, full of this world's glory and of pride. The Jerusalem which he spared when he carried away those distinguished Jewish captives of the "King's seed and of the princes," with whose story the book begins, is now in ruins. And Egypt, which was mightier far than Judah, the rival of the great cities of the Euphrates in wisdom, art, and civilisation, has bowed to his authority. His empire is well-nigh universal, and he imagines that neither God nor man can resist his will.

How soon after his return from his Syrian, Palestinian, and Egyptian conquests he resolved on the erection of a colossal statue in honour of his patron god, to whom he would ascribe his victories, we do not know. Some of the vast structures which he had seen in Egypt, and which were visible at great distances, may have suggested the idea. Whether it was so or not, we are now in possession of some facts relating to the plain of Duva which have an important bearing on the verisimilitude of the story in the book. In the *Speaker's Commentary* on this chapter we are told that during the trigonometrical survey of Mesopotamia, Captain Selby ascertained that in the level plain of Duva the dip of the horizon at twelve miles is fifty-three feet. Now this image was sixty cubits, that is, ninety-five feet, in height, and nine feet in breadth. When the sun struck upon the shining metal in the morning it would be visible all round Babylon to a distance of from fifteen to twenty miles.

"There had probably been long preparations for the eventful day," says Dr. Payne Smith. " The army of veteran warriors had returned and paraded the country, displaying their spoils. The king at its head had been received with humble prostrations, and all that self-abasement and degradation with which an oriental bows before the representative, not of law and righteousness, but of force. The most famous artists had been gathered to decide upon the attitude and features of the god, the size and shape had been carefully modelled, the plates of gold skilfully laid over the frame, and at last all was ready for the feast of dedication. And so, finally, the command goes forth that all the officials of the realm shall gather round the king for the setting up of the image. Having thus provided for a large and glorious concourse of high nobles at this grand ceremony in honour of so many victories, and of the establishment of so vast an empire, as they stood marshalled in order according to their rank, a herald made proclamation as follows: 'To you it is commanded, O people, nations, and languages, that at what time ye hear the sound of the cornet . . . . and all kinds of musick, ye fall down and worship the golden image Nebuchadnezzar the king hath set up: and whoso falleth not down and worshippeth shall the same hour be cast into the midst of a burning fiery furnace.'" *

In all this there is nothing to awaken the slightest suspicion that it is anything but a history of facts. The part ascribed to the king, with all its extravagant assumptions, and all its threatenings of destruction, is the most natural possible in the circumstances. Before his greatness and absoluteness no one had a right to live but as he chose to let him, and as to anyone daring to think and act otherwise than as the king ordained, the idea of it lay in a region of thought of which the despotic mind had no conception. The mad "fury" of the king when he was told that there were three men, and these, men whom he had long favoured, although they belonged to a people whom he had crushed out of national existence, who had absolutely refused to worship his god,—and his equally mad fury in the after decree against such as dared to speak against the God of the men upon whom the seven times heated furnace had no power,—is quite in keeping with all that we know of the man and all that we know of men like him.

The conduct of the three men who would not bow head or heart to the golden image is equally characteristic of *them*. There is no trace of fanaticism in their spirit; it is calm and trustful as was the spirit of the Apostles in a later age, when they stood at the bar of the arch enemies of the infant Church. Shadrach and his brethren knew that their God was able to deliver them, but they did not pretend to know or assume that He would do so. At any rate, from their duty they would not shrink, and the result, a glorious miracle, and more. We do not presume to say that the mysterious person whom the king saw walking in the midst of the fire was He whom we call "the Son of God," or whom even the King of Babylon would call

* *Exposition of Daniel*, chaps. 3 to 6, pp. 87 *seq.*

"a son of God." The Revised Version says, "like a son of the gods." A heathen king could scarcely rise higher than these words indicate, but the miracle suggests to us an anticipation of a most blessed Christian truth—the presence of the Lord of Martyrs with His faithful servants in all their sufferings for His Name's sake, and, indeed, in all the sufferings of this life.

We decline to regard the miracle of escape from the burning fiery furnace as involving any presumption against the literal historic truthfulness of the story, either on the ground of an *a priori* objection to all miracles, or on the ground of any specific objection to this particular miracle. The miracles of the Bible are not arbitrary prodigies. Not only are they all manifestations of Divine power, whether in judgment or in mercy, and attestations of a Divine will, but there is to be seen in them an adaptedness to the circumstances in which they were wrought. This has often been remarked with reference to the redemption from Egypt, and the special miracles which accompanied it. The remark is equally true with reference to the miracles which were wrought in the days of the great crisis of the faith of Israel during the ministry of Elijah. And it is equally true of the famous miracle by which the "three children" were saved from the devouring flames of the fiery furnace. There was now, as in former times, a great conflict, virtually, on the old question: whether Jehovah was God, or whether Baal. Baal, now the Bel of Babylon, seemed the victor everywhere. Neither gods nor men could stand before him. The one people in all the earth who worshipped the Living God were as helpless, to all appearance, before him, as were those who worshipped the works of their own hands. And both the one and the other needed a great demonstration that Jehovah was God; the one to be assured that the calamities which had befallen them were not the result of powerlessness on the part of their God, but rather

MUSIC AND WORSHIP IN ASSYRIAN TIMES.

This illustrates the musical accompaniment of worship in the later Babylonian age referred to in Dan. 3. The King Assur-bani-pal (i.e., Sardanapalus) is offering a libation on returning from a lion hunt.

To face p. 92.

of their faithlessness to His service; the other to be taught the falsity of their boastings in the might of their idols.

However imperfectly the demonstration might be appreciated, it was given in a form that would carry the fame of it far and wide through the dominions of the King of Babylon, and would give courage and comfort to all who might suffer for conscience sake. I am not aware that we have any descriptive record in tablet, or other form, of a Babylonian "fiery furnace," but we have a significant reference to the penal use of fire in Babylon in Jer. 29. 22—"The LORD make thee like Zedekiah and like Ahab [a prophet of lies, *v.* 21], whom the King of Babylon roasted in the fire." We have further evidence that burning alive was, as a matter of historical fact, a Babylonian mode of execution. There is an older notice in the records of Assurbanipal, King of Assyria, who thus revenged himself on his rebellious brother, a viceroy of Babylon about B.C. 648. We dare not moralise on the heathenism of this cruel method of execution, when we remember its adoption and practice for many centuries, by nations calling themselves Christian, and that for no other crime than one identical with the crime of the three faithful ones in the days of Nebuchadnezzar.

The critics have found a very quarry of objections to the historic character of the Book of Daniel, in the names of the musical instruments which are mentioned in this third chapter. But the quarry is now well-nigh exhausted, and, from the first, the arguments which it supplied were based on a strange obliviousness of facts. The assumption which gave them the force they seemed to have, was that the age of Daniel was an age of national isolation—that ancient nations, eastward, westward, and southward, of which history tells us, were so separated and stood so entirely apart from each other, that their languages could not borrow from one another, and that the existence of words in the literature of any one of them, traceable to the language of another, was sufficient to throw doubt on the genuineness of the script in which they were found. But nations which were so intermingled on the battle-field, which were in the habit of transporting captives taken in war from their own lands to the lands of their conquerors, had evidently some means, notwithstanding the diversity of tongues, of carrying on negotiations with each other, and could not save themselves, if they would, from acting and re-acting upon each other, in the use of words, especially such words as might be of frequent and popular use. Perceiving this, any critic, intent only on truth, might be expected to conclude that the occurrence of a word whose root might possibly be traced to another language, say Greek, or Persian or even Sanscrit, was no sufficient reason for questioning the genuineness of a book that was otherwise well attested.

Even if it could be proved, which it has not been, that the names of the musical instruments that are said to have been used in Babylon at the dedication of the golden image, are mostly of Greek origin, it would not prove that the book was not written till the Greek language had been made dominant by the conquests of Alexander. It is now known that Greek trade with the continent of Asia is of vast antiquity, and that caravans carried Greek goods far and wide, carrying their native names with them. It is also known that the names of musical instruments are some of the oldest of all existent words, and their general prevalence is, not without reason, held to be one of the many arguments in proof of a common origin of languages finally so remote as the Semitic and the Aryan family of tongues.*

---

* Dr. Payne Smith, *Exposition of Daniel* chaps. 1–6, pp. 95, etc. Those who are interested in this matter will find it more fully discussed in the Appendix No. 2 on the Early Commerce of Babylon with India 700–300 B.C.

In view of all this, we are not careful to trace the roots and origin of the names of the musical instruments that called the people of Babylon to worship the golden image. The monarch who, with whatever amount of boastful exaggeration, summoned all peoples, nations, and languages, to assemble on so great an occasion, could not fail to have had brought to him from all lands that were known to him, the best they could contribute to his Imperial glory.*

4, The King's Madness (Dan. 4).

Of all the marvellous things recorded in the Book of Daniel, the story told us in this chapter probably appears to many readers as the most strange. It does not take its place with the great miracles of the deliverance from the fiery furnace and from the lions' den. That which is distinctly supernatural in it is the specific foretelling of the judgment which befell the king. As to the nature of the king's affliction, medical science, as we shall see, has thrown such light upon it that all occasion for stumbling has passed away. The date of the occurrence is not known. What we do know is that the affliction lasted seven years, but we do not know how long he lived after.

On the narrative in the Book of Daniel, its verisimilitude, and the possibility of its truth or otherwise, Dr. Pusey consulted a gentleman who in his day was an authority on insanity and kindred questions. In summarising the result he says, "It

---

* Some have compared, or rather contrasted, the gathering of the representatives of Imperial Babylon to celebrate the glory of Nebuchadnezzar and his god, and the recent gathering of the representatives of Imperial England to express their loyalty and affection for Queen Victoria, and to give thanks to the God of Heaven for her long and beneficent reign. I have ascertained that on this occasion there were nearly twenty different musical instruments made use of; the greater number of which are certainly not of English origin.

is now conceded that the madness of Nebuchadnezzar agrees with the description of a rare sort of disease, called Lycanthropy, from one form of it, of which our earliest notice of it is in a Greek medical writer of the fourth century after our Lord, in which the sufferer retains his consciousness in other respects, but imagines himself to be changed into some animal, and acts, up to a certain point, in conformity with that persuasion. Those who imagined themselves changed into wolves, howled like wolves, and (there is reason to believe falsely) accused themselves of bloodshed. Others imitated the cries of dogs; it is said that others thought themselves nightingales, lions, cats, or cocks, and these crowed like a cock. It was no dissimilar form of disease, that others imagined that their bodies were, wholly or in part, changed into some brittle substance, whence they avoided contact with other substances lest they should be broken. Others had similar delusions, varying incidentally from each other."*

There is nothing strange or apparently incredible in the incidents of Nebuchadnezzar's illness that is not paralleled in medical facts which will be found in Dr. Pusey's pages. "My opinion (says Dr. Brown, as the result of 30 years' experience) is that of all mental powers or conditions, the idea of personal indentity is but rarely enfeebled, and that it is never extinguished. The *Ego* and *non-Ego* may be confused. The *Ego*, however, continues to preserve the personality." This even in the case of men who called themselves Angels, Dukes, Christ, and even God. "I think it probable (Dr. Browne continues), because consistent with experience in similar forms of mental affection, that Nebuchadnezzar retained his conscious personality during the whole course of his degradation, even while he ate grass as oxen; and that he

---

* Dr. Pusey on the *Book of Daniel*, pp 427-442.

may have prayed fervently that the cup might pass from him." "That he prayed (adds Dr. Pusey) is related in Daniel with the simplicity of truth; ignorant scepticism pronounces it impossible; true physics and psychology attest the reality of the description." The late Dean of Canterbury (Dr. Payne Smith) was right in saying, "It is one of the many proofs of the credibility of the Book of Daniel that we should thus find in it an account of a strange malady, so described as that the physical facts narrated agree with observations made since by scientific men in modern times. Here we have a species of mania now well known, but then absolutely new (so far at least as we can tell). And the description of it finds its explanation in facts since scientifically observed."

The narrative, intent on its grand moral purpose, does not gratify the natural curiosity which asks, who took care of the *demented* king and of the kingdom during the seven years of his mania? "We may quite believe (with Dr. Payne Smith) that during this time the king was not left without anxious care and attendance. His restoration to his kingdom immediately that he was healed of his disease proves that there were those who maintained his rights. His wife Amyntis, for whose happiness he had done so much, if not Daniel, his faithful visier, would care for him; and so while he supposed himself to be an ox, they may have supplied him with needful food, and encouraged him to remain in some sheltered thicket, where they could take care of him and guard him from molestation, and do all that was possible for his health and comfort."

On a review of this whole story I have no hesitation in saying that it is easier to believe that it is fact than that it is fiction. We may take higher ground than this, and say that as fact it stands any test that can be legitimately applied to it; as fiction its origin is well nigh incredible. That which is avowedly supernatural from its very nature, such as the prophetic character of the king's dream, involves in it nothing that is exceptional or out of keeping with what we are told elsewhere of God's ways of making known His will; while the moral ends contemplated by it are the very highest. The whole spirit of the narrative is *Godly*, and worthy of the great prophetic succession in which Daniel has his place. The parts played in the story by Daniel and by the king are characteristic and significant. Daniel's "thoughts troubled him" (*v*. 19) when he was told of the dream and had discovered its meaning; and with the mingled courtesy and fidelity which distinguished his whole course, he said, "My Lord, let the dream be to them that hate thee, and the interpretation thereof to thine enemies,"—" Wherefore, O King, let my counsel be acceptable to thee, and break off thy sins by righteousness, and thine iniquities by showing mercy to the poor; if it may be a lengthening of thy tranquillity." But the king, Pharaoh-like, hardened his heart. For twelve months, the warning he had received was unheeded. He had " rest " from the many wars which he had waged (*v*. 4), and expended the wealth of which he had robbed many lands, in making his city the wonder of nations. Enthroning himself proudly in his palace, and surveying, as a god among men, the vast structures which he had built at a terrible cost of both " righteousness " and " mercy " (*v*. 27), " he spake," possibly in conscious joy that the threatened doom had not befallen him," and said, " Is not this great Babylon that I have built for the house of the kingdom by the might of my power, and for the honour of my majesty." (*v*. 30). In that very hour, while the word was in the king's mouth, there fell a voice from heaven, saying, "O king Nebuchadnezzar, to thee it is spoken; The kingdom is departed from thee." The voice may have been heard only by the inner ear of the king; but it was unmistakeable and had immediate effect.

INDIA-HOUSE INSCRIPTION,

In which Nebuchadnezzar glorifies himself as the builder of Babylon.

A full translation of it has been published by the Rev. C. J. Ball in the *Proceedings of the Biblical Archæology Society*.

To face p. 74.]

The history of what befell the king comes to us in the form of a decree from the king himself, in which he would show all nations and languages "what God had wrought towards him." In the sentiments of that decree, we may trace, not any dictation from the mouth of Daniel, but the fruit of Daniel's teaching.

5, Belshazzar's Feast (Dan. 5).

There is here another gap in the public history of Babylon on which the Book of Daniel throws no light. That Nebuchadnezzar died in B.C. 561, and that Babylon fell before the arms of Cyrus in B.C. 538, may be taken as an approximately correct statement. But for the history of the twenty-three intervening years, we must look elsewhere. That Nebuchadnezzar was succeeded by his son Evil-Merodach, whose reign was brief, and that, at a later period, the throne was usurped by Nabonidus, the father of Belshazzar, seems well established. The only events with which the personal history of Daniel at this time are connected are two visions with which he was favoured, one in the first year of Belshazzar (ch. 7), and the other in his third year (ch. 8). The prophet was not now in any public service, but was summoned out of his retirement by the terror that was created by the handwriting on the wall.

Assuming for the present that whatever difficulties are connected with the names of Belshazzar and Darius, will be found satisfactorily discussed in a Supplemental Chapter, we read the account of Belshazzar's feast, as it lies before us in the Book of Daniel, to see whether it contains anything that can throw suspicion on its *bona fides*, or anything which we can accept as substantial evidence of its truth.

That Daniel was not at this time the favoured servant of the Sovereign, but was living in privacy and obscurity, excites no surprise. The surprise would have been to find it otherwise. The known caprices of absolute monarchs in raising to power, and casting down from power, whom they would, would itself account for our finding Daniel the greatest man in the empire in the days of Nebuchadnezzar, and neglected and practically forgotten in the days of Nabonidus and Belshazzar. But other reasons may have contributed to the change. If Nabonidus was not the legitimate heir of Nebuchadnezzar, but a usurper, he may have deemed it a wise policy to get rid of the old friends and supporters of the family of Nebuchadnezzar, and surround himself with unscrupulous favourites who owed nothing to the former dynasty. In whatever way the change came about, we may be sure it was very welcome to Daniel. It was not his ambition that raised him to power. In the exercise of power, while he possessed it, he only acted on the instruction which had been prophetically given to his people, to seek the good of the land into which they were to be carried captives. The power to which he was raised, was thrust upon him by an absolute king, and if it was taken from him by an absolute king, it left him what he had been at first, and what he had never ceased to be, the faithful servant of the King of kings. And now while probably having to endure, among those whose exulted over him in his fall, and among the heathen around who hated his nation, the painfulness of the very ancient prediction with which he was familiar (**9. 11**), that his people, unfaithful to their God, should be "a byword among all nations whither the LORD should lead them" (Deut. **28. 37**), he was especially blessed by the God whom he had ever faithfully served, in that he was honoured to receive, by the hand of an angelic messenger, two visions, which are recorded in his book (chaps. **7** and **8**).

We are thus prepared for the part which is ascribed to him in the story of Belshazzar's feast, and which is so characteristic of him, that it can scarcely be other than genuine. When we hear him say to the drunken reveller, "Let thy gifts be to thyself, and give thy rewards to another; yet I will read the writing unto the king, and make known to him the interpretation," and when, after reciting facts in the history of Nebuchadnezzar, which should have been a warning to his successors, he said, "Thou his son,* O Belshazzar, hast not humbled thine heart, though thou knewest all this, but hast lifted up thyself against the Lord of Heaven, ... and the God in Whose hand thy breath is, and Whose are all thy ways, thou hast not glorified,"—we exclaim at once, this is the old Daniel, the man with whom we became familiar long ago, the man who did not shrink from demanding of the mightiest potentate of his age that he should "break off his sins by righteousness, and his iniquities by showing mercy to the poor," (4. 27), the man who was ever faithful to his God in the face of triumphant idolatries,—the same man certainly, whether the favourite of kings or the despised of kings. The least that can be said is, that if the Daniel of Belshazzar's feast be an invention, the Daniel whose acquaintance we first formed nearly seventy years before, must have been an invention likewise; and the inventor has shown great skill in preserving the consistency of the character of which he was the creator. But he is himself involved in an inconsistency which cannot be explained. For (a) he must be regarded as in moral and spiritual sympathy with the character which he has created. But, (b) if so, how could a writer of the high moral and religious spirit which this whole narrative breathes represent as facts what are only the fictions of his own imagination? We find no

---

* How Belshazzar should be called the "son" of Nebuchadnezzar will be fully considered in the Supplemental Chapter.

solution of this moral problem in the supposition that the imagination of the writer had a certain amount of tradition to work upon. He must have been conscious that what he gave to the world as history, was not what it seemed to be.

The pressure of this difficulty becomes still greater when we turn to the narrative of the handwriting on the wall. Let it be read in full with Daniel's interpretation.

"This is the writing that was written, MENE, MENE, TEKEL, UPHARSIN. This is the interpretation of the thing; MENE, God hath numbered thy Kingdom, and finished it. TEKEL, thou art weighed in the balances, and art found wanting. PERES (the U in Uparsin being the conjunction *and*, Parsin the plural of Peres), thy kingdom is divided and given to the Medes and Persians."

We have here not only a translation of the words, but an exposition of what they were intended to intimate. The words themselves being,—*Mene*, numbered; *Tekel*, weighing; *Peres*, divided, perhaps too with a reference to the name of the conquerors.

The first remark that occurs to one on reading this story is that, allowing the "handwriting" to have any meaning approaching to that which is given it in the interpretation of it, the occurrence which it relates must have taken place at the time to which the book assigns it, the time when Babylon fell into the hands of the Medes and Persians. The Persian rule, whose beginning was announced by this mysterious handwriting, passed away two hundred years before the days of the Maccabees. And we cannot imagine a writer in these days having a trustworthy traditional knowledge which could enable him to reproduce the occurrences at the feast of Belshazzar—the hypothesis being that the Book of Daniel had then no existence—nor can we imagine a writer of that time, or indeed of any time, having the genius to invent the sublime and awe-inspiring story of the handwriting on the wall, having no precedent which he could mould to that effect.

But now turn to Daniel and see the perfect verisimilitude of the whole narrative. It was a supernatural intervention for a great moral purpose; and with such intervention Daniel was familiar, both in the age-long history of his people, and in his own life's experience. This handwriting was a providential sequel to God's dealing with Nebuchadnezzar; the dream, which, as interpreted by Daniel, fore-indicated a coming judgment, unless it was averted by the king's repentance of his unrighteousness and unmercifulness (4. 27). Daniel remembered how that the king continued for twelve months in the pride of his power, heedless of the warning which he had received, and how that then, while he was glorying in his greatness and congratulating himself probably, as already remarked, on his immunity from the threatened judgment, the voice of the long-suffering God was heard, as a voice to which no resistance could be offered, "The kingdom is departed from thee?" It was the same God, God of judgment and of mercy, that now sent the mysterious hand to write the doom of Belshazzar on the wall. There was this differerence—to Nebuchadnezzar there was given time for repentance, and a virtual promise of mercy; to Belshazzar there was neither. Daniel understood the whole matter at once.

Out of office in Babylon, he was in prophetic communion with Heaven. In the first year of Belshazzar he had that wonderful vision which revealed to him a succession of four empires, three of which would follow Babylon, necessarily presupposing the ending of Babylon. He "wrote" the vision (7. 1), and he tells us that his cogitations much troubled him, that his countenance changed, and that he kept the matter in his heart (*v.* 27). Two years later he had another vision which caused him great astonishment (**8.** 27). Over these visions, which he "kept in his heart," he must have pored day and night, searching, like other prophets (1 Pet. **1.** 12), what these things might mean. He could not find in them a definite prediction of the revolution which was so near at hand. But this at least he saw, that Babylon was at some time or other to give place to another power. The "heart" in which he kept the things he had seen in vision, was deeply moved as he heard from time to time of the dishonour which was habitually done by Belshazzar to the God of his fathers, the Holy and the True, and many tears must have been shed by the good man as he heard of the king's devotion to idols, and to all the licentiousness of idol worship. He may have often cried "O Lord, how long." The summons to the banqueting hall found him prepared in spirit for all that followed. Therefore, without surprise and without trembling, and, I may add, without rudeness or glorying over a fallen enemy, he charged Belshazzar with the sins which were now to be Divinely avenged, and read and interpreted the fatal words in which was made known his doom and the doom of Babylon.

All this is in keeping both with the Divine providence of which Daniel was the minister, and with the character of Daniel himself. They may object who do not believe in aught that is supernatural. But they who believe in God, and that He concerns Himself with the affairs of men, and that He has actually interposed in men's affairs at sundry times and in divers manners, other than such as we call the action of natural law, see in what is recorded in the Book of Daniel, of the Divine dealings with the kings of Babylon, only reason to rejoice that there is a God that judgeth in the earth.

Now if the history which we have of this writing on the wall is a true history, it must have been recorded at the time of its occurrence. And by whom could it have been recorded? By whom but by Daniel himself? "He wrote," as we have seen, the first vision which he recorded in the days of Belshazzar—and we may be sure he "wrote" the others as well. It was not of less importance that the story of this Divine intervention with the foul revelries of Belshazzar should be recorded, and correctly recorded. And this could be done only by the man who alone understood it. Tradition may preserve some knowledge of palpable outstanding occurrences, and it might long preserve the memory of some mysterious event that had happened during Belshazzar's feast; but it could not have preserved the clear definite statement of the words that were written, with the declared significance of the words, and with the words of the king and of the intrepreter. Carried by tradition through the centuries that separated the age of the historical Daniel from the age of the historical Judas Maccabeus, there would have gathered around the story a cloud of fable and superstition in which the plain facts and the grand moral of the event would have been lost. Preserved, as it has been, in what has been almost universally accepted as a contemporary record, it is true to the period, the circumstances, and the characters of the men whom it concerns. And it is so devoid of any indication, direct or indirect, of more recent events, events of the Persian period, the engrossing events of the conquests of Alexander and of the reigns of his successors, including that bitterest enemy of the Jewish people, Antiochus Epiphanes—one must be excused for saying that it is not possible to believe, at least on such rational grounds as justify historical faith, that it was written in that later age in which Antiochus Epiphanes was the leading actor.

Studying the fifth chapter of the Book of Daniel to see whether it contains anything that can throw doubt on its historical character, I not only fail to find anything of the sort, but I find much to confirm my faith. In this I am not appealing to a purely, or even mainly, *subjective* judgment. The criticism which subordinates external evidence to impressions produced on the critic's mind should be sternly rejected. But our appeal to the impression which the narrative in this chapter produces, presupposes *objective* evidence, and is intended only to confirm it. The external and the internal are in this case mutually confirmatory.

6. The Lions' Den (Dan. 6).

We have here a record which is of immense practical value to the persecuted servants of God in all ages, of a great deliverance wrought by God on behalf of his faithful servant Daniel. We have seen how the father of the Maccabean family drew encouragement from it to stimulate his sons to endeavour to rescue the nation out of the hands of, perhaps, the most malignant persecutor that had ever sought their ruin. He did not venture to predict a great miracle on their behalf, but he saw in it evidence that God does not forsake those "who trust in Him." The story teaches us still the same lesson. Children read it with wonder and interest; older people read it with thankfulness to the God Who has power over the wildest animal passions, even as He has power over the raging of the sea.

Our plea for the historical character of the deliverance of Shadrach and his friends is equally valid in defence of the later miracle, the deliverance of Daniel when cast into the lions' den. This later miracle took place after the Persian conquest of Babylon, in the days of "Darius the Median," who although he had "received" the kingdom from the leader of the Persian hosts, regarded himself as not less "sovereign" than Cyrus himself, and exercised, uncontrolled, all the powers of an

A CAGED LION ABOUT TO BE LET OUT TO BE HUNTED.

This slab illustrates the object for which lions were stowed up in dens or pits.

To face p. 82.

absolute monarch. The miracles of the fiery furnace and the lions' den differ only in circumstance, not in spirit. The absolutism of the decree of Darius was akin to that of Nebuchadnezzar; and the faith which the terror of the lions' den could not shake was akin to that which did not shrink from the fiery furnace.

What information may be gleaned from the now discovered tablets to illustrate the story of the lions' den, I do not know. But if we look forward to the days when a power not yet born when Babylon and Persia were supreme, became the heir of their ambition, we shall very often hear a cry, the very echo of the decree of Darius, " Christianos ad leones." And we shall find men and women submitting themselves to the cruel sentence which sends them into the jaws of lions in the Roman arena, in the martyr spirit which animated Daniel and his friends. Those old-world stories which we have in the Book of Daniel are altogether wanting in the features which usually distinguish legend and fiction. They are told with a severe simplicity which fitly represents their intrinsic grandeur. And one wonders that any Christian should fail to see in them a true, real presence of Him of Whom it was said of old, " In all their affliction He was afflicted, and the angel of His presence saved them."

The author of the Epistle to the Hebrews seems to refer to the story of the lions' den and of the fiery furnace when he speaks of those who through faith stopped the mouths of lions and quenched the violence of fire (11. 33, 34). And it may have been the memory of Daniel's deliverance that suggested to the Apostle Paul the words, " I was delivered out of the mouth of the lion " (2 Tim. 4. 17).

CHAPTER VI.

THE VISIONS IN DANIEL VII.—XII.

WE now come to a portion of the Book of Daniel—from ch. 7 onward to the end—which should be decisive to prove either (a) that Daniel was what Christ called him, a prophet, or (b) that the writer of the book was guilty of a grand imposture. There are four visions, the first in the first year of Belshazzar, the second in the third year of Belshazzar, the third in the first year of Darius, and the fourth in the third year of Cyrus. Not being able to fix one of the dates thus indicated, the first of Belshazzar, the year in which he became co-regent with his father, we cannot determine the age of Daniel, except approximately, when this series of visions began, but he must have been then over 80 years of age. And as we cannot determine how long Darius reigned, we cannot say how much older Daniel was when he had the last vision, in the third year of Cyrus. Between the time when he interpreted the dream of Nebuchadnezzar, recorded in the second chapter, and the time of his first vision, the years must have been nearly seventy.* So that we need not be surprised that after such a lapse of time, further revelations should be given him touching the Divine Kingdom which the God of heaven was to set up by other than human hands (2. 45) and touching events that should greatly affect the condition of the

---

* These dates are known :—Daniel was taken captive in B.C. 606, Babylon fell in B.C. 538, when Daniel had been 68 years in captivity. If he was 18 years of age when taken captive, he would be 86 at the taking of Babylon ; if only 14, he would be four years younger.

Chosen People before the coming of the promised King—the vision stretching forward at the same time, dimly and enigmatically, to the very end of the world (ch. 12). Is the record of these visions true history? Let us see what the book itself avers.

The asserted History of the Visions.

In ch. 7 we read—"In the first year of Belshazzar, King of Babylon, Daniel had a dream and visons of his head upon his bed; then he wrote the dream, and told the sum of the matters. Daniel spake and said, I saw in my vision by night, and behold the four winds of the heaven were upon the great sea" (vv. 1, 2). Then, in vv. 14, 15, "I Daniel was grieved in my spirit in the midst of my body, and the visions of my head troubled me. I came near unto one of those that stood by, and asked him the truth of all this. So he made me know the interpretation of the things." And in v. 28, "Hitherto is the end of the matter. As for me Daniel," and so on.

In ch. 8 we read, "In the third year of the reign of Belshazzar, a vision appeared unto me, even unto me Daniel, after that which appeared unto me at the first. And I saw in a vision, and it came to pass, when I saw, that I was in Shushan in the palace, which is in the province of Elam." In v. 15, "It came to pass, when I, even I Daniel, had seen the vision," and so on. In v. 27, "And I Daniel fainted, and was sick certain days; afterward I rose up and did the king's business, and I was astonished at the vision, but none understood it."

In ch. 9 we read, "In the first year of Darius the son of Ahasuerus, of the seed of the Medes, which was made king over the realm of the Chaldeans; in the first year of his reign, I Daniel understood by books the number of the years, whereof the word of the LORD came to Jeremiah the Prophet, that He would accomplish seventy years in the desolations of Jerusalem. And I set my face unto the Lord God, to seek by prayer and supplications, with fasting and sackcloth and ashes. And I prayed unto the LORD my God, and said " (*vv*. 1, 2, 3, 4). In *v*. 17, " while I was speaking in prayer, even the man Gabriel, whom I had seen in the vision at the beginning, being caused to fly swiftly, touched me about the time of the evening oblation, and he informed me and said, O Daniel, I am now come forth to give thee skill and understanding."

In ch. **10** we read, " In the third year of Cyrus, King of Persia, a thing was revealed unto Daniel, whose name was Belteshazzar, and the thing was true, but the time appointed was long. . . . In those days I Daniel was mourning three full weeks. . . . And I Daniel alone saw the vision: for the men that were with me saw not the vision. In *vv*. 11 and 12 Daniel is addressed, and called "a man greatly beloved."

The last vision begins with ch. **11**. 1, and ends with ch. **12.** 5. where we read these solemn and gracious words: "Many of them that sleep in the dust of the earth shall awake, some to everlasting life, and some to shame and everlasting contempt. And they that be wise shall shine as the brightness of the firmament, and they that turn many to righteousness as the stars for ever and ever." "But thou, O Daniel, shut up the words and seal the book until the time of the end. Then I Daniel looked, and, behold, there stood other two, the one on this side the river, and the other on the other side of the bank of the river" (*vv*. 2-5).

I quote these passages thus fully to help the reader to a just impression of the strength and explicitness of the statements of the book respecting its own contents, and I shall argue that we have no alternative but this, that we have here either plain historic truth or deliberate falsehood. But let us first look at the prophecies, and examine exceptions that are taken to them.

A Preliminary Question.

The prophetic visions of Daniel are neither prefaced nor followed by the Old Testament formula "Thus saith the LORD." Does this suggest any doubt as to their origin or their authority? It is alleged, for the most part vaguely, that it does; and even defenders of the book are sometimes disposed to make a distinction between revelations directly "inspired by the Holy Ghost" and revelations communicated by dreams or by angelic agency—allowing some superiority to the former. But is not this tantamount to a denial of the right of God to communicate His will in what "manner" (Heb. 1. 1) and by what means He pleases? And the student of Scripture must see what havoc this distinction would make of large and precious portions of Holy Writ, including the Apocalypse of St. John as well as that of Daniel.

Contrast with the Older Prophets.

Exception is taken to the visions of Daniel on the ground of a contrast between them and the manner of the older acknowledged prophets. But in taking this exception critics forget not only the general statement that God spake to the fathers of old at sundry times and also in divers manners, but also some plain facts that lie before their eyes even in the prophecies that are nearest to Daniel in time. The prophecies of Haggai and Zechariah are not modelled on those of Isaiah, Jeremiah, Hosea, and others. They differ from the older prophets in their *forms* and *modes* of presenting both present and future truth much more than Daniel does from theirs.

There is nothing so strange, so out of the way, so eccentric (if the expression may be used in a semi-scientific sense), in the symbols of Daniel as in the symbols of Ezekiel and Zechariah, and I might say nothing so hard to interpret. In the very first chapter of Ezekiel we have "animal combinations" such as are found fault with in the visions of Daniel,—even more unnatural, that is less capable of realisation in fact (*see vv.* 5 to 11). And in Zechariah we have a variety of strange symbols such as a flying roll twenty cubits long, and an ephah which was lifted up between the earth and the heaven by two women that had wings like the wings of a stork, who carry the ephah to build a house in the land of Shinar (5. 4–11). Here too we have, what is sometimes objected to in Daniel, angels ministering visions to the mind of the prophet (ch. 5). As to the symbols in the Book of Daniel we may content ourselves with a single sentence from Prof. Robertson: "His predictions are highly symbolical, and in their representation of the future apocalyptical; herein resembling parts of Zechariah, and furnishing a model for the New Testament Apocalypse." [*] The fact that in the great Apocalypse of the New Testament by an Apostle we have "animal combinations" in some of the grandest and most significant symbols (4. 6–11) should silence all objections on this score. In the New Testament Apocalypse likewise we have angels ministering visions of things to come (*see* chaps. **8, 9, 10, 11, 12**). That exegetes are not agreed as to the meaning of some portions of the visions of Daniel is no reason why we should regard these visions as of doubtful authority. It might as well be argued, as we have said already, that because devout and learned men differ in their interpretation of some portions of the New Testament Apocalypse, these portions, or the book that con-

---

[*] *Guild Text Book on the Old Testament*, p. 152.

tains them, should be rejected as of man rather than of God. There is nothing in the great dream which Daniel interpreted to the King of Babylon, or in his own later visions, which divides honest and right meaning men so much as the prophecy of the Thousand Years in the twentieth chapter of the Book of the Revelation. The very symbols in Daniel which perplex interpreters, such as the beast that had ten horns, are repeated in the Book of Revelation (Rev. **11.** 3 ; and **23.** 1), and awaken fresh perplexities there.

Interpreters not Agreed.

In view of these facts the defender of the integrity of the Book of Daniel need not concern himself with the fact that there are differences of opinion as to the symbols and imagery of some portions of the book. Nor is he called upon to interpret them. He may leave it in the hands of exegetes to determine—although he may have something to say on the subject later on—what the four kings, kingdoms, or empires, are that are symbolised by the "four beasts" (**7.** 17), and what the "ten horns" of the "fourth beast" (*vv.* 8, 19, 20). But there is one fact that strikes us as we read these symbols or symbolic prophecies, that, intermingled with them, there are glimpses into the invisible world, and foretellings of the reign of the Christ, which can be accounted for only on the hypothesis (if the expression may be used in such a connection) that he who wrote these passages, these Scriptures, was inspired and instructed of God. Reading some of them, one asks, who but an inspired man could dare even to seem to penetrate into the presence of the Eternal, as this man does ; and reading others, one asks, who but an inspired man *could* foresee and anticipate that glorious future which began to be realised in Him who was at once the Son of Man and the Son of God ?

To see the full force of this averment, one should read vision after vision. But the following passages will illustrate the point :—

"I beheld till the thrones were cast down, and the Ancient of Days did sit, whose garment was white as snow and the hair of His head like fine wool ; His throne was like the fiery flame, and His wheels as burning fire. A fiery stream issued and came forth from before Him : thousands ministered unto Him, and ten thousand times ten thousand stood before Him ; the judgment was set, and the books were opened" (7. 10, 9. *Comp.* Rev. 1. 14).

"I saw in the night visions, and, behold, one like the [*or*, a] Son of Man came with the clouds of heaven, and came to the Ancient of Days, and they brought Him near before Him. And there was given Him dominion and glory, and a Kingdom, that all people, and nations, and languages, should serve Him ; His dominion is an everlasting dominion, which shall not pass away, and His Kingdom that which shall not be destroyed" (7. 13, 14).

"O Daniel, I am now come forth to give thee skill and understanding. At the beginning of thy supplication the commandment came forth, and I am come to show thee ; for thou art greatly beloved : therefore understand the matter and consider the vision" (9. 22, 23).

To these visions should be added the prophecy that was contained in the dream of Nebuchadnezzar, which has been already quoted at length.

It has been argued that even if the Scriptures which contain these mysteriously communicated revelations of the future, date only from the second century before Christ, instead of the fourth or fifth, they prove the reality of prophecy and the reality even of Messianic prophecy. And the argument is good so far as it goes. No human foresight could have anticipated the differences between the kingdoms of this world and the Kingdom of Heaven, with the difference between the kings of this world and the King who appeared in the person of Jesus Christ, as set forth in the dream of Nebuchadnezzar and the visions of Daniel. But the argument cannot rest here. If these are genuine prophecies, or in any true sense genuinely prophetic, they must be older than the second century before Christ, for this obvious reason: that there was, according to the testimony of the Maccabees already cited, no prophet in Israel in the second century before Christ. We have books which have come to us from periods both before and after the wars of the Maccabees, but none of them make the slightest pretension to prophetic authority; and if they did they might soon be condemned "out of their own mouth." Apart from this, admit the reality of the prophecies, and rationalism itself cannot conceive a reason why they may not have been delivered five hundred years as well as two hundred before Christ. In either case they must have come from Him to whom all things were known from the beginning. The bold dictum of a critic that such prophecies were "impossible" in B.C. 536, proves nothing but his own incompetence to judge of such matters, and—his arrogance in view of the fact that tens of thousands of devout and learned men *have* believed not only that they were *possible*, but that they had actually been given.

We shall have to return to the matter of these prophecies at a later point.

CHAPTER VII.

THE THEOLOGY OF DANIEL.

THE assertion is boldly made, and repeated as if it was as obvious as an axiom, that the Theology of Daniel differs from the Theology of the earlier prophets. On the contrary, it will be found on examination that it is demonstrably one with the Theology of all the older prophets, from Moses to Malachi, and that what may be quoted as a difference but grows out of the stage which prophecy had now reached.

As to Theology proper, the doctrine of God, not only is Daniel in accord with Moses, but the historical part of the book is one grand protest against idolatry, and one continuous pleading for the alone Godhead of the God of the people who were now disinherited of their land, while the gods of those who had disinherited them were no gods. In fact, there is a significant analogy between the ministry of Moses and what I venture to call the ministry of Daniel. In the face of a nation steeped in idolatry Moses had it given to him to insist that the God of the down-trodden slaves of Egypt was the true God, and his insistence of this claim was enforced by miraculous visitations, in the form of plagues, each one of which was in its own way an exhibition of the falsity and vanity of the gods of Egypt. In very different circumstances, but in ways equally pertinent and impressive, the events of the life of Daniel and his friends were demonstrations of the vanity of gods made by the hands of man, even when made of superhuman stature and adorned with untold golden splendours. What Isaiah taught in sublime and scornful strains of the folly of the man who makes a "graven image" of his god, and then worships it (ch. 45), was taught by Divine Providence in the events of the burning fiery furnace and of the lions' den. These were palpable demonstrations of the true Godhead of Jehovah. "The doctrine of God" poured into the ears of Nebuchadnezzar and of Belshazzar, both explicitly and implicitly, was that which Moses poured into the ear of Pharaoh. And the humiliation of the Chaldeans, when the falsity of their claims to superhuman wisdom was demonstrated by their impotence and helplessness in the presence of the mystery of the forgotten dream, was such as the magicians of Egypt confessed, when, after frequent efforts to rival the doings of Moses, they exclaimed, in the presence of one of the plagues, "This is the finger of God" (Exod. 8. 19).

But allowing that the great "Doctrine of God" in the Book of Daniel is identical with the teaching of Moses and all the Prophets, and that it is taught and enforced in ways characteristic of the position in which Daniel was placed, there are other doctrines, it is alleged, in which the difference is so marked that it becomes a stumbling-block. Dr. Driver admits that the argument is "sometimes stated in an exaggerated form, as when, for instance, it is said that the doctrine of the resurrection, or the distinction of rank and office in the angels, is due to the influence of Parseeism, or that the asceticism of Daniel and his companions, and the frequency of their prayers, etc., are traits peculiar to the later Judaism." But though for such exaggerations "there is no adequate foundation," nevertheless Driver thinks "that the doctrines of the Messiah, of angels, and of the resurrection, and of a judgment on the world, are taught with greater distinctness, and in a more developed form than elsewhere in the Old Testament, and with features approximating to, though not identical with, those met with in the earlier part of the Book of Enoch, cir. 100 B.C." *

If Daniel, or, rather, the writer of the book if he was not Daniel, was indebted to Parseeism, or was under the "influences of Parseeism," how comes it to pass that the book shows no sign of that "influence" in the matter of the fundamental Parsee doctrine of God—the duality of the eternal principles of good and evil, light and darkness—a doctrine which, though not polytheistic, was essentially contrary to the great Hebrew doctrine of the one eternal, holy God, the one Creator and the one Sovereign of the Universe?

Dr. Driver's questioning of the peculiar theology of the book rests on a fundamental principle which misguides many, and leads them to pose as judges where they should sit as learners. The doctrines of Daniel, he says, "undoubtedly mark a later phase of revelation than that which is set before us in other books of the Old Testament." It is thus we are pulled up again and again by confident assertions that this and that are mistakenly ascribed to a particular author and a particular age—being too advanced for the age in which it is located—and that we must transfer it to a later. It is as if it was given to men to "know the times and the seasons," which, we may say, the Spirit of God "hath kept in His own power."

In the case before us the matter may be easily tested. The doctrines taught in Daniel respecting "the Messiah, angels,

---

* Why should the Book of Enoch be dragged into this matter? Daniel cannot have got his doctrines from a Book which was confessedly not in existence till B.C. 100, and of which able critics believe that important portions are post-Christian. And if the Book of Enoch got its doctrines from the Book of Daniel, it only proves that "Daniel" was before "Enoch;" it does not help in the least to determine whether "Daniel" was two hundred or four hundred years before "Enoch." The constant reference to a book of which ordinary readers know nothing but the name, and around which there is thrown an air of mystery, as if it had some occult bearing on the question, serves no purpose but to create doubt where no doubt is.

the resurrection, and a judgment of the world, are taught with greater distinctness and in a more developed form than elsewhere in the Old Testament." They come to us too early, the prophets did not know them, " they mark a later phase of revelation." But where shall we find this " later phase of revelation ? " A " revelation " later than that which was closed by Malachi—who warned the nation to walk by the ordinances which they had already received, until Elijah should come to prepare the way of the Lord—there was not (Matt. 11. 10). There is no " revelation " to be found in " post-Biblical Jewish Literature." In that literature there is a darkening, rather than a brightening, of the light that had already come to the people through the Old Testament prophets. And if the great dictum of Daniel (12. 2)—professedly uttered by an angelic messenger — " Many of them that sleep in the dust of the earth shall awake, some to everlasting life, and some to shame and everlasting confusion," be considered too "advanced" to belong to the age of the prophets, we are shut up to the concluson that it possesses no authority, being nothing but the imagination, or dream, or guess of at best some uninspired thinker, who perhaps laboured to penetrate into a region of which he had no knowledge.

During the long period which intervened between the latest of the Jewish prophets and the coming of their Lord to His Temple (Mal. 3. 1), there were doubtless many devout men and women who panted after Divine knowledge in the spirit of the writer of the hundred and nineteenth Psalm, and who " meditated on the law of God day and night," and were spiritually taught of the Lord. In answer to their prayer, " open thou mine eyes that I may behold wondrous things out of Thy law," we doubt not their eyes were often opened to see, and their hearts to welcome, blessed truths which were hidden from careless and carnally-minded readers of the sacred page. An experience this, like that of ourselves in these last days, who have been, not four centuries but eighteen, without a living apostle or prophet to speak with authority in "the name of the Lord"; and it is still true, as a modern teacher taught his followers three hundred years ago, that the Lord hath more light to break forth from His holy word. But this is something different from "revelation," and if the age to which the Book of Daniel claims to belong cannot be credited with such advanced teaching as we find in its pages, but must wait for a later revelation, that later revelation did not come till came the Divine Revealer Himself. And it is noticeable that when He had to confront the Sadducees He made His appeal, not to a late stage of Old Testament revelation, but to one of the earliest (Luke 20. 37).

CHAPTER VIII.

THE DOCTRINE OF THE MESSIAH IN DANIEL.

IN an earlier chapter we have remarked on the fact that the term MESSIAH, as the distinctive designation of the long expected Saviour of the world, is found only in the Book of Daniel. The idea of "anointing," and anointed ones, had long been common, until at last it culminated in its being appropriated to One who summed up in His own Person all that Divine anointing could mean. Readers of the New Testament are familiar with the fact that before the appearance of Jesus in the world, this term had already become a household word among not the Jews only but the Samaritans as well. And the question which called for solution on His appearance was whether He was the Messiah, which being interpreted in a language better known at that time than the ancient Hebrew, the Greek, meant the Christ, or the promised Anointed One.

We turn to the book in which the term originated and which gave it currency, to see what manner of man, according to the book, the Messiah was to be, and what was His mission to the world. We shall have to ascertain how far this book's idea of Him accorded with more ancient predictions, and wherein it differed from them.

In order to this we must first of all recall the fact of growth or progress in Old Testament Messianic prophecy, growth, not by way of natural development, but by the Grace of God. In the case of the prophets it is not as when one author or man of science takes up the theory of his predecessor, and, by genius or experiment, confirms it or extends it beyond the point at which his predecessor left it. The advance of Biblical promise and prediction must be accounted for on other principles. To quote from myself :—" We cannot imagine any natural process by which 'the seed of the woman' should, two thousand years later or more, be interpreted to be 'the seed of Abraham'; and by which, nine hundred or a thousand years later, the seed of Abraham should become a son of David ; and by which the Son of David should, some hundreds of years later, be declared to be both human and Divine, and represented as conquering and blessing the world by the virtue of suffering and death ; and by which, hundreds of years later still, it should be foretold that the appearance of the great Deliverer should be preceded by the coming of an Elijah who should prepare his way. In all this we have not a natural development of the seed sown in the primitive promise to our first parents, effected by the genius of thinkers of later ages, but a realisation of the New Testament statement, that God spake to the fathers by the prophets at sundry times and in divers manners."* Thus it was that "prophecy came not in old time by the will of man, but holy men of God spake as they were moved by the Holy Ghost" (2 Pet. 1. 21).

What we have a right to expect then is not that later prophecies should be repetitions of earlier, but that whatever they contain that is new they should be in accord with what is older. And the appearance of the new justifies no suspicion of its genuineness, provided only that it confirms and illustrates the old.

Guided by this principle we ask what older aspects of Messiah's person and character re-appear and are recognised in the Messiah of Daniel. 1. We remark first of all that He

---

* *Handbook of Christian Evidences*, pp. 310, 311.

was to be a *king*. This is not the oldest aspect in which He appears in prophecy, but it is a very old one. Without seeking to determine when we have the first implicit suggestion of it, it is certain that from the time of David it held a prominent place in prophecy and in the national hope. This needs no proof at present. The Messiah was to be the son of David, His throne was to be the throne of David, and on that throne He was to sit for ever; prophecy sometimes using the name of David himself as an appellative of the Messiah, as in Jer. **30**. 9, and Hos. **3**. 5. When the Messiah came to claim His throne, not only was the idea of kingship familiar to the nation, but it had well nigh displaced every other, and in displacing every other it had lost its true spiritual import, and had become miserably secular and selfishly national. But in the face of the falsity of prevailing notions, Jesus did not shrink from asserting this Kingship (John **18**. 33–36).

This doctrine is not wanting in the Book of Daniel. A kingdom implies a king. And we have seen already (ch. **2**) how that the first great prophecy in the book supplied the formula in which both Christ and His herald announced their mission, "The Kingdom of Heaven is at hand." And within the lines of that first prophecy, there was clear intimation of an essential difference between the "Kingdom of Heaven" and the other kingdoms which it foretold (Dan. **2**. 23). Later prophecies, such as that in which Messiah is called by pre-eminence "The Prince" (**9**. 25), made this difference very emphatic and beyond question.

2. What of other aspects of the Messiah's character in Old Testament prophecy? Without any detailed survey of them we find a summary of the very highest of them in the ninth and fifty-third chapters of Isaiah. In the former there is foretold the birth of "a child" in whom should be realised attributes that seem mutually incompatible, that of a human

child and the character of "the Mighty God." And in the latter we are told of His suffering and death, the death being sacrificial and vicarious. It is one of the most painful developments of a certain school of modern critics that doubt, if not even denial, should be cast on what the universal Church has believed from the beginning to be the true import of these great Scriptures. Philip the Evangelist, who accosted the Ethiopian traveller by direct command of "the Spirit" (Acts **8.** 29), did not mislead him when from the fifty-third of Isaiah he "preached to him Jesus."

Turning to Daniel we do not find in his book any such explicit statement of the Divinity of the Messiah as we have in the ninth of Isaiah, but we have sayings which admit of no consistent interpretation that does not involve the idea of a superhuman and pre-existent, if not eternally pre-existent, being. Look at the mysterious words in chapter **7.** 9, 12, 22, where the "Ancient of Days" is described in words which were almost literally adopted by the Apostle John in describing the appearance of the "Alpha and Omega" (Rev. **1.** 11, 13, 14); in *v.* 13 there is a furthur mysterious description of one like a Son of Man, who came to the Ancient of Days, and to whom was given universal dominion and glory—words which when applied by Christ to Himself in reply to the High Priest were regarded as blasphemous. It must not be forgotten that the Divinity of the Messiah appears in prophecy not so much in formal statement, as indirectly, in attributes and works ascribed to Him which could not be ascribed to one who is only human. As to the death of the Messiah we are expressly told "after threescore and two weeks shall Messiah be cut off" (**9.** 26). And in connection with His coming we read: "Seventy weeks are determined upon thy people and upon thy holy city, to finish the transgression and to make an end of sins, and to make reconciliation for iniquity, and to bring in everlasting righteousness, and to seal up the vision and prophecy and to anoint the Most Holy" (v. 24).

It is a matter of no mean consequence that we should find the prophecies of Daniel summing up, gathering to a head, the grandest prophecies of earlier times, and that not by a verbal copying of them or by a literal reproduction of the forms in which they were given of old, but in "a divers manner" (Heb. 1. 1), proper to his own time and to his own special message to the world. The one pregnant saying, "Messiah shall be cut off" re-asserted the grand prediction, "He was wounded for our transgressions, He was bruised for our iniquity, the chastisement of our peace was upon Him." The reader of the Gospels scarcely needs to be reminded that when the Messiah Himself, now Incarnate, began to foreshadow to His disciples the near fulfilment of these and similar Scriptures, His foremost Apostle exclaimed, "Be it far from Thee, Lord" (Matt. 16. 21–23). He could say, "Thou art the Christ, the Son of the living God," but with all the greater vehemence he could say of suffering and death, "This shall not be unto Thee"; and in this he reflected the spirit of his age. It is that spirit, not the spirit of Isaiah and of Daniel, that we find reflected in the book which is so often appealed to, rather referred to, as if somehow it occupied the same plane of thought with Daniel, and might thus be held to neutralise any special claim on the part of Daniel—the so-called Book of Enoch. This book ascribes to the Messiah very high, but not the highest, Divine attributes. He is declared to have existed before all creation—an anticipation of the later Arianism. But it lacks one thing which forms an essential part of the true prophetic idea—it knows nothing of a suffering, far less of a dying, Christ; its Christ is altogether triumphant. The words of our Lord to Peter might be addressed to it—for the occasion is the same—"Thou savourest not the things that be of God, but those that be of man" (Matt. 16. 23).

I repeat that it is of no mean consequence that the doctrine of the Messiah in Daniel is in harmony with the main conceptions of the earlier prophets. It belongs to the age of the prophets, not to an age when the true prophetic conception gave way gradually to conceptions which were hardened into material hopes, or which even in their most spiritual form took such shapes as crystallised in the theories of the Book of Enoch or the vaguer thinkings of even devout men like the disciples of our Lord. Daniel—speaking of him as the representative of the prophecies which have come to us through him—could, while foretelling an everlasting Kingdom and its glories, say, "Messiah shall be cut off." But, though cut off, through Him there shall be "reconcilation for iniquity and the bringing in of an everlasting righteousness" (9. 24)—terms in which we find the very essence of the Gospel of "reconciliation" preached by Christ Himself, and still more fully by His Apostles after the Pentecostal promise had been fulfilled.

And yet there is a speciality in Daniel which differentiates him and his prophecies from those which went before, but it only confirms our faith. He not only foretells a Messiah such as others had foretold, but He intimates the time of His coming with a definiteness which, though veiled in symbolic numbers, sufficed to keep alive the faith of the Church until the hour of fulfilment came. The time, though definitely fixed, might still seem far distant, and in the intervening centuries powers would arise which might seem, but for faith in Him with whom "it is impossible to lie," to gain a mastery before which the light of hope must perish. And thus it was needful, speaking after the manner of men, that to him to whom it was given to tell when the Christ should come, it should be given likewise to tell how it should fare with the world, at least with its dominant powers, during the ages that lay between. In what of this is new, we find no stumbling-block, but a marked advance in the historic progress of Messianic prophecy—an advance most gracious and most seasonable. There were advances in earlier predictions, more marked because they affected the very essence of Messianic prophecy, such as the clear revelation of both the Divinity and the Humanity of the Coming One, in the ninth of Isaiah, and the equally clear revelation of His vicarious sacrifice in the fifty-third—while this of Daniel, confirmatory of that which was old, affected in that which was new only that which was more outward and circumstantial.

In the Divine choice of the man through whom such additional revelations of the future were given, and of the circumstances in which they were given, we cannot fail to see Divine wisdom and grace. They "do greatly err," it is true, who find, not merely the occasion, but the originating cause of prophecy in the circumstances of the prophets, and who regard the horizon of the prophets as bounded by their own times. But it would likewise be an error to overlook the fact that the Divine wisdom may be traced in the circumstances in which prophecies were given, and often in the character, intellectual and spiritual, of the man through whom they were given. For example, it would be difficult to imagine Isaiah and Jeremiah changing places either in the Divine teaching which has come to us through them, or in what we may call the secular duties which Providence imposed upon them.

We can see the Divine wisdom, aye, and the Divine goodness, in the choice of the man Daniel for the prophetic service to which he was called. His position was full of anomalies. He was at once a Jewish captive and a

Babylonian ruler, an anomaly this of a kind not uncommon in Oriental life. He was an earnest worshipper of Jehovah, and for a time at least a member of the Magian or Chaldean college, a position which must often have tried his religious fidelity. He was thus placed in circumstances which fitted him for a task which had not fallen to the lot of any of his predecessors. "Can we wonder," says Dr. Payne Smith,[*] "if he viewed the world with a different eye from that of the exiled priest Ezekiel, living in penury among the poor Jewish colonists planted on the river Chebar—or even from that of Isaiah, whose rapt vision, spurning this poor earth, soared aloft to the spiritual glories of Messiah's reign?" Each of these, and others, had their own special office and message. But the thought present to the mind of Daniel (as we see it in his visions) is "that of the one God establishing His Kingdom on earth, and he sees the world-kingdoms preparing the way for it, but themselves coming to nought as it grows and spreads over all the world. We know how he loved his nation, and how even in extreme old age he still prayed with his face toward Jerusalem; but he places out of sight the work of his country and his church, and sees only the world's history and the share which it has in preparing for the universal dominion of God."

As a corrective to the national form of much previous prophecy, this was not only most precious, but necessary What Daniel's prophecies taught was indeed the true meaning of the whole prophetic choir. "But generations of Jews failed to see this world-wide purpose, not merely because patriotism and national pride closed the avenues of their minds, but because the outer form of prophecy was Jewish, and gave a basis to the narrow interpretation put upon the prophetic

---

[*] *Exposition of Daniel* 1—6, pp. 12, 13.

teaching by the current national thought. But in Daniel the outer form is entirely changed, and the man who was the mighty pillar of their strength in the days of disaster sets the world before them in a completely different aspect, ignores their common standard of thought, and declares that their Jehovah was as much the God and Father of the whole Gentile world as He was their own" (Dean Payne Smith).

"The prophecies of Daniel thus conformed to the times of the Exile and the personal position of the prophet himself in Babylon." "To show the hostility of the world's power to the Kingdom of God," says Dr. S. Davidson, "it was needful to enter into detailed and special predictions respecting the future of that worldly power as embodied in the leading empires which successively prevailed. All is designated by material emblems. The imagery is also cast in a gigantic mould. By this means the haughty rulers of Babylon might be made to see most intelligibly the nothingness of the earthly wisdom and arts of the wise men in whom they trusted, and apprehend the wisdom belonging to the omnipotent Lord of heaven and earth, to whom all are subject." *

As to the definiteness of chronological and other details in Daniel's prophecies of the Messiah and the events which should precede His coming, they differ from other Biblical prophecies, not in essence, but in degree. Other prophetic books contain definite and precise predictions of events in the remote future. There is the prophecy of Micah (5. 1), relating to the Messiah, and specifying the little village of Bethlehem as His birthplace. There is the prophecy of Isaiah (39. 5-7), as well as that respecting the siege and capture of Babylon in Jer. 50 and 51. Isaiah announces to Hezekiah that he should live fifteen years longer (Isa. 38. 5). Jeremiah tells the

---

* *Introd. to the O. T.*, 1856, p. 921, abridged.

false prophet Hananiah that he should die within a year (28. 16, 17), and he foretells the continuance of the Captivity for seventy years. The prophecies of Daniel therefore differ from others not so much in essence as in degree. In definiteness of detail and minute precision they exceed all that preceded them. "This (as Dr. S. Davidson says) must be explained partly by the singular position of Daniel, who was set in opposition to the heathen predictions of Oriental wisdom, and partly by the special wants of the Covenant-people, to whom, during the silence of the prophetic voice in future times, his prophecies were meant to furnish a satisfactory and compensative inheritance." *

As to the use made of *numbers* in Daniel's visions, in which criticism finds some occasion of doubt, we need not give ourselves much concern. They are found in ch. 9. 24–27, and ch. 12. 11, 12. If it was something new in prophetic nomenclature, there was no reason why it should not be adopted if it served its purpose in giving greater definiteness to the Messianic hope. Those who accept the Book of Revelation as apostolic, cannot forget how numbers are used in it. We have first of all that figure "666," the number of the beast, of which it is said "Here is wisdom." And as reckonings of time we have the two witnesses prophesying a thousand two hundred and threescore days (ch. 11. 3); and the woman who fled "into the wilderness," into a place prepared of God, for a thousand two hundred and threescore days (ch. 12. 6); and the notable thousand years of ch. 20. The prophet Daniel anticipated the prophet John.

As to whether the numbers used by Daniel can be verified by the results known to history, our plan and argument do not require us to discuss or to prove. We accept the predictions

---

* *Ibid*, p. 930.

of the Book of Revelation as apostolic, without attaining to clear or definite interpretations of their meaning. And we need not wait for an unquestioned consensus of opinion in regard to all the figures used by Daniel, before we believe that he received them, as he says he did, by the ministry of angels. Not that there is any such scope for doubt or difference of opinion in regard to the Messianic predictions of Daniel, as there may be in regard to the passages referred to in the Book of Revelation. There is no room for doubt as to the substance of the prophecy in the ninth chapter. And if I had doubts I should speedily be delivered from them by the attempts that are made to force into it another than the Messianic interpretation, some of them so offensive that I shrink from quoting them, and all unbiblical and jejune. The only room there is left for question is in the mode of reckoning the seventy weeks and the other periods mentioned, the *terminus a quo* and the *terminus ad quem;* and any differences in the reckoning cannot affect the claim of the prophecy to be considered genuine and Messianic. While my present argument for the book does not require me to take stronger ground than this, there is stronger which it is difficult to invalidate, and Dr. R. Anderson [*] puts it with clearness and force. After a minute examination of dates and a careful reckoning of numbers, insisting that the year was a year of 360 days, he holds that the ancient prediction of the seventy weeks was fulfilled "precisely to the very day upon that Sunday in Passion week when for the first and only time in His ministry on earth, our Lord caused His Messiahship to be openly proclaimed." With unhesitating faith in his reckonings, he says, "the logic of this is inexorable. Either the result is an accidental coincidence, or else it is an overwhelming proof that the visions of Daniel

---

[*] *Daniel in the Critics' Den*, pp. 83, 84.

were a divine revelation." The idea of a coincidence he scouts. "Credulity of the incredulous! we might exclaim." And he concludes, "It is for the reader to judge whether this is an instance of the 'acervation of endless conjecture,' or a legitimate appeal to plain facts and the positive statements of Scripture."

If the reader is not prepared at once to accept this conclusion as established beyond doubt or question—and I do not stake my argument upon it—I submit two considerations which cannot but strengthen faith in the great prediction of the "seventy weeks," on the part of those who cannot verify the figures for themselves. (*a*) If given or written at or about the time at which the book represents it to have been given, no possible reckoning can be made which will not bring us at least approximately to the era of our Lord's coming. (*b*) While if given or written—rather, if imagined and written—in the hypothetic B.C. 164, no possible reckoning can land us in the time of Christ, or carry us forward to any other known epoch of which they might be descriptive. In fact, if they belong to B.C. 164, we can put no rational construction upon them, and cannot understand what the author meant by them, whether he would *pose* as a prophet or was carried away by vagrant fancies that came to him he knew not how. We are thrown back as by the force of a *reductio ad absurdum* on the old and Christian interpretation of Dan. 9. 24-27.

The main difficulty, however, is found in the prophecies with which the Messianic is *associated* and by which it is preceded. These bulk so largely that they seem to fill the entire vision and become the main object of study and inquiry. What the four kingdoms are which are symbolised by the four beasts in ch. 7, what the ram and the goat of ch. 8, who and what the three kings and the mightier King of ch. 11, and how the destinies of Israel and other nations were affected by the reigns and conquests of four or five hundred years, are matters of no mean interest, and are worthy of careful study. But we may lose ourselves in the mazes of theories and hypotheses, and become so absorbed in them that we fail to see or reach the goal of the entire series. The subordinate, the intermediate, the merely instrumental, become the all in all, the very end of the prophetic revelations made to the seer in the days of Nebuchadnezzar and of Cyrus. Thus it is that we are told that "the interest of the book manifestly culminates in the relations subsisting between the Jews and Antiochus." [*] A more entire misreading of the book there could not be. To those who read the predictions of various dynasties merely with the eye of a historian, and who see in them only a symbolic or parabolic " reading " of historic events which filled the space of some centuries—written moreover after, not before, the events had taken place—and who see in the eleventh chapter a picture of the cruel reign of Antiochus Epiphanes, the "interest" of the prophecies may be exhausted or ended in him. But it does not need much penetration or research to discover that the real interest of the predictions, and that which alone makes them consistent and intelligible, "culminates" in the Kingdom which the God of heaven was to set up in the last days, and in the Divine King who was to reign over it for ever,—not in any of the reigns or kings that were to come and go before His appearing. Strange that this should be overlooked, seeing it is revealed unmistakably in the very first of the Daniel prophecies, that which was given through the dream of Nebuchadnezzar, in which four dynasties or rules, described as of gold, of silver, of brass, and of iron and clay, are represented as passing away or being destroyed, giving

---

[*] *Driver's Introd.* p. 477.

place to a kingdom that shall never be destroyed. We have here the key to all the prophecies that follow. And in one of them given in vision to Daniel himself, after his devout and penitent pleading on behalf of his fallen nation, there is made known the time of the advent of the King, the Messiah, the most glorious event in the world's history. "But with what bitter revelations is it combined! What must have been the Jew's feelings when, instead of triumph and victory, and an immediate era of glorious conquest and universal empire, he read that the Messiah was to be cut off, and that the armies of an alien empire would destroy the city and the sanctuary; that the daily sacrifice would cease, and that the abomination that maketh desolate should be set up." This must precede the triumphs of the "Kingdom of Heaven."

CHAPTER IX.

THE OBJECT AND MORAL OF THE BOOK.

WE have now completed our survey of the book, chapter by chapter, in quest of evidence either to nullify or to confirm its claim to be considered historical. And what is the result? The *writer* can only answer for himself; but he *hopes* that the reader likewise has reached the conclusion that there is nothing in the book to justify suspicion of its *bona fides*, and very much to justify the belief that "the hand of God is here." Our first appeal, it will be remembered, was to the direct testimony of Him who is Lord and Master of our beliefs as well as of our actions. Next to the testimony of Christ comes the internal evidence of the book itself. No one, it is true, can study this evidence with a mind entirely unbiassed by conclusions to which he has already come on other grounds. And I must leave my readers to say how far my survey of it has been so fair and honest, as to justify me in saying "I speak unto wise men; judge ye what I say." As to the miracles recorded in the book I need not repeat what will be found in earlier pages. They are very wonderful, but not more so, considering the circumstances, than miracles already recorded in the histories of Moses and Elijah. The most boastful opponent of Christianity to whom these last days have had to listen, confessed that there was nothing puerile in the miracles which the Gospels ascribe to Christ. Had the Gospel narratives been written in the age which produced the apocryphal gospels and under the same influences, "puerility" and absurdity would have been their most prominent characteristics.

The same may be said of the miracles in the Book of Daniel. There is nothing puerile about them. And had they been the fictions of the age which produced Bel and the Dragon and other apocryphal books, "puerility" would have been their least offensive attribute.

As to the great miracle of "prediction" which is implied in the entire series of the visions ascribed to Daniel, nothing need be said, so far as *miracle per se* is concerned, to those who believe that the prophets of the Old Testament were inspired of God. And what of speciality there is, both in the form and in the substance of the predictions of which Daniel was made a medium to the world, if we have interpreted it aright, only confirms our faith. It should not be forgotten that under the Jewish law a false pretension to the prophetic gift was deeply criminal (Deut. **18**. 20), and all the methods by which the heathen sought to penetrate into the invisible and to discover the future, by whatever name they might be called, were forbidden under heavy penalities (Deut. **18**. 9-14). If the visions of Daniel are not genuinely prophetic, it seems to me that their author (who could not be Daniel) must be numbered, in spirit, with the soothsayers of Heathenism.

Thus defending the book as true history we have to inquire into its object or moral purpose, and when we have done so we may perhaps find additional reason for believing that it is of God.

But we are met at the outset with the assertion that its moral purpose, or at least the moral lessons in which we are interested, are independent of its historicity. A parable may be as instructive as a narrative of facts. A fiction may produce as deep a moral impression as a true story. On some such ground as this it is held by those who believe the book to be either in whole or in part fictitious, that so far from being meaningless, as a story told out of the mere love of story-telling might be, it is profoundly instructive, and becomes even more so than on the hypothesis that it is historical. Shut out the idea of history, and not only, it is alleged, does the book lose none of its value, but it acquires fresh beauty and power of instruction. But this seems very like a paradox. How a story which is beautiful and instructive so long as it is considered fictitious—in plain phrase, so long as it is not considered to be true—can become less beautiful when truth is added to its other attributes, it is not easy to understand. The spontaneous experience of children tells the other way. There is no question they ask more eagerly when they have been told a pretty tale, than, "Is it true?" And when they are told that it is not, however much fancy may still be pleased or charmed, the tale loses interest; and if its aim has specially been to teach, its end, instead of being promoted, is frustrated.

What then may we regard as the aim or object of the book? For it cannot be a mere story without an aim. And yet the idea of one grand aim is often lost sight of, and enough is thought to be said and explained by making reference to the examples it furnishes of loyalty to principle. Dr. Driver expands this point. "The aim of these chapters (1—6) is not merely to describe who Daniel was, or to narrate certain incidents in his life; it is likewise to magnify the God of Daniel, to show how He, by His providence, frustrates the purposes of the proudest of earthly monarchs, while He defends His servants who cleave to Him faithfully in the midst of temptation. The narratives in chaps. 1—6 are thus adapted to supply motives for the encouragement, and models for the imitation, of those suffering under the persecution of Antiochus." All true, but for this limitation to the days of Antiochus.

"In chaps. 7—12 (we read) definiteness and distinctness are given to Daniel's visions of the future ; and it is shown in particular that the trial of the saints will reach ere long its appointed term" (pp. 479, 480). True likewise, but for the implied limitation to Antiochus, of which more by-and-by.

A writer of another school of criticism, and one who is consistent with himself, says, "The Book of Daniel has more than one aim. (1) It is essential to complete the continuity of revelation. At the time of the Exile the Israelite had before him the Law, the Prophets, and the Sacred Books, so far as they had been received into the Canon. These were sufficient to teach him the will of God, the certainty of the return from the Exile, and the coming of the Messiah. But it might have been supposed that the Messianic days were to appear immediately after the return from the Exile. The Book of Daniel corrects this impression and prepares Israel for the period that is to intervene between the close of the Captivity and the advent of the Messiah. These glorious days cannot come till a period has passed far darker than any that has yet been known. (2) The Book of Daniel had a very distinct object to fulfil amidst the generation in which it was written. Israel was in captivity. Her last hope at Jerusalem —the Temple—was destroyed. Might it not prove a temptation to the sufferer to think that God's promises had failed ? . . . . Accordingly the Book of Daniel shows by what means Israel's hope was sustained . . . ." (3) "The Book of Daniel had a missionary purpose," etc.

The author from whom I quote (H. Deane in *Bp. Ellicott's Bible*) sums up thus : "It may be said that the object of the book is (1) to supply a missing link in the chain of the continuity of revelation ; (2) to support Israel amid the doubts and fears of the Exile; (3) to reveal to a polytheistic nation the eternal power of the One True God."

The object of the book may be stated in another way, and more briefly: It is to *preserve a record of a remarkable Divine dispensation in the history of God's ancient people.* If we are asked the object of the Books of Isaiah and Jeremiah, we say, in brief, it is to preserve a record of the Divine dispensation towards Israel in the times of these prophets—and if we would know what the dispensation was, and what lessons it contained, in each case, for Israel and the world, we must read their books. Even so with Daniel. If we would know what the dispensation was, in which he was the most prominent figure and minister, we must find it in the book—that is, in the events which the book records, so that ultimately *the object of the book is to be found in the object of the events which it records.* These events must be our teachers. If the hand of God was in them God Himself is the teacher of the lessons which they bring to us. But if the story be of man's invention, the lessons are only man's, and they come far short, as we shall find, of what the book, being of God, really teaches—something far beyond the mere following of noble men, whether real or ideal, in the endurance of wrong for what is right.

We may work our way towards the less obvious end at which we aim, by laying down three guiding principles. (1) That such moral lessons as may be learned from the book, irrespective of the question whether the matter of them is real or fictitious, become far more forcible and effective when they are known to be founded on fact. (2) That lessons drawn from general principles of the Divine government likewise acquire more force and authority when they are given by express Divine intention. And (3) That there are lessons taught in the book which are altogether dependent on their being Divinely taught or given—and this fact, if it be a fact, is dependent on the historic truth of the narrative.

1. Let it be confessed that a tale or novel descriptive of high character, of devotion to duty, of self-sacrifice, may inspire enthusiasm and incite to a noble life. But in order to this the reader must be conscious that while he is reading a work of imagination, the examples which it sets before him are of a kind that has been realised in fact, and *may be*—there being nothing in them that is Utopian or Quixotic. *And*, he will confess that deep as is the impression which the tale has produced on his mind, the impression would have been deeper— following up a position taken on a former page—more effective and more abiding if he knew that the whole story was literal truth. Reduce the example of Daniel and his three young friends in the court of the King of Babylon, and their later examples in braving the terrors of the burning fiery furnace and of the lions' den, to a myth or a legend—come to believe that they are only beautiful conceptions wrought out of a noble brain, and you certainly reduce their power for good, if you do not altogether destroy it. Much, if not the whole, of their value as examples depends on your conviction of their truth.

2. As to my second proposition. We have in Daniel a demonstration or illustration of the general truth of the Divine supremacy over all kings and kingdoms, but here again the practical value of it depends on its being true. We are familiar with the Bible idea of God and man : God, the only God, the one Creator of heaven and earth—man likewise one, all nations "of one blood"—so familiar with this idea that we are unconscious of its grandeur, and forgetful that we owe it not to human discovery, ancient or modern, nor to philosophic speculation, but to Biblical revelation. The idea of the Divine Sovereignty over all reigning powers, kings and

kingdoms, is but an offshoot of the more general idea that God is "Lord of all." The "calling" and "separation" (1 Kings 8. 53 ; Num. 23. 9) of Israel to be for a time, and for educational ends (Gal. 3. 24), a peculiar people, did not involve any abdication of His rule over other nations, or of His claim to their allegiance, or any relinquishment of their responsibility to Him. Whatever mystery there may be in the grand scheme of Divine Providence, all this must be accepted as Biblical teaching, and the denying of it would render no aid to the understanding of "the vast and complicated machinery by which the counsels of the Most High God are carried out."

When God would punish his "peculiar people" for their faithlessness to their calling, as He had solemnly forewarned them He would do, He employed the sword of nations that were themselves idolatrous, such as Assyria and Babylon, and called their kings His servants (Jer. 27. 8 ; Isa. 10. 5, 6) in fulfilling this His awful pleasure. In like manner when He would "turn again the captivity" to which His people were subjected, He used the power of a heathen conqueror, whose personal aims were no holier than those of Sennacherib and Nebuchadnezzar, and called him, not only His servant, but His "anointed" servant, in fulfilling this His gracious pleasure. (Isa. 45. 1). But these His "servants," who had their own designs to serve, not those which were of God, were responsible for the manner in which they executed their mission. (Zech. 1. 15 ; Isa. 47. 8).

Of all this we have demonstration and illustration in the Book of Daniel, especially in the histories of Nebuchadnezzar and Belshazzar. Let us recall the facts briefly. When Nebuchadnezzar returned from conquests which filled him with a pride that would brook no opposition, he required the representatives of his wide dominions to bow down to a golden image of his god. How he was frustrated we read in the story of the burning fiery furnace. At a later period he had a dream which foretold a terrible personal calamity. His faithful adviser, the Prophet Daniel, interpreted the dream and warned him with plain but courteous earnestness. For twelve months the king forgot it, if he could. But God had not forgotten, and a voice then announced that the day of doom had come.

This great lesson was repeated to Belshazzar. The handwriting on the wall has impressed itself on the very language of the world, and may well be recalled, time after time, to warn godless and merciless tyrants. Daniel reminded Belshazzar of what had befallen a greater ruler and a more successful captain of armies than himself, till he knew that the Most High ruled in the kingdom of men, and concluded with an impassioned appeal to his conscience, saying, " The God in whose hand thy breath is, and whose are all thy ways, hast thou not glorified."

Thus God and His prophet would show that Babylon, the patron and upholder of the world's idols, Babylon, the very ideal of the world's despotisms, was not outside the survey of the All-seeing eye, nor beyond the reach of the All-mighty hand. And in the providences towards its kings of which Daniel was the interpreter, God was pleased to assert His claims and His power, and to teach mankind lessons of universal application. Some of these lessons an earnest-hearted moralist might teach, even by fiction or parable, or by indignant persuasion; such as the perils of despotic power, moral and other, even to its possessors, and the wrongfulness of the rule which the despot exercises over his subjects. But what mere teaching could be so effective as the examples which we have in the events which befell these Babylonian monarchs, interpreted as they were to them and to us by Divine authority through the lips of Daniel. These examples and the interpretation thereof stand forth in bold relief on the page of history, for the warning of all ages, "whether men will hear or whether they will forbear."

3. But this does not exhaust the lessons of the book. There are truths taught in it which are entirely dependent on their having been Divinely taught, especially by Nebuchadnezzar's dream and Daniel's visions. "God in history" is now a familiar phrase, and thoughtful men have often confessed that the world's history was unintelligible to them till they saw God in it. But to God in history we now add

Christ in History,

and in doing so, in our present argument, we assume only that He is foretold in the prediction of the Kingdom of Heaven in the king's dream (ch. **2**), and in Daniel's vision of the Messiah in ch. **9**. If our right to assume this is challenged, and the whole thing declared a fiction, we reply that the writer of the fiction must have meant something. What did he mean? In support of our assumption we may plead, before the *Christian bar* at least, that it is in keeping with the New Testament representation of Christ and the Kingdom of Heaven.

With the idea of Christ in History we read the story of the patriarchal age, and of the Jewish age, with its many redemptions and revelations, and come to understand somewhat of the wonderful attributes and functions which an Apostle ascribes to Christ in writing to the Colossians (**1**. 15–18), and how he should designate Him personally, as we believe he does, "the mystery of godliness" (1 Tim. **3**. 16); and how another should call Him "Lord of all." (Acts **10**. 36).

All this is in keeping with the wonderful attributes with which prophecy endowed Him (Isa. **9**), and with the wonderful work which He was to accomplish in the world (Ps. 72; Isa. 11).

When Daniel was called of God to lift the veil more than it had hitherto been lifted off the future, that future was still more than five hundred years distant. But the nation which had been so long favoured with prophetic guides and counsellors was under the hoof of a conqueror; and although "a time to favour Zion" would come, and prophets would come with it, such as Haggai and Zechariah, to aid in the national restoration, the prophetic age would speedily come to an end, and for four hundred years no prophet's voice would be heard in the land. To Daniel it was now given to foreshadow the history of his nation during this period, beginning with the days of the king's dream, until the coming of the Messiah. It would continue to exist as a nation, but in subjection to foreign conquerors and rulers, until what we call the fulness of the times.

It is in connection with this foreshadowing of the events of the five hundred years that came within the purview of the prophet Daniel, that our idea of *Christ in history* becomes a key to the understanding of the book. Using this key, we come to understand that the succession of Powers which the visions indicated, was not the main object of the prophecy—that object was the relation of these Powers to the Kingdom of Heaven, in which they were to culminate. It was of immense consequence to Israel, at least to devout Israel, the "holy remnant" which was destined to survive all calamity and all apostacy (Isa. 1. 9; 6. 13; Mal. 3. 16), to be assured that God had not forgotten to be gracious, that His purpose of mercy was unchangeable, yea, that every fresh revolution which swept over the land, every fresh power that acquired sovereignty, whether Chaldean or Persian or Grecian or Roman, brought the time nearer when the God of Heaven should set up His Kingdom. We may now, as godly men have

THE OBJECT AND MORAL OF THE BOOK.

done of old, inquire into the predicted succession of Powers. These stepping-stones, as it were, across the dreary waste of troubled centuries, and details which appear to us perplexing and difficult of interpretation, may have been necessary to give completeness to the prophetic picture. But the essence of the Revelation was Christ, and the sure fulfilment, in its time, of the promise made to the fathers. To this all was subsidiary. Without this, the prediction would be only a bit of secular history, scarcely enough to gratify curiosity, and certainly unlike the long series of prophecies which, as Christians, we believe to have been fulfilled in Christ. The same Christ who is the key to so large a portion of the world's history before Daniel, is the key to the same world's history in the centuries after Daniel, when the voice of prophecy was silent in the land of the prophets.

The Christian student cannot fail to trace an analogy between Daniel's Apocalypse (if we must adopt this word) * of our Lord's first coming, and the Apostle John's Apocalypse of His second coming. It is more than an analogy, which might exist between two purely human conceptions which had only an ideal relation to each other, the result of the mental or psychological resemblance of thinking on the part of their authors. We have here before us something far more profound, a real, not an imaginary relation, a relation unaffected by time-considerations, springing out of the one purpose of the God of all Grace. And it will not require many words to show, or at least to illustrate, this.

---

* It can scarcely be necessary to remind the reader that the word Apocalypse, although now used technically to describe a special *form* of revelation, really means only "revelation," and its cognates mean "reveal" and "revealer." Ἀποκάλυψις and ἀποκαλύπτειν will be found some forty times translated "revelation" and "to reveal" in the New Testament. Apocalypse is not to be regarded as describing an inferior form of divine prophecy.

Turning to the Christian Apocalypse we are struck at the outset with the fact that there does not once occur in it the prophetical asseveration "Thus saith the LORD"; on the absence of which in Daniel critics remark, as if it involved some doubt of the genuineness of its prophetical character, or at the least reduced its claims to a lower level. But if we have not the ancient formula "Thus saith the LORD," we have more than its equivalent. The Apostle was in the Spirit on the Lord's day, and he heard a great voice as of a trumpet, saying, "What thou seest write in a book." It was "the Alpha and the Omega" that uttered that voice, and He appeared in a vision * which might have reminded the Apostle of the vision of the "Ancient of Days" in the Book of Daniel. "When I saw Him (the Apostle says) I fell at His feet as one dead. And He laid His right hand upon me, saying, Fear not, I am the First and the Last and the Living One; and I was dead, and behold I am alive for evermore, and I have the keys of Death and of Hades. Write therefore the things which thou sawest (the seven candlesticks and the seven stars) and the things which are and the things which shall come to pass hereafter."

This was a Divine command, given in circumstances of more affecting solemnity than any that we read of in prophetic experience, unless it be that of Isaiah recorded in his sixth chapter. The Apostle obeyed the command and wrote " in a book," the visions which made known to him the things which should come to pass hereafter. It is no part of our function at present to defend the forms in which the future was revealed to the seer; the very idea of defence seems to border on the presumptuous, seeing the forms were chosen by Christ Himself. Nor is it any part of our function to attempt, even in the briefest outline, to discuss or to explain the various schools of

---

* Compare Dan. 7. 9, 10, and Rev. 1. 14, 15.

interpretation which have endeavoured to open and expound the symbolic mysteries of the book. There may be more or less of truth in them all—the so-called Præterist, Futurist, and Historical; and none of them, nor all of them together, may contain the whole truth that is veiled in the symbols of the Apostle's visions. What concerns us, in our argument, and what interests us, is this—that this book connects the first coming of our Lord with His second coming; it bridges over the long space, already nearly twenty centuries, between the Apostolic age and the period when it shall finally be said " The kingdoms of this world are become the kingdom of our Lord and of His Christ, and He shall reign for ever and ever (**11. 15**); it foretells revolutions both retributive and merciful, but anticipates a glorious ending in which all " comings " of our Lord shall culminate in a final " Coming," which he foreshadowed Himself when He was with men upon earth (Matt. **24. 37**; **25. 31, 32**),—and which will be followed by the new heaven and the new earth (Rev. **21. 1–5**), where there will be no sin, no curse and no death.

The Book of Revelation may be said to contain the world's history, so far as the Revealer deemed it fit to reveal it, in His own relation to it, from the hour when John was told to " write " it till the Lord shall come as He has promised. " Thus it is seen," says Dr. Boyd Carpenter, "that, though the rise and fall of earth's history is included in it, it is a revelation, also, of a living person; it is not the dull, dead, onward flow of circumstances, but the lives of men and nations in the light of Him who is the light of every man and the life of all history; and thus we learn that only a living person can be the Alpha and Omega, the starting point of creation and its final rest. The testimony of Jesus is the spirit of this prophecy, as of all others." *

---

* *Bishop Ellicott's Bible*, in loco.

We have here the link that connects the Apocalypses of Daniel and of the Apostle John. "Christ in History" is the key to both. In the former He was revealed as ruling over the world's history, amid all its apparent chaos, for five hundred years, until the time of His first coming; in the latter He is revealed as ruling over the world's history—still to the eye of short-sighted sense an apparent chaos—until He shall come the second time, not in humiliation, but in glory: the *when* of that second coming not being definitely made known, as was the *when* of His first coming (Mark 13. 32).

In this comparison we are not indulging our imagination, or framing an unreal analogy. Only admit, as Dr. Driver does —and it is difficult to understand the position of the Christian who does not—that the dream of Nebuchadnezzar, as interpreted by the seer Daniel, was a true prophecy of the Kingdom of the Messiah, and all follows that we have now argued. The great lesson, the main truth, of Daniel's visions is *Christ in the history of all nations*, and in the revolutions of all nations, —working, with a wisdom and a power of which they are unconscious, towards the accomplishment of a great Divine purpose. The analogy seems to me an unanswerable argument for the Divine and historical character of the Book of Daniel.

Let the book be a fiction, more or less—anything but a record of special Divine working and of special Divine revealing—and all the blessed and Scriptural teaching which we thus find in it is entitled to no consideration; it is not of God, but of the writer's brain. And yet, not of his brain, but of some unknown brain to which primarily we owe the book; for these lessons are in the book whencesoever they have come, and some reasonable explanation of their origin must be found. We can imagine none but what we have given.

The object of the book, according to critics who do not see in it what we see, was simply to administer

Comfort under Persecution

in the days of Antiochus Epiphanes, and in order to this it must not be a book four hundred years old, but one written at the time. But we may challenge those who say that the book was written in the days of Antiochus, on the hypothesis that then only could it be of service in strengthening the Jews in their struggle with the tyrant,—to produce evidence from the history of the struggle that the men who were engaged in it were aware that a man of their own age had arisen to write the doom of Antiochus and cheer them with the prospect of victory. We know that their patriotism was inspired by love of their country, by faith in the God of Abraham, and by the heroic examples of their ancestors. The father of the Maccabees, in a passage already quoted, when he would stimulate his sons to arouse themselves for the redemption of their country, after reciting instances of Divine deliverance (the last of which is "Daniel, who for his innocency was delivered from the mouth of lions"), said to them, "and thus consider ye *throughout all ages* that none who put their trust in Him shall be overcome. Fear not the words of sinful man: for his glory shall be dung and worms" (1 Macc. 2. 60, 61). Mattathias made no appeal to any contemporary fountain of strength and comfort which had been opened in his own days, but to the experiences of "all ages." Distance in time had no minimising or neutralising effect on these experiences or on the promises and prophecies upon which they were based. He was no stranger to the spirit of the ninetieth Psalm, and could find strength in the assurance that Jehovah had been the dwelling-place of His people in all generations. And if he turned to the book of the prophet Esaias and read there the words "Comfort ye, comfort ye my people, saith your God," he need not ask the question whether they were written three hundred years before the return from Babylon, or at the time, or whether or no they had a special and exclusive reference to the coming of the long-expected Divine Son of David; he would find within a few sentences sufficient ground for listening to them as a voice from heaven to himself, for there he would read: " Why sayest thou, O Jacob, and speakest, O Israel, my way is hid from the LORD, and my judgment is passed over from my God? Hast thou not known? Hast thou not heard that the everlasting God, the LORD, the Creator of the ends of the earth, fainteth not, neither is weary . . . they that wait upon the LORD shall renew their strength."

Compared with this perennial fountain of strength and comfort, what could any man say or do by writing in the days of Antiochus the story of Daniel as we have it now? We cannot call him a teacher sent from God. He was guilty of forgery, and could not himself take comfort or derive strength from what he wrote. Nor could a few leaves, professedly containing a narrative of what had happened four hundred years before but was all new to the people, dispersed among them for the first time, produce much effect, if any. "Could a sensible Israelite," says Dr. S. Davidson, "believe that several floating leaves, having a fictitious story upon them, could produce the effect which the writer is supposed to have intended? Surely the well-known and genuine history of the people, as presented in the sacred books, contained far more appropriate examples." *

As to consolation from remote ancient prophecy, it is the unfading and undying privilege of the Church of Christ. The Apocalypse of the Apostle John is to-day a perennial

---

* *Introd. to the O.T.*, p. 933 (1856).

fountain of strength and hope, although nearly two millenniums have passed since John heard the voice of his Divine Master.

As to the Book of Daniel, there is reason to believe that it contributed to

A more lasting Service

to Israel than the administering of consolation in the days of Antiochus. But in regard to it we have only indirect and inferential evidence. We have only side lights to guide us in our inquiry how far the books of the prophets collectively, or of any of them in particular, contributed to the weaning of the nation, on its return from exile, from that proneness to idolatry which had resisted prophetic remonstrance for many generations. History bears testimony to the fact that, up to the reign of its last king before the Exile, the nation would have its idols ; and that after its return from Babylon its motto might have been "What have we to do any more with idols?" But how the change was wrought we are not told. It is scarcely enough to refer it merely to the punitive discipline of the bondage to which they were subjected in Babylon. That, doubtless, was great, but it was great not through the mere effect of punishment. Punishment hardens as well as softens. Disaster upon disaster had befallen them in former times, and temporary repentances had followed, especially under the influence of godly kings. But now we witness a great and permanent change. The Divine complaint which was uttered in the days of Jeremiah could be repeated no more (ch. 2. 11), "Hath a nation changed their gods which are yet no gods? But My people have changed their glory for that which doth not profit." Amongst the sins charged against them—and they are not a few—by the prophets who aided in their re-establishment in their own land, Haggai and Zechariah, and by the later prophet Malachi, the worship of idols is not once named. In one of the visions of Zechariah there appears a symbol of "the removal of idolatry from the land of the Hebrews which it had desecrated, to its home in the land of Shinar, to commingle with its native elements, never to return to the land of Canaan" (5. 11.) How remarkably this prophetic symbol has been realised, history attests. From the time of the Captivity to the present, the Hebrew people have never once lapsed into idolatry.

Their renunciation of idolatry and loathing of idol worship was not confined to those who returned to the land of their fathers and enjoyed the re-establishment of ancestral ordinances and privileges as in the ancient time. Those who remained and became naturalised in the land to which their fathers had been carried by force, rivalled those who had returned in their zeal for the worship of the God of Abraham and of Moses. "The singular part of their history (Milman says truly) is this, that while aliens from their native land, they remained Jews in character and religion; they continued to be a separate people, and refused to mingle themselves up with the population of the country in which they were domesticated. . . . . The passionate attachment to their native country, gave place to a more remote, though still profound attachment to the religious capital of their people."* That the memory of Daniel's experiences had never died out is evident from the appeal to them of the father of the Maccabean brothers when he would embolden them to resist, hundreds of years after, at all hazards the heathenish "ordinances" of Antiochus.

Mere punishment, we have said, does not account for the great national change which took place on the return from

---

* *History of the Jews*, bk. xii.

Babylon. But it had to do with it largely, in that it was the final seal of God's providence on what prophets had enforced in vain from generation to generation. This is the keynote to the prophecy of Zechariah. Read ch. **1**, verses 2 to 6. The "former prophets" did not live to see their words fulfilled, but their *words* lived, for they were the words of God, and these "overtook" (R.V.) the fathers, in calamities of which they had been forewarned from the very foundation of the Theocracy (Deut. **28**. 13, 25). And now at last the confession was wrung from the nation, "According as Jehovah of hosts purposed to do to us, according to our ways, and according to our practices so hath He dealt with us." And in the words of Hosea, they were prepared to say " What have we to do any more with idols."

The people would now read with open mind and contrite hearts "the words which the LORD cried by the former prophets when Jerusalem was inhabited and in prosperity," to which their attention is called by this later prophet (Zech. **7.** 7).* And we turn with deep interest to these words to see what we may find in them that must have powerfully affected and influenced the after-condition of the Jewish people, especially in the way of rooting out of them their long and apparently inveterate tendency to idol worship. And when we do so, we find them not in isolated passages merely, like the tender remonstrances of Jeremiah (ch. **2**) and the

---

* This reference to the "former prophets," implying that their writings were in the hands of the people whom he addressed, or accessible to them, throws an interesting light on the gradual growth of what has long been called " The Canon " of Scripture. The only prophecies that were certainly of a later date are those of Haggai, Zechariah, and Malachi. As to Daniel and Zechariah, we can fix these dates, that Daniel was alive in the third year of Cyrus, B.C. 537, and that Zechariah prophesied seventeen years after that, B.C. 520. And whatever may be said of the book which bears his name, the events which it records all took place before the days of Zechariah, covering the long space from B.C. 606 to B.C. 537; and the record of them, assuming the book to be historical, could not be of much later date.

eloquent irony in which Isaiah exposed the folly of idol-making and idol-worshipping (ch. **44**), but in a whole national history from the call of Abraham two thousand years before Christ, which, with many signs and wonders, many visitations of mercy and of judgment, was a continuous, unwearied protest against the world's idolatry.

Coming to the point which has led to this digression, we ask whether we can put our finger on anything in the Book of Daniel, or in books that went before it, that was specially fitted to promote or confirm the recovery of Israel from its ancient tendency to idolatry. We believe that we can. In both Daniel and Isaiah we find not merely a general but a very special adaptedness to promote the return of God's people to the pure faith of Abraham and of Moses. In Isaiah these two things are specially noticeable—the keen irony with which the folly of idol-making and idol-worship is exposed, and the challenge to the gods of the heathen to prove themselves gods by the possession of foreknowledge.

The irony will be found in ch. **44.** 9, 17 and ch. **46.** 6, 7. The Apostle Paul condensed what may be called the argumentative force of these prophetic appeals to the common sense of man, when he said on Mars' Hill "Forasmuch as we are the offspring of God, we ought not to think that the Godhead is like to gold, or silver, or stone, graven by art and man's device."

The appeal to foreknowledge as the exclusive prerogative of Jehovah will be found in ch. **41.** 21-24. "As the raising up of Cyrus (Delitzsch says) evinces the unique power of Jehovah, so the announcement of the deliverance of Judah and Jerusalem, which is now being effected by Cyrus, evinces His unique knowledge." In the Cyrus prophecy there is an appeal to the foreknowledge of Jehovah in evidence of His Godhead, and a challenge to the heathen to produce like evidence to support the claims of their gods. "But (in the words of Prof. Cheyne) judgment goes against the idol gods by default. They can show no prophecies, they cannot so much as speak."

The prophet challenged at the same time "the multitude of enchanters," diviners, astrologers, and others in Babylon, who pretended to superhuman knowledge and power to deliver those that trusted in them (ch. **47**. 12-15).

All this was in the hands of the exiles,* being no doubt included among those "former prophets" of whom Zechariah speaks, and must have been the subject of eager study and meditation by all who "cared for these things." The effect of such study could not but have been profound, and we cannot be wrong in tracing to it, in no small measure, the abhorrence of idols which now took possession of the people.

Turning now to Daniel it seems to me as if Daniel was one long loud AMEN to the teaching of Isaiah. When the book which bears his name came into existence cannot be positively asserted. But the events of the book date from the beginning of the Exile to the end of it. And these events were widely known—some evidence of which has been given in an earlier chapter. They could not be hidden. From Babylon "their sound went out through all the world." Their very first demonstration was of the impotence and utter ignorance of those pretenders to a semi-divinity on whom much of the fame of Babylon rested, and of the existence of a God from whom no secret could be hid and Who could make His faithful worshippers the ministers of His pleasure. Then came the great demonstration of the utter worthlessness of the most colossal and the most splendid deity that human hands could fashion, although every knee should bow to him, and the music of all

---

* The author of this book has no doubt as to the "Unity of the Book of Isaiah." But even on the theory of a second Isaiah the chapters quoted must have come into existence before the end of the Exile.

peoples and nations should celebrate his praise,—the Unseen God of captive Israel delivering His faithful witnesses out of the fire to which they were condemned, in the face of the assembled representatives of the whole empire. These, and later demonstrations to the same effect, were not isolated acts that might be forgotten and leave as little trace as the ripples on the pond into which a stone has been cast. The Israelite witnesses occupied high places, whose authority extended to many lands, and even when Babylon had given place to Persia we find their leader true to his God; and his testimony to that God so well-known that his enemies availed themselves of it to attempt his overthrow,—their scheme being frustrated by a fresh demonstration of the alone Godhead of his God.

We cannot quote chapter and verse to prove that the *events* recorded in the Book of Daniel were the means of weaning his nation from idols. But these following facts need no proof; (1) that the nation was weaned from idols, and (2) that it would be difficult to imagine any process, any series of events, so singularly adapted to contribute to this end as those which we find in this book. Israel needed all the lessons which Providence taught to the Babylonian world, throughout the long life of Daniel, as well and as much as did Babylon itself. And happily Israel's previous training and discipline opened its ears to listen and obey. With all this wondrous adaptedness to the accomplishment of a great end, which we know was accomplished somehow at the very time to which the book refers, and not in the days of Antiochus, it seems strange that men should still be asking whence the book. There is so large a convergence of proofs, direct and indirect, and of moral probabilities, towards one conclusion—one that was not challenged through many centuries, and that comes to us under Christ's own seal—that we entertain no doubt that it will continue to be the faith of the Church of God.

Since the above was written I have met with a striking illustration of the cogency of my argument. J. E. H. Thomson in his Introduction to the "Daniel" volume of the *Pulpit Commentary* says, "The miracles related in Daniel decided the question (the old question of Carmel,—Baal or Jehovah?), *and they alone must have settled it.* The nation that went to Babylon were prone to idolatry, prone to abandon their national God, Jehovah; they came back fanatical monotheists and fanatical worshippers of Jehovah. It could only be some special demonstration of the supreme Godhead of Jehovah that could do this—deeds of wonder like those narrated in the first chapters of the book. It would, however, have value for this end, only if it were a record of facts, not a moral romance. Its popularity is explicable only on the ground that it was regarded as history. No such book as Daniel ever was popular unless on the idea that it was a series of accounts of real events. It is a series of disconnected accounts of events and visions, written some in one language and some in another. It has few graces of composition . . . If it is a record of facts, and regarded as such, this popularity is thoroughly intelligible. No novel of covenanting times in Scotland ever had the popularity among the Scottish people that Howie's "Scots Worthies" had, and that was because, simple and rough in its style as it is, it was looked upon as a statement of facts" (p. xii.).

When those who deny the historical character of the book can account on any other principle for all that has been advanced in this chapter touching the object of the book, its place in the grand scheme of Divine revelation, and its adaptedness to accomplish a great Divine purpose, we may consent to listen to them.

CHAPTER X.

ON COUNTER THEORIES.

1. Dr. Farrar's Defence of Fiction.

WE have had frequent occasion to refer to, and to controvert, recent judgments which have been given to the public respecting Daniel by Dr. Farrar and Dr. Driver; but there are some points in these judgments to which more special attention must be given. We are in some difficulty, however, in doing so—these men, with all their eminence as writers, failing to give us a clear defined verdict, supported by appropriate evidence.

What is this book we have to ask, if it be not genuine history? We are not aware of any attempt to construe it into an allegory, after the modern fashion of dealing with the Book of Jonah. Its contents are far too varied and too little homogeneous to be wrought into a unity in this way. Dr. Farrar himself says, in his new book on *The Supremacy of the Bible*, "Whatever explanation may be offered of the perplexities presented by some parts of Scripture, the fallacious extension of allegory must be rejected as a subterfuge" (p. 71). And of an "allegorical method" he says, "It may, within subordinate limits, be adopted for purposes of illustration, as it was by St. Paul, but cannot be used to set aside plain history" (p. 37). This is a sound principle, but notwithstanding its obvious truth, we find writers of some pretension evading "plain history" by vague references to allegorical or parabolical writing, and even discovering the very fountain of the higher criticism in St. Paul's allegory (Gal. 4. 22-31), overlooking the obvious fact that his allegory is based on the assumption of the literal historic truth of the circumstances on which it is founded.

Shall we suppose the Book of Daniel to be a purely literary effort on the part of someone who had no more serious or practical intention than many a novelist has in our own time, who is moved to his task by the inward promptings of his genius, and hopes at least that others will share the satisfaction he finds in his own creations? Shall we add to this, that the intention of the historical novelist is to reproduce a picture of the times in which the scene of his story is laid? Many writers of this class have succeeded in giving to their readers just and true impressions of bygone ages. But they do not leave on their readers' minds the false impression that what they read is historic fact; or if for a time, by archaic disguises and clever manipulation of names and circumstances, they seek to produce this impression, it is only for a time and for the "greater glory" of their genius. If they attempted otherwise, the deception would soon be discovered. Sir Walter Scott, the chief of historical novel writers, took no small pains to inform his readers wherein his imaginary representations differ from the facts on which they were based.

Whatever explanation may be invented or suggested of the origin of the Book of Daniel, we have to face and consider the one broad distinction between historical and non-historical. And on the hypothesis that the book is non-historical, the first, the deepest, and most abiding impression which it produces, is that it professes to be what it is not, historical. Whether it is a mere achievement of genius, or written with a deliberate untruthful intention—this impression is produced. I do not know that we need labour the question whether we owe this impression only to the genius of the writer, for even then he must have been conscious that he produced it. And we have to fall back on the painful conclusion that if the book is not "plain history," the writer of it was guilty of deliberate untruthful intention.

I know how critics shrink in this and similar cases from admitting a charge of forgery or intentional dishonesty on the part of the writer. And I do not wonder. Because, admit intentional dishonesty, and it would be difficult to maintain the right of the book to the place which it has in the acknowledged Canon of Holy Scripture. *But the charge must be maintained notwithstanding.* And if it can be proved, let the consequence follow. In the case of Daniel the consequence would be that the book which bears that honoured name must descend from the high position which it now occupies, and be classed with Bel and the Dragon, and Susanna, and other books now called Apocryphal. And yet in this we may be giving it a place higher than it deserves. For in these other books, however legendary their contents may be, their writers make no such claims to Divine revelations as we have in Daniel, and are therefore not chargeable with the offence of ascribing to God what they knew to be their own.

Let us turn for a moment to the visions before us. The writer says again and again, "I Daniel" saw; "I Daniel" spake. He specifies the time when, and the circumstances in which, the visions were seen and the words spoken: such as "the first year of Belshazzar," "the third year of King Belshazzar," "the first year of Darius of the seed of the Medes," and "the first year of Cyrus, King of Persia"; and in conclusion the writer represents himself as addressed thus: "they that turn many to righteousness shall shine as the stars for ever and ever. But thou, O Daniel, shut up the words and seal the book."

Submit all this to any jury, learned or unlearned, and what must be their verdict? I answer, either that the writer was

Daniel, or that, not being Daniel, he intended it to be understood that he was.

I have said a jury "learned or unlearned." But I may be reminded that there are learned men who accept neither alternative. It may be offensive to reply that they do so under the pressure of a theory which will not admit the reality of the visions, and yet must find some defence of the position which is assigned to them in a book which is supposed to be inspired. And the defence which they offer only confirms the conviction that their theory is hopelessly at fault. For what is it? Let Dean Farrar answer:—

"When we suppose the name of Daniel to have been assumed, and the assumption to have been supported by an antique colouring, we do not for a moment charge the unknown author—who may very well have been Onias IV.—with any dishonesty. Indeed, it appears to us that there are many traces in the book—φωνᾶντα συνετοῖσιν—which exonerate the writer from any suspicion of intentional deception. They may have been meant to remove any tendency to error, in understanding the artistic guise which was adopted for the better and more forcible inculcation of the lessons to be conveyed."*

The author of the book, we are told, not being Daniel, but possibly Onias IV., is not to be charged with dishonesty: so far from it, there are many traces in the book, intentional of course on the part of the author, which exonerate him from any suspicion of intentional deception, and which should lead his readers to understand that they were reading a work of imagination.

Now let us assume all this. *The author did not mean to deceive* when he wrote of visions and represented Daniel as

---

* *On the Book of Daniel*, p. 85.

asserting, with a speciality that could not be exceeded ("I Daniel"), that he had received them, he did not mean his readers to understand that his tale of these visions was true and genuine. When he told of dreams which he said the King of Babylon had, and which Daniel interpreted, he did not mean his readers to understand that such dreams had really been dreamt, and such interpretations really given. When he told those wonderful stories about the burning fiery furnace and the lions' den, he did not suppose that people would be so simple as to imagine that they were anything but parables. When he closed his book with a colloquy between Daniel and a mysterious person who appeared to him in vision as a man clothed in linen, there was really no Daniel in the matter, nor man clothed in linen. And both the solemn words which go before this colloquy about the awakening of them that sleep in the dust of the earth, and the solemn words of the man clothed in linen, and his foretelling of a time when the daily sacrifice should cease, and the abomination which maketh desolate should be set up, were never spoken. We owe the precious truths which are embodied in these words not to any Divine Source, but to the imaginings of the writer, who we are told, may well have been Onias IV. But in all this Onias IV. had no intention to deceive—no intention to lead his contemporaries to whom the book was first given, or successive ages, to suppose that his book was a history of the doings and sayings and experiences of Daniel—a man of whom neither he nor his contemporaries knew anything beyond a vague tradition, that a man of that name had once been great in the Court of Babylon. The author had no intention to produce any such impression !

But he did. He did not intend to deceive, but he *did* deceive. If he thought that he had succeeded in producing a book which could not be, or was not likely to be, so greatly misunderstood, he was not so successful as he thought—*he even deceived himself*. And the artistic guise with which he is credited was so perfect, it so absolutely concealed the true nature of the book, that it survived the test of the almost superstitious jealousy with which the Jews from the time of Onias, and before, onward to the time of Christ, more than two hundred years, guarded the integrity of their sacred books; its true nature remained undiscovered even in the time of Christ: and was found out at last only towards the end of the third century of the Christian Era!

The discovery, such as it was,—of that by-and-by,—was made at last not by any of the Christian fathers of that period, who instead of suspecting that there was any unreality or untruth in the Book of Daniel, found in its pages arguments to convince the Jews out of their own Scriptures that Jesus was the Christ, but by the bitterest enemy to the Christian faith of whom history has preserved any record. For this discovery, by whomsoever made, we are told to be thankful, for is not the proverb true "Fas est ab hoste doceri." There is another proverb, however, which says in the same tongue, 'Timeo Danaos et dona ferentes." The Christians of the third century did not see with the eyes of Porphyry, and if he was right, their blindness was blindness indeed. The centuries which followed the third, some fifteen in number, inherited the blindness of the third, and continued to believe that the Book of Daniel was historical, failing to find in it those "many traces" by which, we are told, the author meant that the real character of the book should be understood. And even now it is only an *elect* class of critics that perceive what is hidden from all others. It is not through an uncharitableness or a non-appreciation of the powers of these critics that we suspect that they see what they see, not through the clear light of truth, but through the medium of theories, mainly *a priori*, which at the best are hypothetic and uncertain.

As to the one point which I am arguing at present, I do not see how it can be questioned, namely, that the author of the book, not being Daniel, if he did not intend to deceive,—that is, if he did not intend his book to be accepted as a *bona fide* history of affairs in which the Prophet Daniel was the principal figure, failed utterly in his purpose, effectually accomplishing what he did not intend; producing a book which was accepted in his own generation, and has been accepted ever since, with few exceptions, as a true history. In the passage which I have quoted from Dean Farrar, he says, "It appears to us that there are many traces in the book which exonerate the writer from any suspicion of intentional deception." But he does not help us to find these traces for ourselves. And the only indication of their nature is given under cover of a Greek quotation φωνᾶντα συνετοῖσιν, a phrase which in this connection may mean much or may mean nothing. Had the Dean quoted in full the sentence from which he has culled it, he would have answered his own pleading. Let me quote it for him. It will be found in an ode of Pindar's, and, translated, it is this,—"Many swift arrows are there in the quiver by my side (or under my elbow) *sounding to men of understanding*—but for the whole they need interpreters." *
What now becomes of the " traces " which exonerate the author from any charge of intentional deception. Not only are they

---

* Pindar, Ode II. 152. The following metrical version of the words will be found in a translation by I. L. Girdlestone, published in Norwich early in this century:—

" Beside me glittering bright
Full many a shaft of swiftest flight,
Eager to spring, within my quiver lies.
Dull is the vulgar ear
The lofty notes to hear,
Their harmony sounds only to the wise."

discoverable only by *men of understanding*, but even these men cannot understand them without the aid of *interpreters*. And on the strength of *traces* so occult we are asked to exonerate the author from intentional deception.

The suggestion that the author of the Book of Daniel might well be Onias IV. should not pass unnoticed. It is a characteristic of certain critics to laboriously minimise the Biblical evidence that stands in the way of their theories, and to substitute for it, or at least to seem to substitute for it, shadowy suggestions of their own which have no foundation whatever. Here we have, what we are not wrong in calling a reckless denial of an authorship which was believed in by many generations of learned and unlearned men—and a suggestion offered, that the real author might well be a man whose name was never connected with the book, either in his own age or throughout the two millenniums which separate that age from ours. Besides, what is there in the character of Onias IV. to justify the impression that he was either intellectually or spiritually capable of writing the Book of Daniel? Apart from the book, and without taking account of anything the book tells us about Daniel, we have conclusive evidence that *he* was at least spiritually capable of writing it, in spiritual sympathy with the Chosen People and with the Divine purpose regarding them. The reference to him by his contemporary Ezekiel, in the words of God to the prophet, indicates that he was religiously the foremost man of his age, the man of all others whose righteousness might be supposed to avail to avert judgment from the doomed city of Jerusalem. But who was Onias IV. that he should be considered a more probable author of the book, and, if the author, the real creator of the story,—and, like a novelist, the creator of the characters that are found in it?

Onias is a common name of noted men in the age which

preceded Christ by two and three hundred years, and there is only one of them of whom we are told anything that indicates the possession of a really devout spirit. Josephus describes him as a righteous man, beloved of God, who in a certain drought had prayed to God to put an end to the intense heat, and whose prayers God had heard and sent them rain. When he was brought into the Jewish camp during a sedition against Aristobulus, he was required to " make imprecations on Aristobulus and his faction," but his answer so displeased the Jews that they stoned him to death.

But this was not Onias IV. *He* was the descendant of a race of High Priests, under whose corrupt administration, more than through Syrian oppression, the land sank to the lowest depths. Without any attempt to disentangle the intricacies of their lives, enough to say, that Onias IV., to whom belonged of right the High Priesthood, sought refuge in Egypt in the days of Antiochus Epiphanes.

"The fact of his exile and the importance of his being a Jew (perhaps) of royal descent, come out in the foundation of the opposition temple, if we may so call it, in the nome of Arabia, near Heliopolis (about 154 B.C.), where a disused shrine of Bubastis Agria was set up with priests and ritual according to those of Jerusalem,—a day of mourning for the Jews of Palestine who were seriously religious, and saw clearly the danger of disunion and of apostacy if any separate centre were tolerated for the religion of Jehovah. Whether the concession by King Ptolemy VII. (to build this temple) was the result of influence exerted by Onias, or a matter of deliberate statecraft, we can now hardly tell."* Onias was made governor of the nome of Arabia, within which his temple stood. But whatever was his aim, whether, as is believed, to "consolidate

---

* The *Empire of the Ptolemies*, by J. P. Mahaffy, p. 353.

Hellenism," or not, it came to nought. And there is nothing known of the man personally to justify the supposition that he was morally or spiritually capable of writing the Book of Daniel. Nor is there, as already intimated, in the history of his times or of later times, the obscurest intimation that it ever occurred to any man that he was its author. The supposition is entirely gratuitous, a mere makeshift.*

To avoid parenthetic explanations in the last few pages, I have spoken of the "discovery" made by Porphyry in the third century (A.D.). *But it was no discovery.* Porphyry did not profess to have *found out* the real authorship of the book which bore the name of Daniel, and to prove that from the beginning to the end of the book it was a fiction and an imposture. "It was the object of Porphyry (Dr. Farrar says) to prove that the Apocalyptic portion of the book was not a prophecy at all . . . but was written after the epoch which it so minutely described. In order to do this he collected with great learning and industry a history of the obscure Antiochian epoch from authors most of whom have perished." And his conclusion was that the events of the Antiochian epoch were so clearly foreshadowed in Daniel that the "foreshadowing" must have been written not before, but after, the events had taken place. Underlying his argument was the anti-supernatural theory of the impossibility of prediction properly so called. And even with the aid of this theory Porphyry had to put forced constructions on important parts

---

* I have seen the critical process which I call a "makeshift" described somewhere as a "refuge for the destitute," a last resort into which critics flee when argument is exhausted. Bishop Lightfoot in his essays on the book "Supernatural Religion" has given us apt descriptions of it; as when he says, "Our author is content to grope in obscurity : *any phantom can be conjured up there.*" And when he says "The convenience of drawing *unlimited cheques on the bank of the unknown* is obvious."

of the prophecies. If Porphyry's conclusion could have been established, it would of course have convicted the author of the foreshadowing, of imposture, and thus destroyed the credit of the book. But the validity of his argument depends primarily on the soundness of his views of prophecy. And we need not be surprised that the Christians of his own age, who did not accept his theory, and who did not consider it impossible for prophetic inspiration to foretell events at a distance of four hundred years, were not stumbled by the argument of this great enemy of their faith ; nor need we be surprised that the book survived his assault, and was transmitted to the ages following, as we have seen, unaffected by any doubt of its truth.

Besides, we claim one aspect of Porphyry's position as supporting our contention. With lynx eyes, rendered all the more penetrating by a malignant purpose, he failed to discover those "many traces" of "artistic guise" in which the writer intended to reveal to all who had eyes to see, that his book was not historical, but was—what it is difficult to define, but what without definition we may call fictitious—elaborated out of his own brain. Porphyry was as blind to these traces as were the Christians whose faith he laboured to overthrow. Had he discovered them, his argument against the book would have been triumphant and overwhelming. "You claim (he could have said) that hundreds of years before Jesus of Nazareth was born there were predictions of Him, and of what you call His Kingdom, which have been most manifestly fulfilled. These predictions, you say, came partly through the dreams of a Babylonian monarch which were interpreted by a man named Daniel, and partly through visions which, it is said, Daniel himself had. And all this you say has come to you in a book which is now in your hands. But you are labouring under a great mistake. You misunderstand the book. Open it and read, and you will find that the writer never intended you to understand that he was writing a history. There were some lessons which he wanted to teach, and he taught them under the 'guise' of a story of the olden times. That is all, and you are blind not to see it."

This would have been conclusive. How is it that Porphyry did not take this ground? He made inquisition, we are told, such as had never been made before into the history of the days of Antiochus Epiphanes and of the Maccabees, and acquainted himself with all the authors, most of them now lost, and even forgotten, who could throw any light on the subject, and has thus furnished to modern critics the means of proving that certain portions of Daniel are not predictive but historical. How comes it that he did not discover the real author of the book, the *origo mali*, and lay bare the true story of the book? Was Onias so obscure a person that the multitude of authors whom Porphyry consulted knew nothing of him, or so little, that they never suspected him of the authorship of the Book of Daniel or imagined him capable of it? Or, what would have been more to the purpose, did none of these authors furnish a clue to the discovery of the real intent of the author which had been so entirely misunderstood —the discovery of those "traces," which modern eyes have at last found, which go to show that the author never meant his book to be accepted as history? The answer, the only possible answer is this (*a*), that no external trace of contemporary authorship by Onias or any one else was discovered because it did not exist, and (*b*) that no internal or occult traces of any other design than that which appears on the very face of the book were discovered because they had no existence. Porphyry never dreamed that the book was capable of any other construction than that which appeared on the very face of it, and from the standpoint of its own profession he set himself to prove that it was an imposture.* And an imposture it was if it was not a true history. Nothing could save its credit; and out of the maze of unsubstantial hypotheses in which we are entangled by modern criticism, there is no escape but in the receiving of the book as it was received in the early Church under Christ's own sanction.

2. Dr. Driver's View of the Book.

The position taken by Dr. Driver differs almost *toto cœlo* from that of Dr. Farrar. While the latter considers it only possible that Daniel ever existed—so that all that is ascribed to him in the book must be held to be imaginary—the former says, "Daniel, it cannot be doubted, was a historical person, one of the Jewish exiles in Babylon, who with his three companions was noted for his staunch adherence to the principles of his religion, who attained a position of influence at the court of Babylon, who interpreted Nebuchadnezzar's dreams, and foretold as a seer something of the future fate of the Chaldean and Persian Empires. Perhaps written materials were at the disposal of the author; it is at least probable that for the descriptions contained in chaps. 2—7, he availed himself of some work or works dealing with the history of Babylon in the sixth century B.C. These traditions are cast by the author into a literary form, with a special view to the circumstances of his own times. The motive underlying chaps. 1—6 is manifest. The aim of these chapters is not merely to describe

---

* The suggestion that the novelist who wrote the Book of Daniel in the days of Antiochus meant to expose the character and doings of the tyrant under cover of the names of Nebuchadnezzar, Belshazzar, and Darius, is too absurd to need refutation. It is little short of a burlesque on the whole subject. Not one of these, nor all combined, can furnish any likeness to the malignant anti-Judaism and anti-godliness of Antiochus. But the critic who makes the suggestion pays involuntary homage to the fact that these names were the names of real personages, whose history was well known in the days of Antiochus and not the invention of the novelist.

what Daniel was, or to relate certain incidents in his life; it is also (in words already quoted) to magnify the God of Daniel, to show how He by His providence frustrates the purposes of the proudest of earthly monarchs, while He defends His servants who cleave to Him in the midst of temptation. The narratives in chaps. 1—6 are thus adapted to supply motives for the encouragement of those suffering unto the persecution of Antiochus. In chaps. 7—12 definiteness and distinctness are given to Daniel's visions of the future; and it is shown in particular that the trial of the saints will reach ere long its appointed term." *

I quote this passage in full lest by abridgment I should do it injustice. Dr. Driver thinks the book cannot have been written earlier than 300 B.C., that is, about three hundred years after Daniel, (by his own acknowledgment,) was taken to Babylon as a captive, but more probably a hundred and fifty years later, in the days of Antiochus Epiphanes, about 164 B.C. The only material ground on which he bases these dates is that of the style and particular form of expression in the book. He does not fail to recall all the old stock difficulties connected with the names of Belshazzar and Darius and others; but he confesses that "the circumstances alleged will appear improbable or not improbable, according as the critic on independent grounds has satisfied himself that the book is the work of a later author, or written by Daniel himself. It would be hazardous to use the statements in question in *proof* of the late date of the book; though if the late date is established on other grounds, it would not be unnatural to regard some of them as involving an exaggeration of the actual fact." †

I fail to see the meaning of the last few words, but it matters not. The main point is this—Dr. Driver thinks that

---

* *Introd. to the O. T.*, 5th ed., pp. 479, 480.
† *Ibid.*, p. 469.

the late authorship *is* proved on independent grounds, and therefore he feels himself at liberty to give full weight to all that can be said on other grounds *against* the Daniel authorship. And what are the independent grounds on which he takes his stand, and from which he can survey unmoved all that can be alleged in favour of the older theory? They are purely—I think I am right in saying exclusively—philological, or, in his own words, "the evidence of the language of the Book of Daniel." After what seems a formidable list of "words and idioms" taken from both the Aramaic and Hebrew portions of the book, he sums up: "The verdict of the language of Daniel is thus clear." He says, "The Persian words presuppose a period after the Persian Empire had been well established; the Greek words *demand*, the Hebrew supports, and the Aramaic permits a date after the conquest of Palestine by Alexander the Great, B.C. 332. With our present knowledge this is as much as the language authorises us definitely to affirm; although *symphonia* as the name of an instrument (considering the history of the term in Greek) would seem to point to a date somewhat advanced in the Greek period "*

This is clear: that is, he tells us we can "affirm definitely" that the book was written after the conquest of Palestine by Alexander. We cannot go *definitely* beyond this, although there are certain signs of a still later date.

1. But, after all, great names and positive assertions do not satisfy the demands of reason. For first of all, while philological evidence has its place in determining the age of a book, it is far from being conclusive by itself or exclusive of other evidence. It was not by linguistic anachronisms, but by far more palpable anachronisms, that Bentley proved

---

* *Ibid.*, p. 476.

that the so-called letters of Phalaris were forgeries. The linguistic evidence for the alleged age of a book may be faultless, even strongly favourable, while other evidence, both internal and external, may disprove its claim. On the other hand—and this is my contention in the case of the Book of Daniel—the evidence for the age and authorship of a book may be so varied, so conclusive, that the inquirer may feel every confidence when he plants his foot upon it, and from this *independent* ground studies all that can be said against it. To disprove or materially discredit the evidence which justifies us in taking this position with reference to the historical character of the book—this is the real question at issue—is more difficult than to discredit the position of the man who practically stakes the whole case on the linguistic character of the book *as it appears to him*.

2. We can confront Dr. Driver with men who are his peers in learning, and in all departments of scholarship, who are not prepared to call him *Master*, but who on this very question of the Aramaic and Hebrew of the book and of some words of supposed foreign origin, have either delivered verdicts entirely opposite to that of Dr. Driver, or declared that the data are not sufficient to bear the weight of a verdict. I might appeal to such as Dr. Pusey, whom it is easier to push out of the way, by calling him old, than to answer, or to Dr. Samuel Davidson, who wrote in 1856, " The state of the language employed corresponds to the time of the Captivity, when Daniel lived." But it may be enough to quote one more modern than either, and one whose bias cannot help being on the side of the Higher Criticism in everything that is affected by it—Prof. Cheyne. Dr. Robert Anderson quotes him thus : " One of the highest living authorities, who has been quoted in this controversy as favouring a late date for the Book of Daniel, writes, in reply to an inquiry

I have addressed to him, 'I am now of opinion that it is a very difficult task to settle the age of any portion of the book from its language. I do not think, therefore, that my name should be quoted any more in the contest.'" Dr. Anderson quotes, in this connection, Prof. Cheyne's opinion as given in the *Encyclopædia Britannica*, that "from the Hebrew of the Book of Daniel, no important inference as to date can be drawn." *

And yet Dr. Driver rests his whole case upon it. It is his sheet anchor. Others may think as they please, but his confidence in his own judgment cannot be shaken.

Those who are familiar with the history of the Higher Criticism do not need to be reminded of the very different judgments which are pronounced, with a boldness which only inspiration would justify, on the age and authorship of particular books, and even on verses and parts of verses in these books: and how a critic does not hesitate to renounce even an opinion of his own, to which, when held, he could have sworn! —and how he is prepared to demand that his new opinion should be accepted as absolute truth. It is a fit subject for ridicule but for the seriousness of the matter and for its evil consequences. Shall we bow to such teachers, or wait till they agree? In the words of Dr. Godet with reference to New Testament criticism, "The Church would have time to perish for lack of food a hundred times over, before the scientific fluctuations had reached their limit."

3. I now appeal to a learned man who has followed Dr. Driver, step by step, throughout his whole linguistic argument, and has, I think, demonstrated its unsoundness on purely linguistic grounds—J. E. H. Thomson, B.D., in the *Pulpit Commentary* volume on Daniel.† Mr. Thomson traverses the

---

* *Daniel in the Critics' Den*, p. 32.

† This volume, newly published, has come into my hands while finally preparing these pages for the printer.

entire argument of Dr. Driver in regard to words and idioms, foreign words, and the Aramaic and Hebrew of the book. But we cannot even outline in these pages correctly the processes by which he reaches his conclusions, involving, as they do, questions of Hebrew grammar and usage, and that in different ages of the language. We must be content with a bare statement of results. As to the Hebrew of the book, he says, "The whole elaborate list of proofs of the relatively recent date of the Hebrew of Daniel has entirely failed when carefully looked at" (p. xix.). As to the Aramaic portion of the book, he says, "The conclusion we come to with regard to the Aramaic of Daniel, is that, taking all the facts into consideration, the Aramaic is early, but how early it is impossible to say" (p. xxiii.) As to particular words and phrases, Mr. Thomson's discussion of them is involved in, and leads to, the conclusions thus intimated. If only "experts" can follow him in his discussion of Hebrew and Aramaic, non-experts can appreciate his illustrations drawn from English literature. For example: "The argument from the unlikeness of the language of Daniel to that of Haggai, Zechariah, and Malachi, even although that unlikeness were greater than it is, would be unsafe. The language of Spenser's *Faëry Queene* is greatly more archaic than that of Shakespeare's *Midsummer Night's Dream*, yet these two works were published nearly contemporaneously" (p. xix.). And in a more extended illustration, a comparison between Chaucer's *Canterbury Tales* and Langland's *Piers the Ploughman*, he concludes, "Thus it is not a proof that Daniel is later than Haggai and Malachi, that in some respects his language seems more akin to the later Hebrew than theirs. He is, like Geoffrey Chaucer, in the court, and engaged in diplomacies with foreign courts; they are more like Langland, with homelier wits and surroundings" (p. xv.).

But, after all, it will be said, this is only pitting one critic against another. Exactly so; and it is enough. Neither critic may be all right, or all wrong. But the one, assuming that he is all right, absolutely right, right beyond the possibility of question, declares that the Book of Daniel cannot have been written before B.C. 300, very probably not until 150 years later. And on the strength of this assumption he is prepared to reject every argument to the contrary, come from what quarter it may. The other critic comes after him, and, with great elaboration and learning, tries at least to prove that he is all wrong, or wrong for the most part. We listen to both, and if we believe the second we must conclude that the first laid his foundation on the shifting sand, not on the immovable rock. At the very least this follows, that Dr. Driver's right to consider that he has definitely settled the age of the Book of Daniel by his linguistic argument cannot be allowed. *Res non judicata est.* We must look for light elsewhere.

Many readers probably have felt before coming to this point that they could find a shorter, and at the same time a sufficient answer to Dr. Driver's argument. Admitting for a moment the substantial accuracy of his views, as already quoted, what do they amount to? The only *imperative* that he requires of them to accept is in the case of the Greek words, which, he says, *demand* the conclusion of a late origin of the book. The Persian words presuppose the Persian Empire, the Hebrew *supports* (not *demands*), and the Aramaic permits the hypothesis of a late origin of Daniel.

What is there in all this to excite surprise or need explanation? Daniel was carried a captive to Babylon while yet a youth, and never returned to his native land. He spent a long life in Babylon, and during a great part of it occupied a position in the state which brought him into close and intimate relations with the many peoples,* east and west, that were

---

* On the relation of Babylon to other, even distant, nations, something has been said already, and more will be found in the Appendix.

subject to Babylon, and necessarily as well with peoples that were not subject, but that had commercial, and what we call diplomatic, relations with the mighty empire of which we may call him the Prime Minister. In these circumstances, how could he help having some not inconsiderable acquaintance with the languages of the nations around him? And should it be accounted strange if, in writing in his native tongue and in the allied Aramaic, there should be found traces of other languages?

Dr. Driver, it will be remembered, does not regard the Book of Daniel as a work of pure imagination, but as written on a "traditional basis." But what is meant by a traditional basis, and how is the idea applied in this case? Sir William Muir, our greatest living authority on the history of Mohammed, has given us his impressions of *tradition* as illustrated in the history of Mohammedanism, and they commend themselves to common sense. "Tradition," he says, "oral or recorded, is spoken of in the same breath, as if oral tradition and tradition reduced to writing were not two things as far apart as heaven and earth. It seems altogether lost sight of that the value of tradition depends absolutely on the date at which it ceased to be oral by becoming fixed in writing. If so recorded at first hand, or nearly so, it may have all the authority of contemporaneous history; but as generations come and go, and the events recede into the dim past, that which is handed down simply by word of mouth soon degenerates, and, parting with the reality of life, rapidly vanishes into the misty air of myth and fable. After the lapse of a few generations, oral tradition loses all pretence of simple truth. Instead of furnishing any material of fact whatsoever for history, it can be regarded but as the creature of fancy." Of this Sir William gives full illustration, in the history of Islam, from a writer who flourished 200 years after the death of Mohammed, who speaks of 600,000 traditions which he had collected, of which he said only 4,000 were authentic. Other collectors of the same period tell the same story. Quoting some of them, Sir William says, "Such, then, are the nebulous and fabulous results of oral tradition under the most favourable surroundings, and brought to record within a definite period, that is, after the lapse of several generations."

The traditional history that gathered around the name of Mohammed may be considered an extreme case, but it illustrates the utter uncertainty of the results of purely oral tradition. Was it on the *basis* of such tradition that the Book of Daniel was written so many hundreds of years—so many generations, after Daniel was gathered to his fathers? If so, who will winnow its statements and separate fact from fable?

Dr. Driver is evidently conscious that his theory needs better foundation. "Perhaps (he says) written materials were at the disposal of the author; it is at the least probable that for the descriptions contained in chaps. 2—7, he availed himself of some work or works dealing with the history of Babylon, in the sixth century B.C." For this supposition there is not the shadow of foundation in known fact. The only history of Babylon in the sixth century B.C. that has ever been discovered, was written on Tablets which have only been unearthed in these last days of ours. And even if they had been known to writers of the third and second centuries B.C., they would not have furnished "materials" out of which could have been written the "descriptions" contained in chaps. 2—7 of the Book of Daniel. The secular and self-glorifying history of Babylonian and Persian conquerors finds no place in Daniel; nor were the events recorded in his book, the chief aim of which, as Dr. Driver truly says, was to "magnify the God of Daniel and to show how He by His Providence frustrates the purposes of the proudest of earthly monarchs,"—of a kind to find place among the events in which those monarchs gloried.

But the supposition that the writer of the book, not being Daniel, but living hundreds of years after Daniel, may have had the aid of works written in the sixth century B.C., puts into our hands an incidental argument for our belief that the book was really written in the sixth century B.C., and not in the third or second. For it is a confession, a twofold confession, (*a*) that the "descriptions" contained in the book are in keeping with what is known of the sixth century before Christ, and (*b*) that these descriptions could not have been written, or scarcely could, without the aid of written materials which had come down from the sixth. Is not this a proof, as nearly demonstrative as the case admits of, that the book really belongs to the sixth, not to the third, century B.C.? It has been well remarked that to reproduce an atmosphere is as difficult for a historian as for a painter. Now while the mental and moral atmosphere of the book, its entire coloration and its geographical references, are in harmony with the days of the Exile, there is nothing in the letter or spirit of the book to necessitate the location of any part of it in the days of Antiochus Epiphanes.

If the hypothesis of traditional aid in the writing of the book fails to account for its more outward aspects, the failure is much more absolute if we have to ask its aid to account for the prophetic portion. Tradition may long preserve vague memories of facts that are palpable to the senses, especially if they have deeply moved the generation in which they occurred. But what tradition could preserve the memory of the prophetic visions which, according to the book, were vouchsafed to Daniel? Daniel could not trust his own memory to preserve them with accuracy—the difficulty being increased by the fact which he records of some of them, that he did not understand them,—

and so to preserve them he "wrote" them, and only a written record of them could preserve them for after generations. If a man of the third century B.C. wrote the book, his story of the visions did not rest on a traditional basis, but was the invention of his own brain.

Apart from the insuperable difficulty which meets us here, on the hypothesis of a traditional basis, what must the book be? Neither wholly true nor wholly false;—traditions adopted, so far as they served the purpose of the author, manipulated, moulded, and supplemented by his imagination. We hear sometimes of a stream of traditional truth running through history; it reminds one of the junction of the Rhone and Arve, the former flowing pure and clear out of the Lake of Geneva, the latter foul and muddy coming down from the mountain glaciers. For some space the two streams flow side by side, and are distinguishable the one from the other. But by-and-by the waters intermingle and are indistinguishable. And such is the destiny of traditions intermingled with history. If the Book of Daniel be of this order, who will tell us what parts are historical and what are not; and, of matters that are in substance historical, how far is the form in which they come to us, and on which the impression they produce greatly depends, the mere result of the author's imagination and skill? This only is certain, that the reader can never know whether he is reading fact or fiction: this too, that the lessons taught by the book when believed to be historical and therefore Divine, are no longer taught when it becomes a mere composite of fact and fiction—the work of an artist based on tradition.

Besides, this theory leaves the book open to the charge, already urged, of intentional deception. The critic may tell us that the author did not write "as a historian," but put certain traditional materials into "literary form." But this is only the critic's dictum and is of no authority. The phrase "literary form" and its equivalents, often used to cover or account for something that the common eye does not see, is quite misleading. There is nothing literary or artistic in the style of the book or in the arrangement of its materials: it is plain, simple, and straightforward, from beginning to end. And we are bold to repeat what we have already argued, that no one reading the book, unbiassed by theory, can finish the reading without the impression that the author *did* write as a historian; not meaning by this that the book is constructed on a plan in which we can trace a historian's skill or art in working up his materials. He only records in simple and honest words, as matters of fact known to himself, a long train of events without the slightest discoverable indication that they were anything else, and a series of visions which he ascribes to the ministry of angels, and which he represents Daniel as asserting that he had himself received. Of some of these visions Dr. Driver thinks that it is improbable that Daniel received them four hundred years before the days of Antiochus Epiphanes. If he did not, the man who wrote this record of them wrote what he knew to be untrue. So that however offensive the charge of forgery may be, it is confirmed by the failure of every attempt to find some other explanation of the untruthfulness that is stamped on the whole texture of the book, if it be not what it professes to be.

But I have said that after all, Dr. Driver makes admissions or expresses opinions which are sufficient to undermine all the improbabilities and other objections which he alleges against the historicity of the book.

Dr. Driver accepts the dream of Nebuchadnezzar in the second chapter, and its Christian interpretation by Daniel, as genuine. After reciting various opinions with regard to the four "Kingdoms" that were to succeed that of Nebuchadnezzar, he says, "In any case the 'stone cut out without hands' represents the Kingdom of God before which all earthly powers are ultimately to fall" (p. 459). To see the full effect of this belief, the words in which "the Kingdom of God" is represented by "the stone cut out without hands" must be recalled. "In the days of these kings shall the God of Heaven set up a Kingdom which shall never be destroyed: and the Kingdom shall not be left to other people, but it shall break in pieces and consume all these kingdoms, and it shall stand for ever. Forasmuch as thou sawest that the stone was cut out of the mountain without hands, and that it brake in pieces the iron, the brass, the clay, the silver, and the gold; the great God hath made known unto the king what shall come to pass hereafter: and the dream is certain and the interpretation sure."

Here then we have a prophecy not challenged by the critic, delivered four hundred and fifty years before Antiochus, six hundred years before Christ, and stretching forward through we know not how many centuries after Christ, until it attains its final accomplishment. This prophecy we owe to Daniel as much as if he had heard the words of it pronounced from heaven, or as if they were divinely spoken to his inmost consciousness, as such prophecies no doubt often were to other prophets. It is a following up of more ancient prophecies of a Divine Kingdom, under the reign of One who should be at once a son of David and David's Lord, and a presentation of their contents in a form suited to the occasion on which it was delivered, a form which retained its hold upon the heart and hope of the nation until the king's herald announced, "The Kingdom of Heaven is at hand." *The original record of it must have been written at the time of its occurrence.* No imaginable tradition could have preserved it unwritten to the days either of Alexander or of Antiochus, and it is written in that very Aramaic of which Dr. Driver says, "it permits a date after the conquest of Palestine by Alexander." All this has been in substance anticipated in our argument; and it remains now only to point out that on the strength of this one prophecy alone, apart from all that followed it, Daniel is entitled to the designation with which Christ honoured him—" Daniel the prophet."

But this is not the only prophecy in the book which is ascribed to Daniel and which the critic admits to be a prophecy of the Messianic age. With reference to ch. 9. 24–27, he says expressly, " verse 24 describes the Messianic age to succeed the persecutions of Antiochus." " That some of the expressions in this verse describe what was only in fact accomplished by Christ is only natural; though the author pictured the consummation as relatively close at hand, it was actually postponed, and in its fulness only effected by Him " (p. 463). The chief objection he finds is in the figures, seventy weeks, etc., an objection which has been already met and answered. After stating another possible interpretation, he says, " On which side the difficulties are least grave, it must be left for the reader to decide for himself" (p. 466). Acting on the privilege thus graciously allowed to "the reader," I venture to "decide" that there are no difficulties in the Christian interpretation but such as, in their origin at least, were created by a rationalism which aimed at ousting Christ from prophecy. As to any other interpretation the difficulty is fundamental; for no other interpretation can give any reasonable meaning to the words " make an end of sin and make reconciliation for iniquity," or to the words " Messiah shall be cut off "; and even imagination cannot discover any other person than the Christ, or any other event than the great event of Calvary, to which this prophecy might possibly look forward. Edersheim speaks of " the unquestionable fact that no amount of ingenuity can conciliate the Maccabean application of Dan. 9. 24–27 with the chronology of that period, while the Messianic interpretation fits in with it." *Life and Times of the Messiah,* ii. 687.

I claim Dr. Driver then, as at least virtually, accepting this as a genuine Daniel prophecy. That it is a prophecy he does not question; he says that "some of its expressions were only in fact accomplished in Christ," and that "in its fulness it was only effected by Him." Where shall we find the prophet to whom we owe this prophecy? The book says that it was conveyed to Daniel by the angel Gabriel, and it tells us the circumstances in which it was conveyed. Daniel, believing that the seventy years of servitude foretold by Jeremiah were coming to an end, set himself, by prayer and supplication, to plead with God for the pardon and restoration of His people. And then it was that Gabriel was sent to tell Daniel of something far beyond the restoration of his people, both in time and in importance.

If the book does not speak truly in this, I have already argued the consequence. If it speaks truly, can we suppose it probable, or even possible, that the story of Daniel's prayer and Gabriel's revelation was preserved through more than four hundred years by oral tradition, and then reduced to writing by some scribe of whom no indication is given in the book, and of whose existence no indication is found elsewhere?

But be the history of the transmission of this prophecy what it may, we have before us two acknowledged prophecies of Daniel, one in the beginning of his life, "the second year of the reign of Nebuchadnezzar" (ch. 2), and the other in "the first year of Darius the son of Ahasuerus, of the seed of the Medes." Now these being admittedly genuine, *that is, of God,* what becomes of all the objections which the critics elaborate against the series of prophecies of which they are only a part? To insist then on these objections, is it not to fight against God? I have not hesitated to meet them and to repel them. But now I argue that Dr. Driver answers himself, and that his concessions undermine the ground on which he and other critics stand, when they set themselves to dispute the methods in which it has pleased God to reveal His will. If the objections are well founded, the prophecies now acknowledged must be abandoned; if the prophecies are still acknowledged, the objections must be abandoned. *The one or the other must give way.*

In the face of such a dilemma would it not be more conducive to a true conclusion, more likely to end inquiry in truth, if the inquirer, instead of first traversing through a maze of uncertainties, probabilities and improbabilities, possibilities and impossibilities, should begin his inquiry where certainty has been already attained, and make that certainty both his starting point and his guide to other conclusions? In saying this my appeal is only to Christian inquirers and critics. The Kuenens of criticism will scout this counsel, but Christian men, men who believe in Christ, who believe that He was divinely foreshadowed in the prophecies of the Book of Daniel, would not only act logically in the course I indicate, but would be pursuing the only course that is logical. I claim Dr. Driver, whether against his will or not, as an upholder, on his own showing, of the prophetic character of Daniel, and by consequence of the historicity of his book.

Dr. Driver's own formal conclusion respecting the book confirms us in this position. While he holds that the book is to be dated in the days of Antiochus Epiphanes, and that it was written "on the basis supplied by tradition," the writer, he says, "represents Daniel, whose age had coincided with the last great turning-point in the history of his people, when

Israel became permanently dependent upon the great powers of the world, as surveying from the centre and stronghold of heathenism the future conflicts between the world and the theocracy, and declaring the gradual degeneration of the former and the final triumph of the latter. The prophets," he adds, " do not merely foretell history ; they also interpret it (Gen. 9. 25-27 ; Isa. 10. 3-7). And the Book of Daniel does this on a more comprehensive scale than any other prophetic book. It contains a religious philosophy of history. It deals not with a single empire, but with a succession of empires, showing how all form parts of a whole, ordained for prescribed terms by God and issuing in results designed by Him" (p. 481).

What need have we of further witness ? The book is not only a "*prophetic book*," but, in some respects at least, the greatest of prophetic books. Now the book did not write itself, nor did it fall, already written, from the skies. It must have had a human author, and he must be reckoned the greatest of the prophets. He " surveyed " and foretold the history of the world on " a more comprehensive scale than any " of his predecessors. How came he to be able to do this ? Living four hundred years after Daniel, he chose the " age " of Daniel as his stand-point, because it coincided with the last great turning-point in the history of Israel, and, surveying the future from " the centre and stronghold of heathenism," he saw more clearly and fully than any other the outcome of the conflicts of the world with the Divine purpose to establish a kingdom that shall never be destroyed.

With this conception of the book before us, in the main a true conception, there are certain questions which call for answer. (1) How comes it to pass that the name of this great prophetic writer has been lost to the Church and the world ? History has told us more of the age in which he is said to have lived, than of any other of the six centuries which separate

Daniel from Christ. And we know that the patriots who waged deadly war with the cruel oppressor and persecutor of their nation mourned that there was no prophet to counsel them. And all the while there was a great unknown, whose voice was not heard in city or wilderness, in camp or temple, whose prophecy of the coming Saviour should be the joy of all later ages. The scepticism which doubts or denies his existence is fully justified. (2) Assuming the existence of a prophet or author capable, either by inspiration or by genius, of taking a more "comprehensive" survey of the history of the Church and of the world than his predecessors, how comes it that he should ascribe all his knowledge of the future to visions with which Daniel was favoured four hundred years before? Was he fortunate enough to have discovered an ancient Babylonian manuscript or roll written by Daniel himself, in which Daniel was careful to certify certain visions as his, with the prefix "I Daniel?" If so, the real author of the book was Daniel himself, and not some contemporary of the Maccabees. But I am not aware that the recovery of a lost or forgotten book four hundred years old is among the hypotheses of criticism. And the question remains, how did the author—the real author—come to use the name of Daniel as he did, ascribing to him visions which he knew were not Daniel's, and even signing them, as it were, with Daniel's name? Say that it was a literary device to give greater effect to the lessons which he wanted to teach: was this honest? Was this a prophetic practice? To argue that nothing parallel or analogous to such a practice can be found in Biblical prophetic history would be a waste of labour. Should anyone speaking in the name of God—I have not to do with false prophets or heathen soothsayers, but with acknowledged prophets of the true God, the God of Truth—should any such dare such a device he might hear a voice from Heaven saying, "What hast thou to do (thus) to declare my statutes?" But critics cover over this device, when theory requires it, with a veil of fine words, and "so they wrap it up." The author of the Book of Daniel, judging by the aim and spirit of the book, was, we repeat, a man of intense godliness, who "feared God above many," and was morally incapable of ascribing the record of them to Daniel if he did not honestly believe what he said. *All this is logically involved in the honourable title of a "prophetic book," which Dr. Driver gives to the Book of Daniel.*

CONCLUSION.

IT is with pain I note that Dr. Driver entirely ignores the fact that Christ acknowledged the Book of Daniel as a part of His Bible, that He quoted a prophecy which it contains as a prophecy of "Daniel the Prophet," saying to those who had the book in their hands, "Whoso readeth, let him understand," and that He appropriated the language of the book as descriptive of His own glorious second coming. All this is passed by unmentioned, as absolutely as if it were non-existent. In fact, in Dr. Driver's discussion of the question Christ has no *locus standi*. And if He has no *locus standi* in considering the claims of this prophet, neither has He by right in considering the claims of any other; for no other has received from Him a more direct personal recognition than has Daniel. There is no room here for questions of date and authorship. The question is one of substance in the fullest sense; and the claim to interpret the Old Testament in its own light alone, without reference to the new, involves an entire reversal of the aphorism of Augustine, now time honoured and hitherto accepted by all who profess and call themselves Christians, that in the Old Testament there is a veiling of the New, and in the New Testament an unveiling of the Old.

But there is a higher authority than that of Augustine involved in this matter. On the first and on the last of the forty days during which He remained on earth after His resurrection, Christ's theme was of the fulfilment of Old

Testament prophecy. On the last day of His sojourn on earth—for such seems to have been the occasion of the statement in Luke 24. 44–47—He repeated the great lesson which he had so often taught, bestowing on it more pains and care than upon any other. "What weight and worth," says Dr. Hanna, truly, "does this attach to these Old Testament testimonies to His Messiahship? What a sanction does it lend to our searching of their prophetic records in the belief that we shall find much there pointing, in prophecy and type and figure, to the Lamb slain before the foundation of the earth, the Lamb of God, which taketh away the sin of the world!"*

But modern criticism can interpret the law and the prophets, and find very little Christ in them. One of its apostles writes thus:

"Though we find the fifty-third chapter of Isaiah repeatedly applied to our Lord in the New Testament, and commonly regarded among Christians as a prophecy of the Passion, a careful perusal of the whole composition in which it appears shows that the servant of the Lord, of whom the sufferings in this chapter are predicated, is the pious remnant of the Jews, or perhaps some persecuted prophet such as Jeremiah."†

On this bold pronouncement I shrink from comment, except to express wonder that a Christian critic should ask Christian readers thus to read the ancient oracle which, it is confessed, is repeatedly applied to our Lord in the New Testament. I may add that a more untrue statement has never been penned by

---

* *The Early Life of Christ*, complete ed., p. 643.

† The reader will find a careful study of the whole question of the "Servant of Jehovah" in Isa. 42–53, in that admirable work, *Isaiah One and his Book One* by Principal Douglas, of Glasgow, pp. 32–34, 312–318. See also Prof. John Forbes on *The Servant of the Lord in Isaiah Fifty-three*, and a valuable work with the same title by the Rev. W. Urwick, M.A.

Exegete than that a careful perusal of the whole composition of Isa. **53.** shows that the person of whose sufferings it speaks, is either " the pious, persecuted remnant of the Jews " or some prophet like Jeremiah. This is the subterfuge under which unbelieving Jews were wont to shelter themselves from the argument which Christians found in this prediction of the suffering and atoning Christ. But let anyone who is not under the necessity of Jewish unbelief, or who is not the slave of a theory which must be maintained at any cost—such for example as the positively anti-supernatural, or that of Riehm which limits the prophet's vision to his historical horizon, and the contents of a prophecy to the prophet's understanding of it—read the chapter sentence by sentence, and see whether, by any amount of force, he can find it possible to realise its statements in the experience of the Jewish remnant or of any Jewish martyr, with that glorious ending, " He shall see of the travail of His soul, and shall be satisfied ; by His knowledge shall my righteous servant justify many ; for He shall bear their iniquities. Therefore will I divide Him a portion with the great, and He shall divide the spoil with the strong ; because He hath poured out his soul unto death; and He bare the sin of many, and made intercession for the transgressors." "It is," says Delitzch, " as if written under the cross on Golgotha, and illumined by the bright clearness of the now fulfilled exaltation." " That vicarious expiation is here spoken of, cannot be seriously questioned," says Orelli. " As plainly as human language is able, it said and emphasised (*vv.* 4, 5, 6, 10, 11, 12) that the sinless one bore the punishment which else must have fallen on the entire people." Exclude this idea, and this whole Scripture becomes a meaningless mass.

But what shall we say then of this bold setting aside of the authority of the New Testament? The New Testament knows nothing of any fulfilment of this prophecy but in Christ.

John the Baptist's words, "Behold the Lamb of God which taketh away the sin of the world" were founded upon it. The Evangelist Philip taught the Ethiopian that it was of Christ the Prophet spoke in this chapter (Acts **8.** 30—35). Its very specific language respecting the character of the sufferer and the object of His sufferings is adopted by the Apostle Peter, as descriptive of the character and atonement of Christ (1 Pet. **2.** 21—25). St. Mark says that the Scripture was fulfilled which saith, "And He was numbered with the transgressors," when Jesus was crucified between two malefactors (**15.** 28). And Christ Himself quoted these words in Gethsemane as words which "must be accomplished" in Him (Luke **22.** 37). But none of all this was in the original prophecy, we are told, even in a secondary sense or on "the theory of a double interpretation." Let us be thankful, however, that there is a way of escape from an utter rejection of the Christian application of this Scripture. "If Messianic prophecies were realised in their immediate connection, *which was all that the prophets contemplated*,* they still admit of subsequent realisation under other circumstances." Hence it is that while "one hero after another was hailed with acclamation—now Hezekiah, now Cyrus, now Judas Maccabaeus, † none of them realise the hopes that are set upon them." At last Jesus Christ comes

---

* The Apostle Peter had not heard of the Riehm theory! See what he says of the Prophets in his First Epistle 1. 10, 11. According to him the Spirit that was in them testified of things that lay far beyond their "immediate connection" and horizon. And Christ Himself tells us that they "desired to see" these things and did not see them. Daniel himself tells us that he "did not understand" a vision with which he was favoured, and his desire to understand was not gratified (Dan. 12. 8). The critical assumption that the meaning of a prophecy was absolutely conditioned by the Prophet's environments is unscientific and unbiblical.

† Where the critic has found that Hezekiah, Cyrus and Maccabaeus were in their turn or time "acclaimed" Messiahs—or even in germ or in principle shadowy anticipations of the Messiah—I know not, except in his own imagination.

and gathers up in Himself, into Himself, all that was so imperfectly accomplished in the past, "and carries to perfection its latent ideas in a glory never dreamed of by their authors." The reply to all this is obvious. The Messianic prediction of the fifty-third of Isaiah was not one that could be even "imperfectly" accomplished before Christ came, and what He did was not to "carry to perfection its latent ideas," but to do once for all in the end of time the one great thing which it foretold—to offer Himself a sacrifice for sin and thus to bear a world's iniquities. The misleading expectation of the Jews in Christ's time was, that their Messiah was to be a mighty king and conqueror, and of such they *might* find a shadow in Cyrus or Judas Maccabaeus, although there is no evidence that they did. Hence it was that Christ found it so hard to make His disciples understand that it "behoved" Him to suffer ; and when, in proof of this, He appealed to the "Prophets," we know not where He found His proof if it was not in this fifty-third of Isaiah and in the prophecy of Daniel that the Messiah should be cut off. And if He did appeal to this proof—was it proof ? was He really the subject of these prophecies? According to the theory He was not. All that "the prophet contemplated" was "something that was in the immediate connection" of his prophecy. And what we are led to suppose that Christ found in the prophecy for the instruction of His disciples, was not in the prophecy at all !

On this subject nothing could be more to the point or more conclusive than the homely words of a learned divine lately deceased. "I should like," he said, "to ask reverential students whether, if the only way in which a suffering Messiah could be found in the Old Testament, was a roundabout and indirect way of getting Him in,—whether Christ would have been warranted in putting down the two on the way to Emmaus as a set of stupids!—for ἀνόητοι is not 'O fools' nor 'O foolish men,' but 'O stupids' (if we could use such a jibe)—'O silly ones:' meaning, 'where have your eyes been that you could not see what stared you in the face!' Christ made their hearts burn within them by showing that His actual sufferings and His emerging out of them into glory were all written in their own Scriptures. On no other ground could the disciples have been reproached for their ignorance."

I dwell on this particular case as an illustration of how many modern critics not only deny to Christ a *locus standi*, as a factor in determining the question of the genuineness of such prophetic books as that of Daniel, but also minimise to the very verge of extinction, sometimes even to extinction, the most emphatic predictions in which the Christian Church has hitherto seen Christ in the Old Testament Scriptures. If it be an offence to true criticism to force Christ into Old Testament texts in which He has no rightful place, it is a greater offence to true criticism to shut Him out of Scriptures in which by rights He has the first and only place. And this is what is done by interpretations which find Hezekiah rather than Christ in the ninth of Isaiah, and Jeremiah rather than Christ in the fifty-third of Isaiah.

We thus end where we began. The authority of Christ is Alpha and Omega to us on every question on which He has spoken. This is a position from which we dare not depart. "Heaven and earth shall pass away, but My words shall not pass away." They belong essentially, unchangeably, to that "Word of the Lord which abideth for ever." Our interpretation of them may be wrong, and all readers have the right, which we have claimed, to go direct to the Master to hear what HE says. It cannot be denied that He was right in His understanding of all that the Prophets said relating to Himself, yea that He could not be mistaken on the subject. We believe as well that He who knew Himself to be so wonderfully fore-mirrored in the Scriptures, knew the human hands by which the mirror was framed. So that to us He is Alpha and Omega both as the Interpreter and as the Interpretation of the Old Testament. "Without Him (to quote from myself) the Old Testament is an insoluble mystery. Not only do a multitude of passages scattered over its pages lose their meaning, but the Book loses the key to its unity, and no substitute can be found to repair the loss. What makes the wonder of the Book the greater, and the more manifestly Divine, is that the consummation which we find in the Christ of the New Testament was foreshadowed in the very first sentences of the Old, in which we see man separated in his creation from, and raised high above, all living creatures, alone made in the image of his Maker, falling morally from his high estate, but yet not abandoned as a castaway—rather in the very hour of his fall rescued from despair by the hope of a redemption which was made sure by a Divine promise that should be as a golden thread, running through centuries and milleniums until the fulness of the times, when angels should be sent from Heaven to announce the birth of the Promised One. "O the depth of the riches both of the wisdom and the knowledge" and the grace "of God."

CHAPTER XI.

SUPPLEMENTAL : ON ALLEGED HISTORICAL DIFFICULTIES.

By the Editor of "The Babylonian and Oriental Record."

A.
Jehoiakim and "King" Nebuchadnezzar.

THE first charge of historical error which has been preferred against the Book of Daniel relates to the events recorded in chap. 1. 1–4. The charge divides itself into three categorical corrections : (1) that instead of the third year of Jehoiakim, the author should have spoken of the fourth; (2) that Nebuchadnezzar had not then succeeded his father, and is erroneously termed the King of Babylon : and (3) that a deportation of certain persons is said to have taken place in the *third* year of Jehoiakim, when such a deportation was only carried out at a later period.

To discuss the third of these alleged corrections would require a review of the various recorded Babylonian invasions of Palestine and their results, with the history of the sundry deportations which followed; for the Jewish exile was not one event, but several, and such a review would involve a digression which is not needful to establish the *bona fides* of the Biblical history. Enough to say that while one critic, with a confidence which is no sure sign of superior knowledge, declares roundly that no such deportation took place, another candidly admits that it cannot be disproved, although he thinks it improbable. But we may ask wherein the improbability consists. It is far from likely that the author of the

BRICK OF NEBUCHADNEZZAR.

Thousands of Nebuchadnezzar's bricks are in existence, usually stamped with his name and titles as King of Babylon and Firstborn son of Nabopolassar.

To face p. 173.

book, whether he wrote from personal knowledge 500 b.c., or from tradition 250 b.c., should have made so very specific a statement if he had not good reason for the assertion. It can scarcely have been a matter of haphazard, especially as we shall find that the author, whoever he was, was very particular in his statement of dates. The fact of a deportation of Jews at the time of the accession of Nebuchadnezzar to the throne is confirmed by the statement of Berosus that he "committed the captives he had taken from the Jews," to the charge of others, "while he went in haste over the desert to Babylon," to secure his father's Throne.

The second alleged error, viz., describing Nebuchadnezzar as "King," while his father was still alive, involves no real difficulty. Nebuchadnezzar was associated with his father Nabopolassar in the government (as Belshazzar was at a later period with *his* father), and was the monarch's representative in all the lands into which he led his armies. In that position it was not even a popular mistake to call him "King"; he was certainly so to all intents and purposes. The author of the book could not have been ignorant of Nebuchadnezzar's relation to the throne of Babylon.

Then as to the first alleged error—that instead of the *third* year of Jehoiakim the author should have said the *fourth*—one is tempted to say off-hand—if the story is untrue, the author should have said neither the one nor the other, for the events being imaginary or apocryphal, took place neither in the one year nor the other. But happily the tablets furnish an explanation which shows that neither the Book of Jeremiah was in error when it called a certain year the fourth of Jehoiakim, nor was the Book of Daniel in error when it called the *same year* the third of Jehoiakim. The fact is that the Babylonians and the Jews reckoned the beginning of a king's reign *from different starting points*. The Babylonians, instead of reckoning a king's reign from the day of his accession, counted from the following New Year's day, until which his first year did not technically begin, the last broken year being assigned to the former sovereign.

The Jews on the contrary reversed this process; and as we know from familiar usage—"three days and three nights," etc.—gave the monarch who succeeded the credit of the whole year of his accession, although he had only begun to reign near the end of the term. This explanation not only meets the entire difficulty, but furnishes an independent argument in fixing the date of the Book of Daniel; for it tends to prove that the book was written in Babylon, and by someone who was familiar with the Babylonian method of numbering the years of their kings' reigns, and that at a period when this method was familiarly and universally known as it could not have been if the book had been written hundreds of years later in Palestine.

It may be added that so careful is the author to keep his dates in order, and so important does he appear to consider them, that after stating that Nebuchadnezzar had in that 3rd (*i.e.* 4th year) of Jehoiakim, carried away certain princely captives who were put under linguistic and other training for *three years*, he asserts that the events recorded in ch. 2 took place in the second year of Nebuchadnezzar, which would have been a contradiction of himself, but for the method of computation which he adopts, and to which we have just referred.

B.

Belshazzar.

One of the most determined and confident points of attack upon the veracity of the Book of Daniel is that which concerns the position and career of Belshazzar. The manner in which that attack recoils on those who deliver it, may be regarded, however, as a considerable triumph for the defenders of the sacred narrative. Never does the meretricious method of statement and argument to which we are accustomed, on the part of our most recent English critic, appear so glaring as when he proceeds practically to eliminate the Babylonian Prince from the page of serious history, and boldly asserts that there was no "King" Belshazzar.

1. By an unaccountable obliquity of vision, Dr. Farrar seems to see that shadowy personality (as he chooses to regard him) acting, not as viceroy in the capital, but as the leader of a portion of his father's army in the field, and at length "conquered in Borsippa" (p. 54).* If this critic can make the Prince's habitat anywhere except Babylon, he knows that he will have accomplished two things, (1), he will have proved that the *res gestæ*, as described by the Biblical writer, never took place ; and, (2), that the author of the "religious novel," as he describes the work, has deliberately, and for some unimaginable purpose, altered and even reversed the positions of Belshazzar and his father, Nabonidus. But what are we really entitled to affirm on the subject ?

It requires no proof to show that any man (*à fortiori*, any hereditary prince), acting as a viceroy, would in the East be popularly known as "king." Recent discoveries, besides, have made it clear that Belshazzar was formally associated with his father in the Royal Government, and that a great deal, unmistakeably historical, is known both of him and his father, Nabonidus. The latter made a fair show of devotion in his earlier days. In an inscription obtained a few years ago by Mr. Hormuzd Rassam,† he is stated to have given in the eighteenth day of Nisan, in the year of his accession (B.C. 556),

---

* *The Book of Daniel.*
† *Bab.* and *Oriental Record,* vol. i., p. 209.

a very rich offering to the Sun-god, in the temple at Sippara. And another inscription,* discovered in the ruins of the temple of Mugheir (Ur of the Chaldees), makes Nabonidus pray piously regarding his heir : "and for Bel-sarra-utsur, my firstborn son, the offspring of my heart; the fear of thy mighty divinity cause thou to dwell in his heart; may he not be given to sin or favour untruth." But this "religiousness" was only transitory; and, at the time of the invasion by Cyrus, he was openly neglecting the gods and their offerings, incurring thereby the hatred of the priest caste, which indeed is supposed to have conspired against his dynasty.

Belshazzar, on the contrary, appears to have been a devotee throughout. Early in his father's reign (5th year B.C. 550) he had, as crown-prince, a separate household, with a scribe and a major-domo, the latter of whom had filled the same office to Lubasi-Kudur, the son of the former king, Nerighssar, whom Nabonidus had dethroned and succeeded. In a most interesting inscription in the British Museum (S.+329, 76, 11, 17) we have a detailed account of the munificent gifts which Belshazzar, "the son of the King," bestowed on Bel, Nebo, Nergal, and the Lady of Erech, in the 7th year of his father's reign. In No. 1043 of Dr. Strassmaiers's *Inscriptions of Nabonidus* there is a record of a tithe paid for his daughter by her brother Belshazzar, showing his regard for these religious duties so neglected by his father. And we also possess a statement as to the dowry given by the crown-prince on the occasion of his own daughter's marriage. Moreover Canon Rawlinson † unhesitatingly affirms that it is proved historically that Belshazzar was co-sovereign with Nabonidus, and he even adds that "Bel-shar-uzur, *who was the grandson of Nebuchadnezzar*, in his father's absence, took the direction of affairs within

---

* *W. A. I.*, I. 68, vol. ii., 24-31.
† *Ancient Mon.*, vol. iii., p. 70.

CLAY CYLINDER OF NABONIDUS,
containing a prayer for his son Belshazzar (Belu-Shar-uzur, *i.e.*, Bel protect the King).

To face p. 176.

ALLEGED HISTORICAL DIFFICULTIES. 177

the city." He carried out all the functions of the Babylonian monarchy, and prayers were offered for him in this capacity. For about four years Nabonidus is said to have been in Tema, either because of bodily or mental sickness (the latter would present an interesting comparison with Nebuchadnezzar's insanity) or having vowed himself to the life of a solitary (as Winckler believes, but as seems improbable for many reasons).* He did not even take part in the New Year's Festival, when the presence of the monarch was demanded. Doubtless Belshazzar acted throughout for his father.

2. Dr. Farrar objects to any proof of the prince's viceroyalty being gathered from the words of his promise to Daniel (ch. 5. 7): "He shall be the third ruler in the Kingdom."

The critic is so confident here that he flatly declares the translation "third ruler" to be "utterly untenable." But so far from this being so, we find the R.V. adhering to this rendering—the phrase "rule as one of three" in the margin being admitted only on the final revision, and even that representing a very different idea from "a board of three," as suggested by Dr. Farrar. The Jewish Rabbis have nearly unanimously translated the words "third ruler"; and Winer—an almost indisputable authority on such points—affirms this to be correct. Kautzch and Behrmann, in their most recent works, give the same decision. The Chief Rabbi says, in a note addressed to Dr. Anderson and published in "*Daniel in the Critics' Den*" (p. 26): "I cannot absolutely find fault with Archdeacon Farrar for translating the words 'the third part of the kingdom,' as he follows herein two of our commentators of great repute. . . . On the other hand, others of our commentators . . . translate this passage as 'he shall be the third ruler in the Kingdom.'" This rendering seems to be more strictly in accord with the literal meaning of the words, as

---

* *See* Thompson's "*Introd. to Daniel*" in the *Pulpit Commentary*, vol. xxvii.

shown by Dr. Winer in his "*Grammatik des Chaldaismus.*" In the face of this and other evidence, is not the expression "utterly untenable," as applied to the usual rendering, a little too sweeping?

3. Several critics, among whom is Professor Sayce, appeal to the (supposed) silence of the Annalistic Tablet of Cyrus concerning Belshazzar as indicating his probable death; and Dr. Farrar thinks this shows that the *Chasid*, who wrote this pious fiction (the Book of Daniel), must have kept him alive merely for the dramatic purposes of the scene in ch. 5! But what are the ascertainable facts on this point?

In the first place, as Dr. Anderson has remarked in his trenchant exposure of so many sophistries ("*Daniel in the Critics' Den*," p. 28) the document was written by the Persian Monarch expressly to show that his mission was divine, and not even contrary to the wishes of the Babylonians themselves. We therefore very strongly decline to admit (as is too often demanded in similar cases) that if any statement there seems to be, or even is, irreconcilable with the record of Scripture, the latter must on that account be held to be untrue. But such a quite legitimate defence as this is happily unnecessary here. For the tablet in question is *not* silent regarding Belshazzar. Only one authority (Prof. Sayce) reads an expression in that document as to the demise of a certain personage as referring to "the wife of the King." Pinches, Boscawen, Ball, Hagen, and others assert very strongly that it should be read "the king," or rather "son of the king."

The Tablet says that "on 14th Tammuz (June–July) Sippara was taken without fighting, and Nabonidus fled." The fallen monarch afterwards, according to Berosus, surrendered to Cyrus at Borsippa and was awarded estates and probably even a government in Carmania. The document proceeds: "On the 16th Tammuz Gobryas (note the special mention

ALLEGED HISTORICAL DIFFICULTIES.

here of the conqueror's general) and the soldiers of Cyrus entered Babylon (but are not said to have taken complete possession of it) without fighting." On the 3rd day of Marchesvan (Oct.-Nov.) Cyrus himself arrived; then follows the statement : "*and the son of the king died.*" That this was Belshazzar is made more likely by the statement that Akkad lamented greatly for him, he having formerly held a military command in North Babylonia, where he was much beloved. A week of mourning ensued, and a state-burial was conducted by Cambyses, the son of Cyrus, in person—a not incredible statement when we consider the generous treatment which, from motives of policy or otherwise, was extended to Nabonidus himself.

Notwithstanding the assertion that the entry of the invaders into the capital was bloodless, we may doubt whether the whole vast metropolis was at once surrendered. We certainly know that for a whole year (covering the personal arrival of the Persian conqueror), the commercial tablets of Babylon were still dated "in the reign of Nabonidus," and only those from Sippara bear the words "in the reign of Cyrus." It is more than likely that the subjugation of the city was only completed on the 3rd or 11th Marchesvan, when also Gobryas was installed as the supreme prefect or viceroy.

A most interesting reading of a sentence in the Nabonidus-Cyrus Chronicle has been recently suggested by Dr. Hagen in the *Beiträge zu Assyriologie*, 1896, p. 293. It is as follows : " In the night of the 11th of Marchesvan, *Gobryas fell upon the son of the King and killed him.*" If this eminent scholar's rendering be correct, it would appear, as is very probable, that a portion of the city had held out until after the arrival of Cyrus himself on 3rd Marchesvan, although he boasts *more suo* that "dissensions were allayed before him." Belshazzar, who was, we have reason to believe, a brave soldier, along with a desperate band, may have defended the palace for eight days longer, until on the 11th Marchesvan, in the fury of a closing struggle, the Median general may have slain him with his own hand, or at least boasted that he did so. The dramatic dénoûement would thus be complete : the Babylonian Viceroy slain, the great Median soldier at once receives his vice-royalty !

4. Dr. Farrar must have allowed considerably for the extreme credulity of his readers, when he pressed so strongly the argument that Belshazzar having been termed Nebuchadnezzar's *son* in this book proves it therefore to be unveracious. For (1) the word translated " son " may quite as well bear the interpretation " grandson " or " descendant " ; (2) Assyrian kings are known to have unblushingly declared their pedigree to be derived from Sargon and other illustrious monarchs of former ages, with whom they had no blood relationship whatever ; (3), it may have been a customary although high-flown compliment, to describe both Nabonidus and Belshazzar as " sons " of Nebuchadnezzar, their predecessor on the throne ; and (4), the greatest possible likelihood exists that the prince whom " the queen " and Daniel thus addressed, was actually descended from the mighty king. The Babylonian records lead us to believe that a daughter of Nebuchadnezzar, was married to Nabu-baladh-su-ikbi, the father of Nabonidus, so that on the maternal side Belshazzar was thus really a " son " of Nebuchadnezzar. And it is not at all unlikely that when Nabonidus usurped the Kingdom, he sought—as was common in such cases—to make it more secure to his dynasty by a similar alliance, so that Belshazzar would in that case be really the grandson of the great monarch. Mr. Boscawen says * that from the 7th year of Nabonidus' reign to the fall of the empire

---

* *Trans. Vict. Inst.* vol. xviii., p. 117.

the crown prince "seems to have been the leading spirit and ruler of the kingdom; and this may account in some measure for his prominence in the Book of Daniel."

A few words may be said here regarding the great feast which, begun and carried on with blasphemous revelry, had such a tragic termination. Unlike the Persians,* the Babylonians admitted their women to many of their public carousals. The king's wives and concubines are said to have been present on this occasion, while "*the* queen," whoever she was, had possibly declined to be a party to the orgy of the viceroy and his *convives*. She may have been the daughter of Nebuchadnezzar and the wife of Nabonidus; for it is unlikely that she was the mother of the latter, as that royal personage seems to have died at Sippara in the seventh year of the king, while he was at Tema, "the king's son" and the soldiers mourning her for three days in Akhad. This princess, who was drawn suddenly into the banquet-house by the loud voices of Belshazzar and his nobles, and probably the screams of the terrified women, was thoroughly conversant with past events in the Babylonian court, and especially with Nebuchadnezzar's part in them, while it is to be observed that she has implicit faith in the power of Daniel to read the writing which flashed across the " plaster," such as we know, from recent discoveries, to have been on the walls of this particular palace.

The feast which had such a terrible conclusion was, it would appear, that annually celebrated on the 15th Tammuz in honour of the name-god of the month and Istar, his bride. Belshazzar, with his superstitious devotion, would see that the lascivious rites were punctiliously observed, and the gold and silver vessels of Jehovah's temple were requisitioned to make this occasion one of special magnificence, and, as some believe,

---

* *See* the Book of Esther, *passim.*

of deliberate insult to the Hebrews, who were suspected of complicity with the invaders. At this high festival the Babylonian Adonis was supposed, first, to die, when the simulated grief of the men and women would be intense ; then, as he rose to life and embraced his beloved Istar, the wild shouts of joy would be heard throughout the palace. It was probably at that moment, when the holy vessels of the living God were raised to the lips of this half-drunken company, under the gorgeous golden candelabra, to celebrate the resurrection of Tammuz, and when the men and women "praised the gods of gold," that " the fingers of a man's hand " wrote across the wall the fateful words : *Mene, mene, tekel, upharsin.*

Thus it was at midnight, between 15th and 16th Tammuz, that, as Greek authors as well as the tablet have asserted, Babylon, or part of it, was taken—and that practically without resistance—by Gobryas, the Median General of Cyrus.

Belshazzar, according to the Book of Daniel, had sufficient time to confer the honours he had promised. But is it at all necessary to suppose that the expression "In that night was Belshazzar the Chaldean king slain " compels us to believe that this event took place immediately after the royal debauch ? He was doubtless killed either at the instance of Gobryas (possibly, as Dr. Hagen reads, by the general's own hand), or by some priestly conspirator ; and the event may have taken place when Cyrus arrived, on 3rd Marchesvan, or more probably later, if the above reading be correct, viz., on 11th Marchesvan, when the tablet declares the death of the king's son took place, and goes on to describe his state funeral, which was conducted by the Persian Crown Prince, Cambyses. The division of the Book of Daniel into chapters and verses, as we possess it, is admittedly not of Divine authority, and just as *v.* 31 in the Hebrew Bible is taken from ch. **5.** and stands as the first verse of ch. **6.**, we might possibly, if there seemed to be good reason for it, close ch. 5. with *v*. 29. and commence ch. 6. with *v*. 30, (which, in the A.V., begins a new paragraph = ¶). By this simple arrangement the text remains absolutely untouched, but we are introduced to a new series of events by a section of the book which would begin thus : "In that night (in which) Belshazzar the Chaldean king was slain, Darius the Mede received the kingdom," &c.* In some recensions these words occur after the description of Daniel's decoration : "And the interpretation came upon Belshazzar the king, and the Kingdom was taken from the Chaldeans and given to the Medes and Persians," leaving the date of the fulfilment of the fatal writing indefinite. But the treatment of the received text which I have suggested above makes our acceptance of this view quite unnecessary, while it completely harmonizes with the conclusions from the Cyrus tablet, which have been thus summarized by Mr. T. G. Pinches † : "Tammuz (June—July) 16th ; Gobryas, general of Cyrus, goes down to Babylon. Marchesvan (Oct.—Nov.) 3rd : Cyrus arrives at Babylon and promises peace to the city. Gobryas appoints governors there. *Marchesvan* 11*th* : Action of Gobryas and *death of Belshazzar during the night.* Adar 27th, Nisan 3 (Feb.—March) : Mourning for Belshazzar. . . . . . . From the above," Mr. Pinches adds, "we see that Belshazzar was practically king when Babylon was taken. The *final* action took place, and Belshazzar was killed during the night. The city was taken by Gobryas, not by Cyrus. Moreover,

---

* We know that such writers as Rev. E. H. Thomson, B.D., who zealously support the authenticity of the Book of Daniel, have doubts as to the genuineness of *v*. 30 because it is omitted in certain versions of the Septuagint, thus differing from the Masoretic text. The writer of this chapter offers the suggestion in the text as a possible alternative, if thought necessary, to reconcile the author of the Book of Daniel with the author of the Tablet. Mr. Pinches gives his opinion that it seems a reasonable reading of the Chaldee. And other good Hebrew scholars concur in the opinion.

† In *The Guardian*, Oct. 14, 1891.

Gobryas appointed governors in Babylon. It can hardly be regarded, therefore, as unreasonable to identify Gobryas and Darius as being one and the same person."

It is to be borne in mind that Nabonidus had only two sons: Belshazzar, the elder, crown prince and viceroy, and the younger, named Nebuchadnezzar, who lived to lead an unsuccessful revolt a good many years later. If a "son of the king" was slain on the 11th Marchesvan, as the tablet asserts—and there is no reason to doubt the statement as historical—it must have been Belshazzar, who therefore cannot have been killed, (as we have hitherto concluded—without any grounds for questioning it such as we possess now)—on 16th Tammuz, the night of the festival and the miraculous writing on the wall.

If a close grammatical and exegetical examination of the received text should compel scholars to conclude that, according to that version, it was certainly on the night of the feast, and not later, that Belshazzar was slain, then there still remains the alternative of asserting that the statement on the Cyrus tablet does not refer to that prince, or, *which is surely quite possible, that it is incorrect. It is as likely that the royal Persian chronicler should err in regard to a date as the author of the Book of Daniel, whoever he may have been:*—a suggestion, this, which is in no way gratuitous or groundless, the proclivity and practice of Oriental chroniclers to magnify their heroes at the expense of truth being well known, whereas there is nothing more striking in Hebrew history than its unvarnished truth-telling, even at the cost of the honour of those who might be considered its heroes.

C.
Darius.

But if the critics make such a confident assault in regard to the personality and career of Belshazzar, what must be the triumph with which they hail the difficulties which everyone readily admits beset the question as to the identity and historical position of the ruler named Darius by the author of the book of Daniel?

At the outset we must entirely demur to any demand that those who take the Biblical author seriously are bound to solve this hard problem, or to extricate the exact truth from the numerous suggestions made alike by assailants and apologists; or, failing this, to suffer judgment to go by default against the sacred book.

On the other hand, we maintain that if such statements of facts and such cogent considerations can be advanced as may make it *not incredible* that the writer was referring to an inner circle of Babylonian government under the Persian conqueror, which, although it did really exist, does not appear on the face of contemporary records so far as those have yet come to light; that is all that is needed to arrest a verdict of unveracity against the Book of Daniel. And, indeed, the lacuna before referred to in the Cylinder of Cyrus occurs exactly where a reference might have been expected to such a viceregal arrangement as would leave room for the " vassal-king " we presume Darius to have been.

Moreover, even a "religious novelist" was not likely to gratuitously intercalate a new and impossible sovereign into the list of known monarchs, and that without attributing to him any specialty more than a kindheartedness such as might have been found in some other real despot.

If Darius be a mythical personage, it is perfectly inconceivable : (1) why the author should have introduced him at all, inasmuch as Cyrus (whose existence is not denied by any one) would have served equally well the dramatic purposes for which he uses the other ; (2) why he should have been so careful to describe him as "the Mede" (ch. **5.** 31), and "the son of Ahasuerus, of the seed of the Medes, which was *made king* over the realm of the Chaldeans" (ch. **9.** 1) ; or (3) why he should have fixed his age exactly at 62.

An English romance writer, wishing to invent a sovereign, *e.g.*, between Edward II. and Edward III., would surely never startle his readers by describing him as a Frenchman or a Burgundian, or as the son of some well-known foreign prince ; nor would he, except for some fictitious purpose which does not appear in *this* book, have fixed on the prosaic age of 62 for his hero !

But is it really impossible to find a clue to Daniel's Darius, or a place for him in history ? On the contrary, some of the most recent investigators (*e.g.*, Mr. Pinches and Mr. St. Chad Boscawen) insist that, if the reading of the Babylonian chronicle be as they believe it to be, then it is impossible to do otherwise than identify Gobryas with Darius the Mede. Mr. Pinches says that "This identification (though not without its difficulties) receives a certain amount of support from Daniel **6.** 1, 'It pleased Darius to set over the kingdom 120 satraps' ; an act that finds a parallel in the chronicle which states that after Cyrus promised peace to Babylon, 'Gobryas his *governor* appointed governors in Babylon.'"

Mr. Boscawen says that Gobryas (Ugbaru) was formerly prefect of Gutium (Kurdistan) and "was appointed on 3rd Marchesvan B.C. 538—after taking the kingdom on 16th Tammuz—'prefect of the prefects' ; and he appointed other prefects over the kingdom. . . . . His reign lasted only for one year. There is nothing against his being a Mede ;

and Gobryas was probably the leader of the conspiracy against Astyages who was deposed and given over to Cyrus.* . . . Indeed (adds Mr. Boscawen) he seems to me to fulfil *in every way* [the italics are ours] the required conditions to be Darius the Mede."

We ask, moreover, if it was at all unlikely that Cyrus, retaining the real power of empire in his own hands, should be willing to ingratiate himself with his trusty allies, the Medes, by appointing one of their race (who was also *his own* victorious general in the campaign), as the vassal-king in the newly acquired realm? And if this Persian sovereign did not for some time at least cease to reside in his own capital, Susa, must there not have been some high official appointed to rule in his name at Babylon?

Several statements in the Book of Daniel seem to give reply to these questions. (1) Darius is said to have been about 62 on his accession to power, obtaining as a veteran leader, popular with the officers and soldiers (a contingency which may have counted for more than we think), this elevated rank; (2) he is said to have "received" the kingdom, an expression also used (ch. 2. 6, and 7. 18), and more suitable to describe a delegation of royal authority than an inherited succession (Lenormant emphasises this); and (3), as before quoted, he was "*made* king over the realm of the Chaldeans."

Again, if this Median general was just as truly "King of Babylon" as Belshazzar is now proved to have been, we need not wonder if we have no commercial tablets bearing his name, any more than that we have none bearing the name of Belshazzar; because in the one case Cyrus, and in the other, Nabonidus, were the imperial sovereigns themselves.

---

* This identification, however, is open to question.

But it is to be noted that in all the documents of the first two years of Cyrus's reign he is only styled "King of Nations" (and in his first year all tablets from Babylon still bear Nabonidus's name, and all except one of the tablets with the name of the Persian conqueror are dated from Sippara); and, that it is only in the third year of his reign, when Darius had undoubtedly ceased to rule, that he is named fully "King of Babylon" as well as "King of Nations."

Is it not, besides, very probable that when Daniel speaks of the first year of Darius he refers to (*a*) the brief period during which that personage ruled in Babylon, and (*b*) the first year of Cyrus, concurrently, as his suzerain, and in whose *third* year (doubtless dating from 16th Tammuz, 538 B.C.), the prophet declares he saw another vision?

Whatever be the value of these suggestions, one thing, we maintain, cannot possibly be disputed in the face of the conclusions arrived at by eminent experts in Assyriological history and literature (who certainly hold no "brief" for the *opponents* of the advanced school). It is that Gobryas is probably identical with—according to one of them, "*can be no other than*"—"Darius the Mede, the son of Ahasuerus"; and, moreover, that there is certainly room in history for such a viceroy at Babylon. In view of this fact no critic, whose "wish is" not "father to the thought," is entitled to assume, or to invite others to believe, that the statements of the Book of Daniel are irreconcilable with history, on this point at least —whatever they may be in regard to others.

Even Canon Driver, who goes so far as to say that in his opinion "there is no room for such a ruler" as Darius, is careful to add (although now he seems to accept Prof. Sayce's single and unsupported reading "wife of the king" in the Annalistic tablet): "A cautious criticism will not build too much on the silence of the inscriptions, where many certainly remain yet to be brought to light." But Dr. Westcott, the learned Bishop of Durham, maintains that Darius is identical with Astyages, the last king of the Medes, "Astyages" being a national and not a personal cognomen; while, according to him, Ahasuerus (the name also of the father of Daniel's viceroy) represents Cyaxares, the father of Astyages, whose own personal name, it is suggested, was Darius. But this Greek equivalent of Ahasuerus may be gravely questioned.

Again, does it not seem remarkable that the Scriptural author, whether pre-Maccabean or post-Maccabean in date, should have chosen to give one of his alleged fictitious characters the name of a prince so well known in Jewish annals—that borne by "Darius the Persian" (Darius Hystaspes, the founder of the Perso-Aryan dynasty), who years afterwards carried out the decree of Cyrus for the rebuilding of the Temple? That he does not mean his readers to believe them to be the same, and that there is not here an intentional or undesigned anachronism, is clear; because he is careful to describe the Babylonian ruler as "the Mede," "of the seed of the Medes," and the later Darius (the Persian) was certainly not "the son of Ahasuerus."

But it must also be noted that the word Darius (Persian Cuneiform = Dariyavus) is quite as impersonal as Astyages, and seems originally to have only meant "King," "Ruler," or "restrainer," and it certainly has been assumed as a throne-name by several monarchs. Would it be hard, therefore, to believe that Gobryas on his elevation assumed it as a title, or, more probably, had it conferred upon him by his suzerain Cyrus, as sounding somewhat more royal than "Ugbaru" —as his new Babylonian subjects would pronounce his name?

It has been very strongly urged that it is quite inconsistent with the position and authority of the most exalted viceroy to act as Darius did in the matter of the "royal statute" and "strong interdict" (R. V.) that "none should ask aught of any God or man save of himself for thirty days," and of the decree commanding allegiance to Jehovah from all peoples, dominions, etc.

But if we look closely into the Sacred narrative, and mark the repeated and honourable conjunction of the Medes with the Persians in conquest and government (notably in ch. 5. 28, and ch. 6. *passim*); and if we give weight to certain considerations which arise out of the relations borne by the two nations to each other in this confused period of history,* we shall be almost forced to believe that there were some high reasons of State or military expediency why a *Median* ruler should first govern Babylonia, although this was followed by a speedy and complete reversion of the whole power into the hands of Cyrus.

And apart from such an argument, surely it is not too much to suppose that if Darius was the Median General Gobryas, who was unquestionably made "governor" or "prefect" of Babylon, whatever that title may have meant; and if he had authority, as we know he had, to create a large number of prefects or satraps, his sovereignty must have been quite as absolute, *e.g.*, as that of Herod the Idumean, who was "made" king by Antony and "received" the kingdom of Judea at his hands, with large additions afterwards from Augustus. This prince "killed and made alive"; he massacred the Innocents of Bethlehem; he slew almost all the members of his own family, so that Macrobius asserts that Augustus jested coarsely that it were better to be Herod's "sow" than his "son"! But the Cæsar, as his suzerain, never seems to have in any way interfered with his cruel and despotic exercise

---

* Cyrus himself, *e.g.*, was really not a Persian but an Elamite.

of power. Darius was doubtless fully as irresponsible a ruler as the Judean prince, and made his "royal statutes" and issued his "strong interdicts" at Babylon almost, if not quite, as freely as Cyrus himself did at Susa.

Hugh M. Mackenzie.

D.

Summary.

Before dismissing the subject which Mr. Mackenzie has so ably discussed in the preceding chapter, it may be well, even at the cost of some repetition, to restate the true relations of Biblical to extra-Biblical history, especially as it concerns the Book of Daniel.

We have two histories in our hands which are independent of each other, although they touch each other at a few points and throw side-lights upon each other. The one is partly Biblical and partly extra-Biblical. By the Biblical part I mean the Bible histories, in "Kings" and "Chronicles," and in the "Prophets," especially Isaiah and Jeremiah, of the Assyrian and Babylonian invasions of Palestine; and by the extra-Biblical, such references to the same times and events as are found in ancient history and especially in the tablets which modern exploration has discovered and modern learning has deciphered.

Confining our attention, as we do in this book, to the period of the conquest of Babylon by the Medo-Persian army, these tablets furnish materials for a history of that period, not in a continuous writing, but in unconnected portions or fragments which it is far from easy to form into a unity. We have another history, more limited in its scope, in itself a unity, compressed within a few pages, known to us as the Book of Daniel. But this book, let it not be forgotten, does not profess to be a history of the times of Daniel, either Babylonian or Persian, or even a history of the relations of Babylon or Persia with the Jewish people.

The fairest method, and the most logical, of studying these two distinct histories, would be to assume the genuineness of both, to compare them and to combine their lights. As to the newly-discovered tablets, there is no question as to their genuineness. They are certainly not manufactured by their discoverers. This however has to be said, that for the interpretation of them we are dependent on experts, and there are few experts who will claim to be infallible. This too must be said, that even if we could be sure that we have a perfect translation and a perfect interpretation of the tablets, we are not required to give them an unlimited credit for veracity and fairness. Not a few ancient inscriptions have been proved to be far from fair or veracious, especially in matters in which personal or national honour was involved. And great wrong is sometimes done to other, especially Bible, history, when it seems to be contradicted by inscription or tablet, by assuming that the inscription or tablet is necessarily right, and the other necessarily wrong. Still, notwithstanding this, we hold that in beginning our historical inquiry it is logical to assume that the tablets, which are certainly ancient and original, contain genuine history. And we claim the same privilege and honour for that other history which we have in the Book of Daniel, and which covers a considerable portion of the same time, though not recording, except to a very small extent, the same events. We might ask this even if we regarded the book only as a piece of ancient literature, considering the many centuries through which it has lived unchallenged. Much more may we ask this of critics who believe that the book is inspired, (whatever value they attach to Inspiration), and that it has had and has a rightful place among the sacred and authoritative books of both the Jewish and the Christian Church from time immemorial.

But there are critics who, instead of approaching the book in a friendly, or even judicial spirit, expend their learning and dialectic skill in finding out, as with the aim of a "cross-examiner," everything that can wear a doubtful aspect. And yet the "force of truth" constrains not a few to make admissions that are more than sufficient to neutralise all the difficulties on which they stumble.

Our main defence of the Book of Daniel to which we have given prominence throughout, rests on grounds which are independent of our being able to provide an absolute solution of every difficulty that may be raised—grounds which, if they are rejected, will land us in difficulties immensely greater than those with which this chapter deals. Meantime, supported by the argument furnished in this chapter, which, be it observed, is the argument, not of the writer of this chapter alone, but to a large extent of such eminent scholars, in this department of study, as Mr. Boscawen and Mr. Pinches, we boldly challenge a verdict in favour of the historical accuracy of the statements of the Book of Daniel, on *all the points whereon it touches or comes into any connection with the general history of the times in which Daniel lived.* One need feel no surprise that even with the aid of Tablet revelations it may still be difficult to construct a definite and perfect story of the Perso-Median conquest of Babylon, with all the incidents of the taking of the city and what befell its rulers, father and son, and the Perso-Median government which immediately followed. The wonder is that so little remains unexplained. Enough is known to justify the assurance that whatever further explanation may be forthcoming, the *bona fides* of the Book of Daniel is already established and cannot be shaken.

J. K.

APPENDIX I.

OUR LORD'S INTIMATE KNOWLEDGE OF OLD TESTAMENT SCRIPTURE.

The most cursory reading of the Gospels leaves on the reader's mind the impression that Jesus was very familiar with the holy books of His nation. But this impression will be greatly strengthened if we take the trouble to trace His references to them in their historical order.

I. The creation of man and the law of marriage recorded in Gen. 1. 27 and 2. 24, are referred to in Matt. 19. 4: "Have ye not read that He which made them at the beginning made them male and female, and said, For this cause shall a man leave father and mother, and shall cleave to his wife, and they shall be one flesh."

II. In Gen. 4. we have the sad story of the death of Abel, and two of the Evangelists represent Christ as uttering these solemn words : "Behold, I send unto you prophets, and wise men, and scribes; and some of them ye shall kill and crucify, that upon you may come all the righteous blood shed upon the earth, from the blood of righteous Abel unto the blood of Zacharias, whom ye slew between the temple and the altar" (Luke 11. 51, Matt. 23. 35). Abel is the first martyr recorded in the Old Testament, Zacharias is the last. It is evident that our Lord had the whole written history of the sacred books before His mind when He "thus swept the thoughts of His hearers across the centuries from the first to the last of the recorded righteous martyrs."

III. In Gen. 6., 7., 8. we have the history of Noah and the Flood, and in Matt. 24. 37 and Luke 17. 26, 27, Christ is recorded to have said: "As the days of Noah were, so shall also the coming of the Son of Man be. For as in the days that were before the flood they were eating and drinking, marrying and giving in marriage, until the day that Noah entered the Ark, and knew not until the flood came and took them all away; so shall also the coming of the Son of Man be."

IV. The history of Abraham occupies a large space in the Book of Genesis, some fourteen chapters. Among our Lord's recorded words we do not find reference to specific events in the life of Abraham, but we find abundant testimony to his personal existence, and to his relation to the Jewish people, and the importance which had always attached to his position in Jewish history. The memorable conversation with the Jews in John 8. is proof of all this. "We be Abraham's seed," the Jews said, "and were never in bondage to any man" (*v.* 33). "I know that ye are Abraham's seed," Christ said (*v.* 37). "Art thou greater than our father Abraham, which is dead, and the prophets which are dead?" the Jews said (*v.* 53). The significant words, "before Abraham was I am," closed a colloquy in which the Genesis story of Abraham, with all its significance, is implicitly accepted both by Christ and by the people.

V. Following the sequence of the books we come to Exodus, in the third chapter of which we find the account of the mystery of the Burning Bush (*vv.* 1–6). The comments of Christ on this mystery is recorded by three Evangelists, Matt. 22. 31–33, Mark 12. 26, Luke 20. 37 : " As touching the dead, that they rise [that they live after death]: have ye not read in the book of Moses, how in the bush God spake unto him, saying, I am the God of Abraham, the God of Isaac, and the God of Jacob. He is not the God of the dead, but the God of the living." How far Moses apprehended the great truth that was involved in the words, "I am the God of Abraham," we are not concerned at present to inquire. But if he reflected—and could he fail to reflect?—he must have felt that there was more in the words than if these had been "I *was* the God of Abraham." Our present concern is with the fact of Christ's recognition of the story as He *read it*, and as we read it in the "book of Moses."

VI. In the sixteenth chapter of Exodus we are told how God provided for the wants of the people in the wilderness by a daily supply of manna. In the sixth of John we are told how that the Jews said to Jesus, " Our fathers did eat manna in the desert; as it is written, He gave them bread from heaven to eat." The fact of the manna, and the fact as written, was acknowledged by Jesus; but He would have them to understand that the manna was in no sense the work or gift of Moses, but of the Father, and that the Father had now sent to them in him the Bread of Life: " Moses gave you not that bread from heaven, but my Father giveth you the true bread from heaven."

VII. We find sundry of the special laws which the Book of Leviticus ascribes to Moses referred to by Christ as such, *e.g.*, circumcision on the eighth day. Comp. Lev. 12. 3 and John 7. 22, 23, where the fact of the Mosaic enactment, and the fact that the rite was older than the enactment, are explicitly asserted. The law of leprosy recorded in the thirteenth chapter of Leviticus is recognised by Christ with equal explicitness. To a leper whom He had healed He said, " See thou tell no man; but go thy way, show thyself to the priest, and offer the gift which Moses commanded for a testimony to them " (Matt. 8. 4; Luke 5. 14).

VIII. In Numb. 21. we read the story of the fiery serpent by which came death, and the serpent of brass by which came healing. In this story our Lord found an act illustrative of His own great work of salvation; "As Moses lifted up the serpent in the wilderness, even so must the Son of man be lifted up, that whosoever believeth in Him should not perish, but should have eternal life" (John 3. 14).

IX. To the contents of the last book of the Pentateuch we find several references in the sayings of our Lord. In Deut. 6. 4, 5, these great words are written, "Hear, O Israel, the Lord our God is one Lord; and thou shalt love the Lord thy God with all thine heart, and with all thy soul, and with all thy mind." Christ found in these words an answer to the lawyer who asked Him, "which is the great commandment in the law?" (Matt. 22. 37). From the same chapter of Deuteronomy Christ quoted two of His replies to the tempter in the wilderness (*vv.* 13 and 16), in each case saying, "*It is written*"— "Thou shalt worship the Lord thy God, and Him only shalt thou serve;" "Thou shalt not tempt the Lord thy God." In the eighth chapter, verse 3, we have other words quoted by our Lord in reply to the tempter, and these, too, are prefaced by "*It is written*"—"Man shall not live by bread alone, but by every word that proceedeth out of the mouth of God" (Matt. 4.)

It is noticeable that Christ repelled all the temptations of the devil by quotations from the written Scriptures, and that all His quotations were from the Book of Deuteronomy.

In the same book (24. 1) we find a law of Moses which gave occasion to Christ's re-assertion of the original law of marriage. The Pharisees tempted Him with the question, "Is it lawful for a man to put away his wife for every cause?" (Matt 19. 3, 4). And in reply to His answer they said, "Why did Moses then command to give a writing of divorcement and put her away?" "Moses" (Christ said) "because of the hardness of your hearts, suffered you to put away your wives."

The enactment of Moses was not a repeal of the original law; it was a restraint on an evil practice, but at the same time a concession to it. Both the Jews and Christ—and this is our point—were familiar with the law of Moses on the subject as written in the Book of Deuteronomy.

X. Passing out of the Pentateuch we find our Lord referring to recorded facts in the histories of David and Solomon. "Have ye not read what David did when he was an hungred, and they that were with him, how he entered the house of God and did eat the shewbread, which was not lawful for him, but only for the priests" (Matt. 12. 3, 4; Mark 2; Luke 6). The law which David set aside appears in Exod. 25. 30, and more fully in Lev. 24. 5-9; and the record of David's action is in 1 Sam. 21. The knowledge of it came to the Jews in Christ's day, not by tradition, but in a book with which they were familiar—"*Have ye not read?*"

The same is true of our Lord's references to Solomon, though not implicitly asserted. When He said, "Solomon in all his glory was not arrayed like one of these lilies of the field" (Matt. 6. 29), He was referring to a history of magnificence which was the nation's boast and pride. And when He referred to the visit of the Queen of the South to hear the wisdom of Solomon (Matt. 12. 42), He referred to a written history with which the people were familiar (1 Kings 10).

XI. The whole history of Elijah and Elisha stands out in bold relief before our minds, when we read the words which Christ spoke in the synagogue of Nazareth—"many widows were in Israel in the days of Elias, when the heaven was shut up three years and six months, when great famine was throughout all the land; but unto none of them was Elias sent, but only to Zarephath in the land of Sidon (R.V.), unto a woman that was a widow. And many lepers were in Israel in the time of Eliseus the prophet, and none of them were cleansed, but only Naaman the Syrian" (Luke 4. 25-27; 1 Kings 17. and 18.).

There is another incident in the life of Elijah referred to in Luke 9. 53-56, "Wilt Thou" (said James and John) "that we command fire from heaven and consume them" (Samaritans who would not receive Christ because His face was as though He would go to Jerusalem), "even as Elias did?" (2 Kings 1). Our Lord's reply recognised the fact to which His disciples referred.

XII. Our Lord's references to the Psalms have important bearings, some of which will have to be considered; but at this point we confine attention to the fact that He spoke of a "book" which He called the "Book of Psalms." He said to certain scribes, "How say they that the Christ is David's son? For David himself saith in the Book of Psalms (110. 1), The Lord said unto my Lord, sit thou on my right hand till I make Thine enemies my footstool" (Luke 20. 41, 42; Matt. 22. 41-45; Mark 12. 35-37). On the same occasion Christ spoke a parable, in which he referred to the same book, replying to a "God-forbid" of His hearers, "what is this, then, that is written, The stone which the builders rejected, the same is become head of the corner" (118. 22).

XIII. Our Lord's recorded quotations from, or specific references to, the books of the prophets are few, but they are very significant. Taking them in the order of time, not in the order of the positions of the books in our Canon, Jonah comes first. He stands in immediate succession to Elijah and Elisha. And although Christ does not name the *book* of Jonah, He quotes and reasserts the most important facts recorded in it: "As Jonas was three days and three nights in the fish's belly, so shall the Son of man be three days and three nights in the heart of the earth. The men of Nineveh shall rise in judgment with this generation, and shall condemn it, because they repented at the preaching of Jonas, and behold a greater than Jonas is here" (Matt. 12. 40–42). The two facts asserted by Christ are the chief wonders in the book, one physical and the other moral; and they presuppose what goes before: a Divine commission to the prophet to preach in Nineveh, the casting of the prophet into the sea, and his being saved from death by means of a great fish, so that they carried the whole book along with them; and that irrespective of all questions as to whether the writing of the book was Contemporaneous with the occurrences which it records, or a hundred years after.

XIV. Coming to the greatest of the prophets, we find two specific references to words in the Book of Isaiah. In Matt. 15. 7, Christ is reported to have said, "Ye hypocrites, well did Esaias prophesy of you, saying, This people draweth near me with their lips, but their heart is far from me. But in vain they do worship me, teaching for doctrines the commandments of men." The words of Isaiah (29. 13) are not a prophecy, in the sense of a prediction, of what was to be in the days of Christ; they are a prophetic, *i.e.*, divinely inspired, description of what was in Isaiah's own days, and so a prophetic description of things which existed in many ages, and never more painfully than in Christ's time, and in the case of the men with whom He had to do. The Lord saw in the words of the prophet a mirror of what was now before His eyes.

In the sixty-first of Isaiah, Christ found words of which He said boldly, "This day is this Scripture fulfilled in your ears." The Gospels record no scene in the life of Christ more significant or more memorable than that which we find in the fourth of Luke. Standing up to read in the synagogue of the town in which He had spent His early life, there was delivered to Him the synagogue copy of the roll which contained Isaiah, with which His eyes had been long familiar; and, unrolling the book, He found the place where it was written, "The spirit of the Lord is upon me, because He hath anointed me to preach good tidings to the poor. He hath sent me to preach release to the captives and recovering of sight to the blind, to set at liberty them that are bruised, to proclaim the acceptable year of the Lord" (R.V). Closing the roll and giving it back to the attendant, He sat down and said, "To-day hath this Scripture been fulfilled in your ears" (R.V.). Never before, by priest or prophet. Inspired men had often spoken "gracious words" to afflicted Israel, and even from the reading-desk of the Nazarene Synagogue spiritual Israelites may have spoken words of comfort to their neighbours. But not until now had the prophet's words been "*fulfilled.*" Ask the Ethiopian question, "Of whom speaketh the prophet? Of himself or of some other?" And Christ will reply, "To-day *in me* is this Scripture fulfilled."

XV. In the Gospels we find two references to the Book of Daniel, one of them express, the other not. The former is in Matt. 24. 15, and Mark 13. 14.

The latter is in Matt. 26. 64, Mark 14. 62, and Luke 22. 69. The occasion was most solemn. "I adjure thee by the living God" (the High Priest said to Him) "that Thou tell us whether Thou be the Christ the Son of God." Jesus saith unto them, "Thou hast said; nevertheless I say unto you, Hereafter ye shall see the Son of man sitting on the right hand of power, and coming in the clouds of heaven." Both Christ and the High Priest were familiar with the remarkable passage in Daniel 7. 13: "I saw in the night visions, and, behold, one who like the Son of man (or, "a Son of man," R.V.) came with the clouds of heaven, and came to the Ancient of days, and they brought him near unto Him." Whether this passage is to be regarded as the ground, or genesis, of the title by which Christ usually designated Himself "the Son of man" does not concern us at present, but that it was in our Lord's mind and its language used with intention, cannot be reasonably doubted. The appropriating to Himself of the mysterious language of the prophet's vision gave emphasis to His unqualified affirmation that He was "the Christ, the Son of God," and left no room for the High Priest to doubt that He claimed attributes and functions which in his judgment justified the charge of blasphemy—a charge which would have been true if these attributes and functions were not really His.

XVI. Christ had the book of Malachi in His mind when He said, "The law and the prophets prophesied until John, and if ye will receive it this [John] is Elias that was to come" (Matt. 11. 13, 14). The only foretelling of an Elijah to come is in the last words of the Book of Malachi; "Behold, I will send you Elijah the prophet before the coming of the great and dreadful day of the Lord. When Christ said to the three favoured disciples who had seen the Transfiguration, in which Moses and Elias talked with Jesus of His coming "decease" (Luke 9. 31), "Tell the vision to no man until the Son of man be risen from the dead," they asked Him, "Why then say the scribes that Elias must first come?" Jesus answered, "Elias truly must first come, and restore all things. But I say unto you that Elias is come already, and they knew him not, and have done unto him whatsoever they listed." The disciples then understood that He spoke of John the Baptist (Matt. 17. 9–13).

On these illustrations of Christ's familiar acquaintance with what was the Bible of His nation, we remark :—

1. Our Lord's references to facts and sayings, which we find in our Old Testament, are based on *books ;* by which we mean that they were not based on unwritten traditions nor supernaturally revealed by Him to His hearers. This appears plainly on the face of the Gospel narratives. His appeals were

to books that were well known and constantly read by His hearers. "Have ye not read?" He said with reference to the law of marriage (Gen. 1. and 2.), and with reference to the burning bush (Exod. 3.). Sometimes the formula is, "It is written" (Mark 11. 17; John 10. 34). The subject-matter of remark by our Lord was thus based on ground common to speaker and hearers.

2. That there are books in the Old Testament to which we find no reference in our Lord's recorded sayings it is true, but it must be remembered that these sayings were purely incidental, *i.e.*, as occasion arose through questions and objections on the part of the people. Even in the few cases in which he appears, not as a respondent, but as originating or volunteering Old Testament references, as when He asked the Pharisees, "What think ye of the Christ?" (Matt. 22. 42), and quoted Psalm 110., there was an immediate *occasion* for it in the hostile attitude assumed by the Pharisees and Sadducees, and the questions that were asked by the one and the other to draw Him if possible into compromising answers.

3. Christ neither quoted from nor referred to any book later than that which contained the prophecy that Elijah should come to prepare the way of the Lord. There were books written after that time, and with some of them at least we are familiar in the collection known to us as the Apocrypha. Josephus refers to them in the well-known passage in which he describes the books which constituted the Jewish Canon and which constitutes ours. "From the time of Artaxerxes, moreover" (he says), "until our present period, all occurrences have been written down, but they are not regarded as entitled to the like credit with those which preceded them, because there was no certain succession of prophets." There was no *prophesying*, no prophetic ministration, no one entitled to say, as prophets said, "Thus saith the Lord," from the time when

Malachi said "The Lord shall suddenly come to His temple" until Elijah appeared in the person of John.*

In Dr. Stanley Leathes' book, entitled: "The Law in the Prophets," which will be found in the series to which the present volume belongs, the reader will find tables of passages illustrating our Lord's appeal to Scripture: in S. Matthew nearly thirty, in S. Mark seventeen, in S. Luke twenty, and in S. John nine. Dr. Leathes sums up in these words: "It is impossible to survey this body of evidence and doubt the character of our Lord's appeal to Scripture. If He was mistaken in one point He may have been mistaken in any; and, if so, is there any in which we can implicitly trust Him? Shall we say that the channel through which we receive the Scriptures, the agency of Moses and the Prophets, is natural or supernatural, that its message is human or divine, that the recognition of it given by Christ is conditional or absolute, provisional or final?" (p. 243.)

To this I may add a passage from Canon Girdlestone's book, "Doctor Doctorum." "Modern criticism barely refers to the Lord's teaching, and thus cuts itself adrift from any definite ground on which to proceed. Christ leaves many things open; there is manifestly plenty of room for higher criticism within the bounds fixed by Him. Every Biblical question is open just so far as Christ has left it open, but no further. It is here that the real point of divergence comes in. We are told to dismiss prejudice, or, as the critics kindly put it, *praejudicium*. We are to approach the Old Testament as if Christ had neither come nor taught. We are not even to read the books from a Jewish point of view, but simply as critics. This we decline. The books of the Old Testament are not only to be read in connection with

---

* From Essay by the Author in the *Evangelical Magazine*, 1896, on "Christ the True Interpreter of the Old Testament."

one another, but are to be studied in the light of the New. The dispensations of which they speak are related. We might as well study the bones of the body without reference to the head as study the Old Testament without reference to the New. Criticism without Christ is shifting sand. We have not enough materials to go upon without taking Him and His words into account. We must view the Old Testament from His point of view rather than from the German critical point of view. Germans may err, and have erred. Christ has not erred, and cannot err." . . . "Men are slow to give way; but few of our English critics are so pledged, or have so far committed themselves, that they cannot introduce new safeguards into their books. Why should they not consent to abide under the shadow of the Lord's teaching?" (pp. 183-184.)

APPENDIX II.

NOTES ON THE CONNECTION OF BABYLON WITH OTHER NATIONS, EASTERN AND WESTERN, ILLUSTRATIVE OF SOME PASSAGES IN THE BOOK OF DANIEL.

By JAMES KENNEDY, ESQ., *late Bengal Civil Service.*

THE author of this work has pointed out that unless the Jews lived in a state of complete isolation at Babylon, they could not fail to pick up words current among the Gentile population; and it would therefore be no cause for surprise if foreign words were found in the Book of Daniel. I propose in the following notes to show that the relations of Babylon in the days of Nebuchednezzar extended westwards as far as the Ægean, and eastward to the coasts of India and China.

Babylon was from the earliest ages a sacred city. But in the 6th and 7th centuries B.C. it became proverbial for its riches and magnificence. This grandeur was sudden in its origin, and lasted in full splendour for less than 150 years, commencing with the reign of Nebuchadnezzar's father, Nabupolassar, the founder of the new Chaldæan Dynasty, and ending with the death of Darius. During the earlier part of this period Babylon was the seat of empire; but its riches were obtained, not so much from empire as from commerce. It was the discovery and monopoly of the sea trade with India that brought it unparalleled wealth. And the circumstances of this discovery were as follows :—

The kings of Assyria had long held Babylonia in a kind of uneasy vassalage. But their rule was continually disputed by the Chaldæans and Elamites as well as by the Babylonians themselves; and the greater part of Sennacherib's reign (704–681 B.C.) was employed in suppressing these persistent revolts. He succeeded at last in driving his chief enemy, the Chaldæan Mardukbaladdin, out of Babylonia. Mardukbaladdin sailed with his followers to Elam, and settled at the mouth of the Ulai River. He could be reached only by sea, and Sennacherib equipped a fleet—the first and last Assyrian fleet which ever sailed upon the Persian Gulf. Ship-builders were brought from the Syrian coast to the Euphrates, and the ships were manned by Phœnicians and Greeks—the latter probably Cypriotes. These ship-builders and sailors were revolted subjects—prisoners of war, and we may be assured that they never returned to their native land. In the art of ship-building and in boldness and nautical skill they were far superior to the Chaldæans, the principal maritime people at this time on the Persian Gulf. But whether it was these Phœnicians and Greeks or others, it is certain that the sea route to India was opened up in the 7th century B.C. by men who possessed sea-going vessels, and who did not hesitate to venture from the easternmost promontory of Arabia to the West coast of India across the open ocean. Before the middle of the 7th century B.C. sea-traders from the West had introduced a coinage based on Babylonian standards into Kiaotchou in the South of China, and imitations of the Lydian and early Æginetan coinage were common in the Shantung Peninsula before the end of the century. There are abundant traces in Babylon of the trade with India during the 6th century B.C. Logs of Indian cedar have been discovered in the palace of Nebuchednezzar at Barsippa; and Nabonidos employed Indian teak in rebuilding the temple of the Moon-god at Ur. We know that among the imports by sea were sandal wood, rice, and peacocks; and rice and peacocks under their Tamil names must have reached Greece either before or shortly after the end of the century.

The whole of this lucrative trade with the East centred in Babylon. The Arabians were not at this time a sea-going folk; and there is nothing to show that the Egyptians had any share in it. On the contrary, the efforts of Pharoah Necho to reopen the Red Sea Canal, and the voyages of exploration on which he sent his Phœnicians along the coast of Africa, were probably due to a spirit of emulation. Thus Babylon became the great centre of trade, and a multitude of foreigners came to reside there. So great was the concourse of strangers and captives that Nebuchadnezzar added an entirely new quarter to the town. Egyptians, Phœnicians, Syrians, Jews, and Cappadocians were to be found in the streets; and among the merchants, sailors, loafers, and captives we must number the Asiatic Greeks.

Greeks had frequented the coast of Syria from the earliest times. A Greek is mentioned in the Tel Amarna tablets: bands of Greeks had invaded Egypt in the time of Rameses III., and the Greeks in Cyprus formed the bulk of the population, and had come by turns under the rule of Egyptians, Assyrians, and Babylonians. If the peoples of the Levant had little acquaintance with the Greeks of the mainland they were intimately acquainted with the Asiatic Greeks, and islanders, the Ionians and Cypriotes who swarmed among them as merchants or mercenaries. Indeed, the Greeks in Egypt were popularly known only as "Ionians" down to the days of the Mahomedan conquest—Hellen signifying not a Greek, but an idolator. We might therefore conjecture with probability that Asiatic Greeks made their way to Babylon, but we are not left entirely to conjecture.

1. We find that Sennacherib employed Greeks—perhaps Cypriotes—to man his fleet in the Persian Gulf; and these Greeks being prisoners of war, must have been settled there after the campaign, according to Assyrian usage.

2. It is difficult to trace foreigners in the contract tablets, the practice being to assimilate their names or to give them new ones. Daniel and his companions are an instance in point. Another case is that of the Egibi, the great bankers of Babylon. The women have often Hebrew names, the men purely Babylonian ones. We are not surprised, therefore, at the absence of Greek names, but such do occur. Mr. Pinches has furnished me with a couple of instances. He says:—" The Greeks that I had in my mind are named on Tablet K 281 (W.A.I. III. Pl. 46, No. 5, lines 30 and 33). The first (the first witness to the contract) is given simply as *Yamannu* (= *Yawannu*), and the second (the fourth witness to the contract) is called *Yamannu*(= *Yawannu*) *rab ḫanšāa*, apparently ' the Greek (who is) captain of fifty.' The date of this tablet is 640 B.C., or later, and it was found at Kouyunjik. Istar of Nineveh is referred to therein, implying that the transaction took place in that city." If Greeks are found at a non-commercial city like Nineveh in 640 B.C., we may be sure that they were to be found at Babylon when it had become a great emporium half a century later.

3. We know from excerpts of Berosus given by Josephus, that Nebuchadnezzar settled the captives taken in his Egyptian wars in Babylon, and employed them on his public works. The Ionians formed the flower of the Egyptian army defeated by Nebuchadnezzar, and large bands of Greeks must have been included among these captives. The Branchidae, whom Darius transported to the Persian Gulf, assuredly found compatriots on their arrival.

Three Greek words, "citharis," "psanterin," and "symphonia," occur in the list of musical instrument given in Daniel 3. 5 and 7, and on the strength of these words it is sought to assign the book to a date after the age of Alexander the Great. "Citharis" is admittedly indecisive, and the identity of "psanterin" with the Greek psalterion is doubtful. The question turns on the crucial word "symphōnia," which is certainly Greek, and which the A.V. translates by "dulcimer." The word first appears in Plato as a technical term of music; and in Polybius as the name of a musical instrument. The adjective symphōnos is as old as the Homeric hymns, and is (with the corresponding verb) continually used both in a general and a technical sense. Symphonia, as a technical term, meant (1) the unison or concord of sounds. Symphōnous intervals in music are opposed to diaphōnous ones according as the chords are harmonious or discordant. (2) Symphōnia may mean a musical instrument, possibly "the oriental sephonya, called by the Italians zampogna and in old French chifonie It seems to have been a sort of reed-pipe." (3) It means a concert or concerted music. The word appears to be used in Daniel in the second or third sense.

The fact that a primitive kind of pipe is incidentally mentioned for the first time by a late author, affords no proof that it was of late invention. Our knowledge of the every day life of antiquity is extremely fragmentary and limited, and Mommsen has pointed out that the stepping-stones which were found in every street of every Italian town are mentioned only once by any Latin author. Our knowledge of life in Mesopotamia is immensely less, and our knowledge of Babylonian music is *nil*. The Ionians who wandered to Babylon were not great folk like the political exiles, soldiers-of-fortune (*condottieri*), and physicians who visited the court of the great king, and wrote accounts of their travels. They were humble men, captives, mercenaries, artisans, merchants, at the best—doubtless much of the same class as the Europeans who traversed India in the days of the Great Moghul. But these vagabond Europeans, artillerymen, artificers, contributed more words for common objects to the native languages than the English have done since Plassey. The "symphōnia" pipe is precisely one of the things that would pass—word and thing—from one to another in this stratum of society.

It is however far from certain that "symphōnia" was used either by Daniel or Polybius to denote a musical instrument at all. It may have been used in the sense of a piece of concerted music. Certainly some kind of concerted harmony would be required amid the 'horrid clang' of instruments with which the worshippers greeted the colossus of Dura. Every traveller to the East has heard the word 'fantasia'; it means anything from a ballad to a play, and is used by Arabic-speaking people innocent of Italian, and in senses which never entered an Italian mind. "Symphonia" perhaps served a somewhat similar purpose.

The presence of Greek words in Daniel is fraught with difficulties if we look only to the Greeks of Europe. But the Asiatic Greeks of the sixth and seventh centuries B.C. surpassed the European Greeks not only in commerce and philosophy, but in music. The story of Apollo and Marsyas, the adoption of the Lydian measure, the improvement of the lyre, were all due to them. They had founded a colony in Egypt, and supplied her army with mercenaries; they were to be found all along the Syrian coast, and in Syria and Cyprus they were subjects of Assyria and Babylon. They visited Babylon as prisoners of war; they must have visited it as traders also. That they should have introduced some rude but popular musical instruments into Babylon is not in itself improbable. It is dangerous to found an argument on our ignorance where our knowledge is so scanty, and as Dr. Salmon has justly remarked " conclusions drawn from the study of the character of an entire book are not to be lightly displaced by an argument founded on a single passage."

INDEX.

"Abomination that maketh desolate, The" . 6, 12, 13, 36
Ahasuerus, father of Darius 21, 189
Alexander the Great . . 148
Anderson, Dr. R., on Cyrus's
 Annalistic tablet . . 178
—— —— on Dan. 9 . . 107
—— —— quotes Prof. Cheyne 149
—— —— quotes the Chief
 Rabbi . . . 177
Animal combinations in visions 88
Annalistic tablet of Cyrus, 178, 183
Antiochus Epiphanes: his persecution . . 11, 36, 113, 128
—— —— in relation to date of
 Daniel 3, 81, 132, 146, 157, 161
—— —— in relation to object
 of Book of Daniel . 109, 125
Apocalypse. *See* Revelation of
 St. John.
—— The word . . . 121
Apocrypha, The
 35, 54, 112, 136, 203
Aramaic portion of Daniel 1, 151
Arbitrary criticism . . 8, 143
Artaxerxes Longimanus . . 46
Assurbanipal 69
Astyages 189

Augustine, St.: an aphorism
 quoted 165

Babylon conquered by Cyrus 75, 178
—— Foreigners in . . 69, 208
——: intercourse with China
 and India 207
——: its Greek subjects in Cyprus 208
——: period of its greatness . 206
Babylonian way of dating a
 reign 173
Bel and the Dragon
 50, 55, 112, 136
Belshazzar in light of recent
 research 176
—— related to Nebuchadnezzar? 180
Belshazzar's death . . 178, 182
—— feast . . . 75, 181
"Benedicite," The . . . 54
Berosus on Egyptians in
 Babylon 209
—— on Nebuchadnezzar's "deportation" 173
Biblical and non-Biblical history 191

INDEX.

Boscawen on Belshazzar . . 180
—— on Darius . . . 186
Burning as a punishment in Babylonia, &c. . . . 69

Cairns, Dr., on dulness of rationalistic criticism . . 53
Cambyses, son of Cyrus . . 179
Canon of the O.T., The 38, 46, 50
Canonicity of Daniel acknowledged by Jews . . . 49
Carpenter, Dr. Boyd, on the Apocalypse 123
Chaucer and Langland: a philological contrast . . 151
Cheyne, Prof., on the philological argument . . 149
—— on prophecy and idolatry 131
Christ in history: the key to Daniel 121
—— ——: the Apocalypse . 124
Christ: "Interpreter and Interpretation" 171
—— "not in the Old Testament"? 166
—— the final authority . 170, 204
Christ's explicit references to two prophets . . . 52
—— references to Daniel 12, 16, 28, 51, 165, 201
—— way of alluding to the O.T. . . . 10, 166, 202
Christian critics appealed to 4, 61, 161
Citharis (Dan. 3) . . . 209
Commercial tablets and name of Darius 187
Cyaxares 189
Cyprus under Babylon . . 208
Cyrus, Annalistic tablet of 178, 183

Cyrus, as fulfilling prophecy . 130
—— takes Babylon . 75, 178
——: when first called King of Babylon 188

Daniel, Book of, acknowledged by Jews 49
—— —— author could not remain unknown . . . 162
—— —— instructiveness dependent on truth . . . 115
—— —— not a biography . 1
—— —— not a secular history 2, 192
—— —— true or fictitious as a whole 156
—— —— wanting in "literary form" 156
"Daniel in the Critics' Den" 107, 149, 150, 177
——: most comprehensive of prophets 162
Daniel's character: its consistency 77
—— life, Dates in . 1, 84, 129
Darius compared with Herod the Idumæan . . . 190
——: his "decree" . 82, 189
——: meaning of the word . 189
—— not an imaginary person . 185
——: precision of Daniel's statements 186
——: recent identification with Gobryas . . . 184, 187
——: why not named in tablets 187
Darius Hystaspes . . . 189
Davidson, Dr., on date of Daniel's prophecies . . 105
—— on futility of a "late" Daniel 126
—— on language of Book of Daniel 149

INDEX.

	PAGE
Deane, Rev. H., on the objects of Book of Daniel	114
Delitzsch on Isa. 53	167
—— on prediction	130
Den of lions, The	39, 82, 125
Deportation of Jews in Jehoiakim's reign	1, 173
Destruction of Jerusalem	5, 11, 37
Divinity of Messiah: how far predicted in Daniel	100
Douglas, Principal, on "The Servant of Jehovah"	166
Driver, Dr., grants a "historical basis"	146, 154
—— grants Daniel to be a prophetic book	164
——: his admission respecting Dan. 2	64, 124, 157
——: his evidence of "late authorship"	148
——: his views and Dr. Farrar's compared	146 (and Preface)
—— on Dan. 9	159
—— on Daniel's visions	109
—— on Darius	188
—— on date and authorship of Daniel	3, 147
—— on doubtful tablet-reference to Belshazzar	188
—— on "late Jewish" doctrine	93
—— on object of Book of Daniel	113, 154
Ecclesiasticus, Book of	39, 41, 51
Edersheim on Daniel and the O.T. Canon	48, 49
—— on Daniel 9. 24–27	159
—— on the Haggadah	53
Egyptians in Babylon	209
Emmaus: Christ and prophecy	169
Enoch, Book of	10, 94, 101

	PAGE
Esdras, Book of: reference to Daniel	41
Ezekiel and Daniel compared	104
Ezekiel's reference to Daniel	29, 141
"Fäerie Queene, The": its language	151
Farrar, Dean, on allegorical interpretations	9, 134
—— on Belshazzar as "son" of Nebuchadnezzar	180
—— on Belshazzar as "King"	175
—— on *bona fides* of author of Daniel	137, 140
—— on canonicity of Daniel	10
—— on Christ's reference to Jonah	8
—— on date and authorship of Daniel	3
—— on Mat. **24**. 15	7
—— on Porphyry	143
Fiction-theory: as regards *bona fides* of author	49, 135
——: *partial* application impossible	156
——: use of historical names	146
—— uselessness of a "Maccabean" author	126
——: why pretend to be Daniel?	163
Forbes, Prof., on "The Servant of the Lord"	166
"Forgery and dishonesty"	136
"Four Centuries of Silence"	45
Fulfilment of prophecy in Christ, claimed by Himself	16, 169, 200
Furnace, Nebuchadnezzar's	39, 67, 82
Gabriel, The Angel	18, 86, 160
Girdlestone, Canon: "Doctor Doctorum" quoted	204

	PAGE
Girdlestone, Canon: "Foundations of the Bible"	46
Girdlestone, Rev. I. translates Pindar	140
Gobryas, General of Cyrus	178
—— Governor of Babylon	190
—— same as Darius?	184, 187
Godet, Dr., on the fluctuations of criticism	150
"Golden image, The"	65, 131
Gore, Canon, quoted	12
Greeks in Babylon	208
Greeks in Cyprus, subject to Babylon	208
Greek trade with Babylon	70, 208
Greeks of Asia pre-eminent in the arts	211
Hagen, Dr., on Belshazzar's death	179
Haggadah and Halakhah, The	52, 53
Hanna, Dr., on Messianic prophecy	166
Heliopolis	142
Hezekiah	105, 168
Higher criticism, The, both positive and fluctuating	150
Historical accuracy *professed* in Book of Daniel	135
Historical novel, The, characterized	135
History of the world, how regarded by Daniel	120, 124, 162
Horns as symbols	34, 89
Identity, Question of: "two Daniels"?	29
Idolatry, Jewish: influence of Book of Daniel	130

	PAGE
Idolatry, Jewish: Isaiah's attacks upon	130
—— its cessation	127
Isaiah: chap. 53, as used in the N.T.	166
——: his attacks on idolatry	130
——: his irony	130
——: his precise predictions	105, 130
——: if two Isaiahs, both were prophets	131
—— named by Christ	52, 200
Jehoiakim, King of Judah	1, 173
Jeremiah's precise predictions	105
Josephus on the O.T. Canon	46, 203
—— refers to Daniel	47
—— refers to Onias	142
Judas Maccabæus	40, 81, 168
Kennedy, Dr. J.: "Handbook of Christian Evidences" quoted	98
Kennedy, James, on Babylonian trade, &c.	206
Kenotic theory	11
Kingdom of Heaven: Daniel and the N.T.	22, 62
Language of Book of Daniel	1, 69, 148, 206
Leathes, Dr. Stanley, on "Christ and the O.T."	204
Lightfoot, Bishop, on arbitrary criticism	143
"Literary form" of Daniel	156
Lycanthropy	71
Maccabean age, The, in relation to Book of Daniel	58, 91, 125, 155, 162

INDEX.

Maccabæus, Judas and Simon . 40
Maccabees, Book of, quoted . . 35
Mackenzie, Rev. H. M., on
  "historical difficulties" . . 172
Magians, The, in Babylon . 30, 60
Mahaffy, I. P., on Onias IV. . . 142
Malachi, Date of 48
——: his book referred to by
  Christ 202
——: last of the prophets . . 44
Mattathias refers to Daniel
  . . . . 38, 82, 125, 128
Messiah: as expected by devout
  Jews 23, 25, 27
—— as expected by Jewish
  nation . . 25, 101, 110, 169
—— in the older prophets . 98
—— His divinity implied in
  Daniel 100
—— His sufferings . 25, 100, 168
—— His two-fold character . 99
—— in Book of Enoch . . 101
—— in Dan. 9
  . . 23, 27, 102, 107, 159
——: meaning and use of word
  . . . . . . 23, 97
Messianic element in prophecy
  . . . . . 16, 169, 200
Milman, Dean, on cessation of
  Jewish idolatry . . . 128
Miracles in Book of Daniel
  . . . . . 68, 83, 111
Mohammed 154
Mommsen referred to . . . 210
Moses and Daniel: an analogy . 92
Muir, Sir W., on oral tradition . 153
Musical instruments in Dan. 3
  . . . . . . 70, 209

Nabonidus, King of Babylon
  . . . . 75, 175, 178, 207
Nabopolassar 173

Nebuchadnezzar: date of death . 75
Nebuchadnezzar deports Jews . 173
—— "King" in his father's
  life-time 173
——: Madness of . . 71, 118
——: the "golden image" . 65, 131
Nebuchadnezzar's dream (Dan. 2)
  . . . . 14, 25, 59, 157
—— reign, Daniel not a history
  of 2, 64
Nehemiah's prayer 34
Nerighssar 176
New Testament: references to
  Book of Daniel . 6, 12, 28, 83
Noah and Job, why mentioned
  with Daniel 31

Object of Book of Daniel: not
  merely encouragement under
  persecution 125
—— not merely to predict . 121
—— not Babylonian History 64, 194
—— stated in one sentence . 115
—— to complete chain of revelation 114
—— to keep alive expectation
  of Messiah 120
Onias mentioned by Josephus . 142
Onias IV., alleged possible author of "Daniel" . 137, 141, 145
Oral tradition: its uncertainty . 153
Orelli on Isa. 53 167

Parseeism 93
Payne-Smith, Dr., on Daniel
  and Ezekiel 104
—— on the "golden image" . 66
—— on Nebuchadnezzar's madness 73
Persian words in Daniel . . 152
"Phalaris, Letters of " . . 148

S 7431.   P

	PAGE
Philological evidence alleged for "late" Daniel	148
"Philosophy of History" in Daniel	162
Phœnicians employed by Sennacherib	207
"Piers the Ploughman"	151
Pinches, Mr. T. G., on Gobryas,	183, 186
—— on Greeks in Nineveh	209
—— on the taking of Babylon	183
Pindar quoted by Dr. Farrar	140
Porphyry: his "discovery" respecting Daniel	139, 143
Prediction contrasted with "soothsaying"	112, 130
—— of precise events	105, 130
Predictions containing "numbers"	106
—— in Daniel: if not Messianic, what?	108, 119
Prophet, Was Daniel a?	13, 52, 90, 124, 164
Prophets: their characters and circumstances	103
—— their varied manner of teaching	87
Providence of God over all nations	117
Psalms referred to by Christ	199, 203
Psanterin (Dan. 3)	209
Ptolemy VII.	142
Pusey, Dr., on Nebuchadnezzar's madness	71
Pye Smith, Dr., on the "Son of Man"	17
Queen, The, at Belshazzar's feast	181
Rabbi, Chief, on "third ruler" question	177

	PAGE
Rationalistic criticism: its dulness	53
Rawlinson on Belshazzar	176
Redford, Rev. R. A., on "Four Centuries of Silence"	45
Revelation in abeyance in Maccabean times	95
—— not the same as spiritual discernment	95
Revelation of St. John compared with Daniel	100, 106, 121
—— how far "based" on Daniel?	42
—— its main object	123
Riehm theory	167
Robertson, Prof., on Daniel's visions	88
—— on Septuagint	49
Salmon, Dr., on arbitrary criticism	8
—— on canon of the O.T.	47
—— on disproportion in criticism	211
Sayce, Prof., on Cyrus and Belshazzar	178
Sennacherib employs Greek and Phœnician sailors	207
Septuagint, The	49
"Servant of Jehovah, The"	166
"Son of Man, The"	15, 201
Song of the Three Children, The	54
Strassmaier, Dr., on Inscriptions of Nabonidus	176
Subjectivity in criticism	82
"Sundry times and divers manners" of Revelation	60, 87, 101
Supernatural intervention	80, 117
Susanna, Story of	55, 136
Symbolism in Daniel and otherwise	88

"Symphonia" (Dan. 3) . 209, 210

Tablet-history of Babylon, etc. 175–193
"Third ruler in the Kingdom, The" 177
Thomson, Rev. J. E. H., on Daniel and Jewish idolatry . 133
—— on date of Daniel . . 46
—— on the fiction-theory . 133
—— on the philological argument 150
Trade of Babylon with Asiatic Greece 208
—— with the far East . . 207
Tradition an impossible basis for Book of Daniel . . 154

Urwick, Rev. W., on "The Servant of the Lord" . . 166

Visions of Daniel: difficulties of interpretation . . 108

Visions of Daniel: how prefaced 85, 136
—— not invented . . . 89
—— their main theme and object 109
——: validity as Revelation . 87
Visions of Zechariah . . 88

Walter Scott, Sir, and the historical novel . . . 135
Westcott, Bishop, on Darius . 189
Winer, Dr., on "third ruler" question 177
Wisdom of Solomon, The . 41
"Writing on the wall, The," not an invention of a later age 78

Zechariah and the "former prophets" 129
—— date of his life . . 129
—— his visions . . . 88
—— key to his book . . 129

HER MAJESTY'S PRINTERS' Special Publications.

SPECIAL EDITIONS OF THE HOLY BIBLE.
THE HEBREW MONARCHY.: A Commentary.
OUR BIBLE AND THE ANCIENT MANUSCRIPTS.
THE BIBLE AND THE MONUMENTS.
LEX MOSAICA; OR, THE OLD TESTAMENT AND THE HIGHER CRITICISM.
THE BIBLE STUDENT'S LIBRARY.
THE STUDENT'S HANDBOOK TO THE PSALMS. Memorial Edition.
SPECIAL EDITIONS OF THE BOOK OF COMMON PRAYER.
&c. &c.

EYRE & SPOTTISWOODE,
Her Majesty's Printers:
LONDON—GREAT NEW STREET, FLEET STREET, E.C.
EDINBURGH, GLASGOW, MELBOURNE, SYDNEY, AND NEW YORK.

For an Illustrated Catalogue, or other Information, apply to any Bookseller or to the Publishers.

Dan.

CONTENTS.

	PAGE
THE QUEEN'S PRINTERS' Special Editions of the Holy Bible:—	
THE NEW ILLUSTRATED TEACHER'S BIBLE	
,, ,, AIDS TO BIBLE STUDENTS	4, 5
,, ILLUSTRATIONS	7
THE TEACHER'S ROLL OF BIBLE ILLUSTRATIONS	8
THE VARIORUM ILLUSTRATED TEACHER'S BIBLE (Large Type)	9
,, ,, REFERENCE BIBLE (Large Type)	10
,, ,, REFERENCE APOCRYPHA (Large Type)	11
Description and Opinions of the Variorum and other Teacher's Bibles	12–15
THE HEBREW MONARCHY: A COMMENTARY, WITH A HARMONY OF THE PARALLEL TEXTS	16, 17
OUR BIBLE AND THE ANCIENT MANUSCRIPTS	18, 19
THE BIBLE AND THE MONUMENTS; OR, PRIMITIVE HEBREW RECORDS IN THE LIGHT OF MODERN RESEARCH	20
LEX MOSAICA; OR, THE OLD TESTAMENT AND THE HIGHER CRITICISM	21
THE QUEEN'S PRINTERS' Bible Student's Library	22
VOL. I. THE FOUNDATIONS OF THE BIBLE	23
VOL. II. THE LAW IN THE PROPHETS	24
VOL. III. THE PRINCIPLES OF BIBLICAL CRITICISM	25
VOL. IV. SANCTUARY AND SACRIFICE	26
VOL. V. HEZEKIAH AND HIS AGE	27
VOL. VI. ABRAHAM AND HIS AGE	28
THE STUDENT'S HANDBOOK TO THE PSALMS (Second Edition, *with Memoir of the Author*)	29
THE QUEEN'S PRINTERS' Special Editions of the Book of Common Prayer:—	
THE ANNEXED BOOK OF 1662 IN TYPE (*with Appendices*)	30
THE HISTORICAL PRAYER BOOK	30
BARRY'S TEACHER'S PRAYER BOOK (*with Glossary*)	31
BARRY'S PSALTER WITH COMMENTARY (Large Type)	32
THE "E. F. G." DICTIONARIES	32

Special Publications.

NEW ILLUSTRATED EDITION.

The EYRE & SPOTTISWOODE
TEACHER'S BIBLE.

Published, 1875. Enlarged, 1877. Variorum Editions 1880 and 1890.
Extended, 1893. Revised and Illustrated, 1897.

EDITED, WITH

AUTOTYPES OF ANTIQUITIES AND PHOTOGRAPHIC VIEWS,

SELECTED AND DESCRIBED, BY THE

Rev. C. J. BALL, M.A.,

Chaplain to the Honourable Society of Lincoln's Inn; Member of Council of the Society of Biblical Archæology, &c. &c.; Author of A Commentary on the Books of Chronicles; The Inscriptions of Nebuchadnezzar the Great; The Variorum Apocrypha, &c. &c.

ALSO WITH

PHOTOGRAPHIC REPRODUCTIONS OF MANUSCRIPTS AND VERSIONS

SELECTED AND DESCRIBED BY

F. G. KENYON, M.A.,

Of the Manuscript Department of the British Museum; Author of Our Bible and the Ancient Manuscripts.

FIFTEEN EDITIONS.   Prices from 2s. 6d. to £2 2s.

(*Illustrated Catalogue, or other Information, from any Bookseller or the Publishers.*)

IN this series of Editions of the Authorised Version—several of them page for page—are combined—

I.—The Queen's Printers' Reference & VARIORUM Reference Bibles.
II.—The Queen's Printers' "AIDS to the Student of the Holy Bible."
III.—The Queen's Printers' "MONUMENTAL ILLUSTRATIONS OF THE HOLY SCRIPTURES."

Academy.—"The Queen's Printers have gone the right way to produce a valuable book. They have selected for treatment important subjects, and then entrusted them to the hands of always trustworthy, and sometimes eminent specialists. Thus we have admirable papers."

The Christian.—"The Bible student cannot afford to be indifferent to the advantage of having the aids to which he commits himself written by scholars eminent in their various departments. The 'Aids to the Student,' published by Messrs. Eyre & Spottiswoode, Her Majesty's Printers, are beyond comparison more trustworthy and more complete than any other similar book."

EYRE & SPOTTISWOODE.

"Magnificent collection of plates."—*Guardian.*
"Nothing could be better."—*Church Times.*

THE
New Illustrated Aids to Bible Students.

WITH COLOURED FRONTISPIECE, "A ROYAL HITTITE."

The Second Part of the Queen's Printers' Teacher's Bibles.

Separate Issues, Prices from 1s. to 12s. 6d.

THE Queen's Printers were the FIRST TO ISSUE what was known as *the Sunday School Teacher's Bible* in May, 1875. It was not until 16 MONTHS AFTERWARDS that a Bible issued from the Oxford University Press, bearing on its title page "The S. S. Teacher's Edition," and closely following the model of the Queen's Printers' Teacher's Bible; this brief statement is necessary to remove misunderstandings.

The "Aids to the Bible Student," which are approaching their 23rd year of publication, were prepared by the most eminent specialists, and have been from time to time enlarged and brought up to date with the utmost care, in order that every intelligent reader of the Bible might have at his disposal the BEST and SUREST information from the pen of the most Eminent Authority on each of the principal subjects.

The resulting compendium of Biblical information has throughout been admitted to be not only the largest and fullest work of the kind, but also the best. The most competent judges have drawn attention to the compass and thoroughness of the "AIDS"—none of which are anonymous—and to the eminence and authority of the contributors.

The Publication of the Queen's Printers' **VARIORUM** Bible, and of the Revised Version which followed it, called popular attention to the sources from which we have received the Sacred Text, and the quotations in the **VARIORUM** Notes of Manuscripts, Versions, Ancient Fathers, etc., aroused a spirit of enquiry as to their relative importance. To meet this, the Rev. Professor Swete wrote for these AIDS a new Article entitled,

The Bible: its History, which has now (1897) been supplemented by Dr. Kenyon, of the Manuscript Department of the British Museum, who has selected and described specimens of MSS. and Versions (reproduced in *facsimile*) to illustrate the Transmission of the Text.

The following are the

ADDITIONS TO THE 1897 EDITION.

A Comprehensive Series of Illustrations (*upwards of* 170 *Plates, comprising more than* 200 *subjects*), selected and described by   Rev. C. J. BALL, M.A.

References in the New Testament to Passages in the Apocrypha and other Jewish Writings, by   Rev. C. J. BALL, M.A.

The Period between the Testaments, a comprehensive article by
    Rev. G. H. BOX, M.A.

A Combined Index to the Proper Names, Places, and Subjects of the Bible, by   Rev. C. HOLE, M.A.

EYRE & SPOTTISWOODE,

Special Publications.

NEW ILLUSTRATED AIDS—*continued*.

Some of the Contributors to the AIDS:

REV. PROFESSOR SWETE, D.D., *Regius Professor of Divinity, Cambridge.*
REV. PROFESSOR SAYCE, M.A., LL.D., *Professor of Assyriology, Oxford.*
REV. PROFESSOR W. SANDAY, D.D., LL.D., *Dean Ireland's Professor of Exegesis, Oxford.*
REV. PROFESSOR STANLEY LEATHES, D.D., *Professor of Hebrew, King's College, London, &c.*
REV. C. H. H. WRIGHT, D.D., *Examiner in Hebrew, Universities of Oxford, Durham, and London.*
REV. PROFESSOR CHEYNE, D.D., *Oriel Professor of Interpretation, Oxford; Canon of Rochester.*
DR. F. G. KENYON, *of the MSS. Department, British Museum, late Fellow of Magdalen College, Oxford.*
REV. CANON TRISTRAM, D.D., LL.D., F.R.S., *Durham.*
REV. S. G. GREEN, D.D., *Co-Editor of the Revised English Bible.*
REV. C. HOLE, M.A., *Professor of Ecclesiastical History at King's College, London.*
PROFESSOR N. STORY MASKELYNE, M.A., F.R.S., *Professor of Mineralogy in the University of Oxford; Hon. Fellow of Wadham College, Oxford.*
SIR J. STAINER, M.A., Mus. Doc., *Professor of Music in the University of Oxford.*
F. W. MADDEN, M.R.A.S., *Author of " History of Jewish Coinage," &c.*
W. ST. CHAD BOSCAWEN, Esq., *Fellow of the Royal Historical Society; Member of the Society of Biblical Archæology.*
REV. G. H. BOX, M.A., *Hebrew Master at Merchant Taylors' School.*
REV. C. J. BALL, M.A., *Chaplain to the Honourable Society of Lincoln's Inn; Member of Council of the Society of Biblical Archæology; Editor of the Variorum Apocrypha, &c., &c.*
&c. &c. &c.

SEPARATE ISSUES. NEW ILLUSTRATED AIDS.
WITH COLOURED FRONTISPIECE, "A ROYAL HITTITE."

	PEARL 24mo. Size, 5¾ × 4 × ¾ in.		RUBY 16mo. Size, 6¼ × 4¼ × ¾ in.		MINION 8vo. Size, 7¾ × 5½ × ⅝ in.
	s. d.		s. d.		s. d.
Cloth, red edges	1 0 (net)	..	1 6	..	2 6
French Morocco, red edges	1 6	..	2 3	..	3 0
Paste Grain Morocco, gilt edges	1 9	..	3 0	..	4 0
Turkey Morocco, gilt edges	4 0	..	5 0	..	6 6

THE VARIORUM (Large Type) AIDS
With Special Glossary.
Price 5s.

Bourgeois 8vo., uniform with the Variorum Bible and Apocrypha.

	s. d.
Cloth, bevelled boards, red edges	5 0
Paste Grain Roan, gilt edges	8 3
Morocco, gilt edges, gold roll inside cover	12 6

GREAT NEW STREET, LONDON, E.C.

SOME OPINIONS
OF
THE QUEEN'S PRINTERS' NEW ILLUSTRATED TEACHER'S BIBLE.

THE RIGHT REV. BISHOP OF EXETER:—"Beautifully executed."

THE RIGHT REV. BISHOP OF BATH AND WELLS:—
"Confers a great benefit upon all engaged in teaching the Holy Scriptures."

THE RIGHT REV. BISHOP OF GLOUCESTER:—"A good guide."

THE RIGHT REV. BISHOP OF WORCESTER:—
"A great improvement on all previous editions."

THE RIGHT REV. BISHOP OF CHICHESTER:—"A handsome volume."

THE RIGHT REV. BISHOP OF TRURO:—"Much pleased with it."

THE RIGHT REV. BISHOP OF LICHFIELD:—
"A mine of information indispensable to students."

THE RIGHT REV. BISHOP OF MANCHESTER:—"Very interesting."

THE RIGHT REV. BISHOP OF ST. ASAPH:—"Most instructive."

THE RIGHT REV. BISHOP OF CHESTER:—"Very valuable."

THE RIGHT REV. BISHOP OF KILLALOE:—
"A wonderfully extensive compilation."

THE RIGHT REV. BISHOP OF CARMARTHEN:—
"A reliable handbook of Biblical Archæology, with its splendid series of monumental illustrations, is a most opportune contribution to the study of Holy Writ."

THE VERY REV. DEAN OF CARLISLE:—
"The new matter which has been added is most interesting, and has been wonderfully well selected."

THE VERY REV. DEAN OF DURHAM:—
"A lovely book. Will be of great service for our Divinity students."

THE VERY REV. DEAN OF GLOUCESTER:—
"A marvellous book. Shall be glad to see it in the hands of foes as well as friends of the Book of Books. Such a treasury of Biblical lore has never been dreamed of before. As instructive as it is intensely interesting."

DEAN OF WORCESTER:—"Should be in the hands of every diligent student."

DEAN OF ROCHESTER:—"Most comprehensive."

DEAN OF WELLS:—"Excellent in design and execution."

DEAN OF ST. PAUL'S:—
"Invaluable. The names of the writers are a guarantee of accuracy."

DEAN OF CHICHESTER:—"Of great use."

DR. FRITZ HOMMEL, *Professor of Semitic Languages in the University of Munich; Author of* "*The Ancient Hebrew Tradition as Illustrated by the Monuments*":—"Dr. Ball's book deserves the palm."

EYRE & SPOTTISWOODE,

Special Publications. 7

Latest Addition to the Queen's Printers' Teacher's Bible.

ILLUSTRATIONS,

Monumental, of Manuscripts and Versions, and of Biblical Sites and Cities,

SELECTED AND DESCRIBED BY THE

Rev. C. J. BALL, M.A.,

Chaplain to the Hon. Society of Lincoln's Inn ; Member of Council of the Society o Biblical Archæology; Editor of the Variorum Apocrypha, &c. &c.,

THIS systematic and comprehensive Selection of more than 200 Subjects, reproduced by Photographic Process in upwards of 170 Plates, is offered to the general reader as a "Handbook to the Science of Biblical Archæology," as well as an Aid to the intelligent reading of the Bible.

I.—The Series is divided thus:—

Part 1.—The History of Writing, *or*, The Origin and Development of the Written Characters by means of which the Holy Scriptures have been Preserved and Transmitted to Modern Times. (*Plates* I.-X.)

Part 2.—The Transmission of the Text in Manuscripts, Versions, and Translations. (*Plates* XI.-XXIV.)

Part 3.—Illustrations of the Religious Phraseology, Traditions, Ideas, and Practices of Contemporary Nations and of Ancient Israel; of the Contemporary Knowledge of the Arts of Life; and of the Course of History as recorded in the Old Testament from the Monuments of Assyria, Babylonia, and Egypt, and from those of the Hittites and Phœnicians: to which are added Autotype Representations of Important Sites, Cities, and Personages mentioned in the Old and New Testaments. (*Plates* XXV.-END.)

II.—The following is an Analysis of the Subjects:—

Babylonian . . . 40	Hittite 11
Egyptian 44	Persian 7
Assyrian 41	Greek 16
Phœnicio - Hebrew and } 9	Latin 10
Hebrew . . . . }	Views of Sites, &c. . 26

III.—The Selection has the following Special Features:—

1. The Subjects have been carefully selected from the entire area of available material.
2. Autotype reproductions have been preferred to drawings of the originals, but the Drawings included have all been made specially for this Work. The whole is executed in sepia.
3. Running heads at the top of each page indicate the Scriptural connection, and the Subjects are arranged chronologically, *i.e.* in the order of the Canonical Books.
4. Of the Monumental Subjects more than a third appear for the first time in such a Publication; the selection includes the most recent discoveries, *e.g.*, THE GOSPEL OF ST. PETER, and a few Subjects hitherto unpublished.
5. Complete Series are given of (i.) The Cherubic Figures of Babylonia and Assyria; (ii.) The Races of the Bible; (iii.) Of the Hittite Remains; (iv.) Of the Lion Hunts of Assyrian and Persian Kings; (v.) The Monumental Names of Babylonian, Egyptian, Assyrian, and Persian Kings, named or alluded to in Scripture; (vi.) The known Portraits and Busts of Kings and Emperors.
6. Subjects are, as a rule, reproduced complete and not in part ; some are illustrated by the addition of a second, or even of a third, specimen ; in the case of the Moving of Colossi and of Sieges of Cities the Assyrian and Egyptian representations are given for comparison.
7. Seals are much used to illustrate Archaic Religion and Mythology.
8. Translations, original or revised, are given: (i) COMPLETE, of the shorter Inscriptions which appear in the Plates, and (ii) IN PART, as specimens of the longer, *e.g.* of *The Deluge Tablet containing the Chaldean History of the Flood* (translated in full in the VARIORUM Edition).

GREAT NEW STREET, LONDON, E.C.

NOW READY.

THE
TEACHER'S ROLL
OF
BIBLE ILLUSTRATIONS

CONSISTING OF

THE PLATES

FROM EYRE & SPOTTISWOODE'S

TEACHER'S BIBLE.

Arranged on Sixteen Sheets. Size 17½ by 22½ inches.

Separately Issued and Mounted on Roller – – –
– – – With accompanying Pamphlet of Descriptions.
Price **3s. 6d.**, complete.
Also Mounted on Linen, with Roller, **7s. 6d.**

These Illustrations, arranged chronologically, exhibit the main results of Modern Research in Biblical Archæology, and throw a welcome light on the Sacred Records. An Enlarged Edition of the Table which traces the Phœnicio-Hebrew Alphabet to the Archaic Babylonian script rather than to the Egyptian hieratic occupies the first page. Adapted for use in class.

Selected and Described by the
Rev. C. J. BALL, M.A.,
Member of the Council of the Society of Biblical Archæology, &c., &c.;
Author of The Inscriptions of Nebuchadnezzar; The Variorum Apocrypha, &c., &c.

The Illustrations—Autotypes of Antiquities, Manuscripts, and of Important Biblical Sites and Cities—have been produced in our "Woodbury" Works.

RETAIL OF ALL BOOKSELLERS.

EYRE & SPOTTISWOODE,

Special Publications.

THE BIBLE READER'S VADE MECUM.

THE VARIORUM TEACHER'S BIBLE.
LARGE TYPE VARIORUM BIBLE AND AIDS,
WITH THE
NEW ILLUSTRATIONS.

Bourgeois 8vo. (BIBLE and AIDS, 1894 *pages, Size*, 9¾ × 6¾ × 1¾ *inches.*)

This novel and comprehensive Edition of the Authorised Version—the climax towards which the Queen's Printers have consistently developed their Series of Teacher's Bibles for nearly 23 years (1875-1898)—combines—

I.—The VARIORUM Reference Bible. (*See p.* 10.)
    With Apocrypha. (276 *pages.*) *See p.* 11.
II.—The "AIDS to the Student of the Holy Bible." (*See pp.* 4, 5.)
III.—ILLUSTRATIONS—MONUMENTAL, OF MANUSCRIPTS & VERSIONS, AND OF BIBLICAL SITES. (*See p.* 7.)

The most competent judges have drawn attention to the compass and thoroughness of the "Aids" (none of which are anonymous), and of the Illustrations; as well as to the eminence and authority of the contributors.

Special Subjects.	*Authors.*		*Special Subjects.*
HISTORY OF BIBLE.	SWETE.		PLANTS.
	BALL.	LEATHES.*	
MUSIC.	BOSCAWEN.	LUMBY.*	METALS, &c.
	CHEYNE.*	MADDEN.	
POETRY.	DRIVER.*	MASKELYNE.	ANIMAL CREATION.
	GIRDLESTONE.	MAYHEW.	
MONEY.	GREEN.	SANDAY.	PROPER NAMES, &c.
	HOLE.	STAINER.	
ETHNOLOGY.	HOOKER.	TRISTRAM.	CHRONOLOGY.
	KENYON.	WRIGHT.	
BIBLE & MONUMENTS.		SAYCE.*	HISTORICAL EPITOME.

* Members of Old Testament Revision Committee.

PRICES, Finest India Paper, from 27s. to 52s. 9d.; with APOCRYPHA, 6s. 9d. additional.
Thin White Paper, in various leather bindings, from 24s. to 47s. 3d.
SCHOLASTIC EDITION, bound in cloth, 18s. 9d.;
with APOCRYPHA, 4s. 6d. additional.

SCHOOL EDITION (without APOCRYPHA or ILLUSTRATIONS).
Nonpareil 8vo. (*Size*, 7¾ × 5½ × 1¼ *inches.*) 1250 *pages.*
PRICES (Finest India Paper or Thin White Paper), from 7s. 6d. to 38s. 6d.

GREAT NEW STREET, LONDON, E.C.

Special Publications.

THE NEW BIBLE FOR PREACHERS, TEACHERS, & STUDENTS.

Large Type VARIORUM Reference Bible,

(Size, 9¾ × 6¼ × 1½ inches. 1308 pages.)

WITH APOCRYPHA.

(Size, 9⅜ × 6¼ × 1¼ inches. 276 pages.)

For the TEACHER'S EDITION see page 9.

The **VARIORUM** Edition of the Authorised Version has a great and independent value, whether for daily use or as a standard work of Reference. It meets the wants of every grade of student, from the intelligent reader to the learned reviser.

In style and appearance the **VARIORUM REFERENCE BIBLE** was assimilated to the familiar 8vo. Reference Bible to make its utility no less universal. But it is distinguished from all other Reference Bibles by the addition, *on the same page as the Text*, in Foot-notes, of a complete digest of the chief Various Renderings and Readings of the original text from the very best Authorities. The sources from which the Annotations are taken comprise, in the

OLD TESTAMENT.	APOCRYPHA.	NEW TESTAMENT.
90 Commentators, 14 Versions, including the Revised Version, AND R.V. Marginal Readings.	49 Commentators, 20 Versions, AND 15 Manuscripts.	78 Commentators, 6 Ancient Versions, 23 Ancient Manuscripts, 11 Critical Editions of the Text, AND Revised Version & Margin.

The **VARIORUM** Notes, therefore, lay open to the ordinary reader of Scripture stores of information hitherto confined to great scholars or to the owners of very costly Libraries, and comprise the quintessence of Biblical Scholarship in the most convenient form.

The Commentary here is strictly textual (with Brief Explanatory Notes); and the names of the Editors—Professors CHEYNE, DRIVER, SANDAY, the late Rev. P. L. CLARKE, and the Rev. C. J. BALL—are sufficient guarantees for its accuracy and completeness.

The numerous Commendations of the completed Work include :—

The Rev. Dr. Wace, *late Principal of King's College, London :—*

"It is a work of incalculable usefulness, for which the warmest gratitude is due alike to the editors and yourselves."

The Rev. Canon W. J. Knox Little :—

"It is a beautiful and valuable work. I think it the most satisfactory copy I have ever had. I like it more, the more I make use of it."

EYRE & SPOTTISWOODE,

Special Publications.

THE VARIORUM APOCRYPHA:
EDITED WITH VARIOUS RENDERINGS AND READINGS FROM THE BEST AUTHORITIES,

BY THE

REV. C. J. BALL, M.A.,
Member of the Council of the Society of Biblical Archæology, &c., &c.

Large Type.   Bourgeois 8vo.   Superfine Paper.   276 Pages.
Cloth, Bevelled Boards, Red Edges, 6/6.
(*May also be had in Leather Bindings.*)

COMMENTATORS.

R. Arnald, St. Athanasius, C. Badwell (in "Critici Sacri"), Prof. R. L. Bensly, Dr. E. C. Bissell, Dr. J. F. Böttcher, Dr. C. G. Bretschneider, Rev. W. R. Churton, St. Clement of Alexandria, St. Cyrillus of Alexandria, Rev. W. J. Deane, Dr. T. A. Dereser, Dr. W. M. L. De Wette, Drusius (in "Critici Sacri"), Dr. Alfred Edersheim, Dr. J. G. Eichhorn, Eusebius, Dr. Heinrich Ewald, Very Rev. Dr. F W. Farrar, Dr. O. F Fritzsche, Prof. J. M. Fuller, Dr. J. F. Gaab, Dr. Abraham Geiger, Dr. W. Gesenius, Ven. Dr. E. H. Gifford, Dr. H. Grätz, Dr. C. L. W. Grimm, Hugo Grotius (in "Critici Sacri"), Dr. C. Gutberlet, Dr. M. Gutmann, Dr. L. Herzfeld, Dr. A. Hilgenfeld, Dr. F. Hitzig, Dr. J. H. Holtzmann, Pastor J. J. Kneucker, Dr. J. G. Linde, Rev. J. H. Lupton, Prof. D. S. Margoliouth, Dr. F. E. Movers, Origen, Rev. G. Rawlinson, Dr. F. H. Reusch, Dr. H. Rönsch, Prof. H. B. Swete (Cambridge Sept.), Dr. Const. von Tischendorf, Dr. C. J. Van der Vlis, Dr. G. Volkmar, Dr. C. A. Wahl, Dr. B. Welte.

VERSIONS.

Aldine Edit. of Greek Bible (Sept.), Arabic Version, Armenian Version, Complutensian Edit. of Greek Bible (Sept.), The Apostolical Constitutions, Coptic Version, Ethiopic Version, Walton's two Hebrew Versions of Tobit, Itala or Old Latin Version, Old Latin Version, Septuagint Version, Symmachus, Syriac Version, Hexaplar Syriac, Walton's Syriac Text, Walton's two Syriac Versions of Susanna, Theodotion, Vulgate.

MANUSCRIPTS.

Latin MSS. of 2 Esdras, Codex Sinaiticus, Uncial MSS., Cursive MSS. collated by Holmes and Parsons, Codex Alexandrinus, Codex Vaticanus, Amiens MS., containing 2 Esdr. (= A), Codex Chisianus, Codex Corbiensis, Codex Sangermanensis, Codex Venetus Marcianus, Chaldee, Hebrew, India House Inscription of Nebuchadnezzar, Vol. I. of the Cuneiform Inscriptions of Western Asia.

SOME OPINIONS.

Academy.—"Excellently adapted to its purpose; there does not exist a commentary upon the Apocrypha which is at once so concise and helpful."

Athenæum.—"A difficult task satisfactorily accomplished, it will be a great help to those who write on Apocrypha literature."

Saturday Review.—"The books of the Apocrypha, containing as they do much splendid literature, should have the long standing neglect they have suffered removed, by such an edition."

Church Quarterly Review.—"One of the greatest difficulties in dealing with the Apocrypha consists in the endeavours to restore the lost original text of books which, for the most part, once existed in the Hebrew tongue. In his preface Mr. Ball points out numerous instances where confusions of similar Hebrew letters have made sheer nonsense of the Greek text.

"The book is a welcome addition to the well-known Variorum Reference Bible."

Guardian.—"Mr. Ball has worked through a large number of authorities—forty-nine; he has not however confined himself to quoting their opinions, but has added throughout many suggestions of his own, both critical and explanatory.

"The information which he has given is judiciously selected, and the advance marked by his work, on previous works upon the Apocrypha, is exceedingly great."

Recommended also by the
Record, Expository Times, Church Review, Literary World, &c., &c.

GREAT NEW STREET, LONDON, E.C.

THE
ADVANTAGES OF THE VARIORUM
Above every other Bible.

For the Variorum TEACHER'S Bible, see page 9.

1. "It is the only edition of the English Bible in which the details of textual criticism are made accessible to the ordinary reader" (*Dr. Kenyon; see p.* 18),—including the evidence for and against the Revised Version.

2. **THE GENERAL READER** unacquainted with the original languages, Hebrew and Greek, is enabled to arrive at a *truer, fuller,* and *deeper* meaning of Scripture than he could obtain from any other published work. The **VARIORUM** foot-notes correct, explain, unfold, and paraphrase the text; indeed, the alternative versions of obscure or difficult words and phrases often render further note or comment needless.

3. **THE SUNDAY SCHOOL TEACHER** will find the use of the **VARIORUM** foot-notes of the utmost value to him in the preparation of his lessons. And, whilst teaching, a glance at the foot of the page will enable him to give the *best* alternative reading or translation of the original text, or to explain phrases or special words in the A.V.

   REV. DR. PARKER *says that it is quite as valuable for preachers and hearers as for teachers and scholars. It is a library in itself, containing everything that is immediately needed for the elucidation of the sacred text.*

4. **THE MODERN PREACHER** finds every passage ear-marked of which the text or the translation is considered by scholars defective, and in the corresponding foot-notes he finds the evidence, for and against alterations, judiciously digested from the most authoritative Versions and Editions, including the readings and renderings adopted in the Revised Version and its margin. This discrimination of sources and of authorities saves him infinite time and labour. Where all scholars agree upon a rendering the names of authorities are omitted.

   THE LATE ARCHBISHOP OF CANTERBURY said: "*It is so useful that no apology is, I am sure, needed for commending it.*"

5. **THE PROFESSIONAL STUDENT** of the original texts will find in this conspectus a more careful selection of critical data, especially as regards the Old Testament and authorities, than is elsewhere accessible. He will have at hand the very essence of textual criticism, extracted from the most reliable sources, ancient and modern.

   DR. WESTCOTT (LORD BISHOP OF DURHAM) says *I constantly use the Old Testament, and find it a great help to have at hand a brief and trustworthy summary of facts and results. Nothing could be better done than the Psalms.*" He also informed the Archbishop of Canterbury and the Conference at Lambeth that he considered that this **VARIORUM** Edition of the Authorised Version "*was much the best edition of the kind.*"

EYRE & SPOTTISWOODE,

The Queen's Printers'
VARIORUM and other TEACHER'S BIBLES.

OPINIONS OF THE CLERGY.

THE LATE ARCHBISHOP OF CANTERBURY (DR. BENSON):—
The Archbishop said, at a Diocesan Conference:—"I should like to call the attention of the Convocation to the New Edition of the 'Variorum Reference Bible,' published by Messrs. Eyre and Spottiswoode. I will just read an account of what it contains. The whole book has been revised. It was laid, I may say, before the Lambeth Conference—the promise of it—and now it is finished. The old edition forms the basis of the new edition; it is printed in larger type; and every passage which has been disputed by great scholars as to its correct translation or rendering, is marked by a figure before and after the sentence or word, these figures referring to the foot-notes, which give the alternative renderings or readings, together with the authorities for the same, abbreviated to save space. The collection of these notes from 69 commentators for the Old Testament, and 73 for the New, has occupied many years close study and preparation. The New Edition is much amplified as compared with the old one, and you may like to know that the opinion of Dr. Westcott is that it is much the best edition of the kind that has appeared."

THE LATE ARCHBISHOP OF YORK (DR. THOMSON):—
"The names of the authors guarantee its excellence. A miniature library of illustrative matter. If such a book is carefully and generally used, there must be a great improvement in Bible knowledge in this generation. The critical matter at the foot of the columns is remarkably complete. *The last feature gives it special value.*"

THE LATE ARCHBISHOP OF ARMAGH:—
"I have carefully examined the 'Variorum Teacher's Bible' published by Messrs. Eyre and Spottiswoode. The varied and valuable amount of information it contains is most remarkable. There are few subjects connected with the Bible left unelucidated. The Student of the Bible will find the Variorum Edition a treasury replete with instruction."

THE BISHOP OF DURHAM (DR. WESTCOTT):—
"Admirably done. I constantly use it."

THE BISHOP OF LIMERICK:—
"The Variorum (Teacher's) Bible, with its References, Concordance, Various Readings and Renderings, and supplemented by its Aids to Students, serves as a Biblical Encyclopædia, useful by its compactness and the value of its contents, to Biblical Students of all grades."

THE BISHOP OF EXETER (DR. BICKERSTETH):—
"I am much gratified with it . . . eminently fitted for teachers, and all who desire in a clear and compendious form very full information respecting the sacred Scriptures.
"A most valuable work, and will greatly enrich the library of Biblical Students."

THE BISHOP OF LLANDAFF:—
"An immense amount of information, a great help to Teachers, and to Bible readers generally.
"The names guarantee the value of the information. I trust it will be largely circulated."

THE LATE BISHOP OF ST. DAVID'S (DR. W. BASIL JONES):—
"I have delayed . . . until I could find more time to look into the volume; it contains so large an amount and variety of matter in a very small space. But its contents appear to me of the highest value and admirable in arrangement. I would refer especially to the various Readings and Renderings in the foot-notes."

GREAT NEW STREET, LONDON, E.C.

THE BISHOP OF GLOUCESTER AND BRISTOL:—
"A very valuable work, well suited for those for whom it is designed, and for all earnest students."

THE BISHOP OF LIVERPOOL:—
"I admire it very much, and think it a most valuable edition of the Holy Scriptures. I shall be glad to recommend your work."

THE LATE BISHOP OF WAKEFIELD (DR. WALSHAM HOW):—
"I have carefully examined the (Variorum) Teacher's Bible published by Messrs. Eyre and Spottiswoode, and I consider it a most valuable work. Believing that the Bible is its own best interpreter, I am sure that the Aids to an intelligent understanding of the text itself, together with the assistance given to students who desire to have an accurate conception of the purest form of that text, will prove of inestimable service to all Bible readers."

THE BISHOP OF DOWN AND CONNOR:—
"I consider the Variorum Teacher's Bible highly useful both to Teachers and Students. The various readings in the foot-notes largely increase its usefulness, placing before the professional Student an amount of information and research which to many would otherwise be inaccessible."

THE BISHOP OF CORK:—
"The eminent names of those who have contributed Articles to the Teacher's Aids are a guarantee for the accuracy of the information, which will be found most valuable to those who wish to understand or teach, or first to understand and then to teach, and help to provide that skilled and accurate teaching, which is not only the true antidote to prevalent unbelief, but the great preventive of it."

THE LATE BISHOP OF KILLALOE (DR. FITZGERALD):—
"I find it to be a most perfect compendium of information on almost every Biblical matter that could be comprised within such a compass, and it seems marvellous how much has been introduced and how varied the topics. It will, I am sure, prove a most important aid to Clergymen, Sunday School Teachers, and many others, and I hope to avail myself of it yet in that direction."

THE BISHOP OF TUAM:—
"I admire greatly the most valuable contents."

THE LATE BISHOP OF KILMORE (DR. DARLEY):—
"I have looked through it carefully . . . a most valuable edition of the sacred Scriptures. The Variorum foot-notes represent much critical research, very carefully arranged; the Aids to Bible Students contain a mass of interesting information in a convenient form; useful alike to Teachers and Students."

THE BISHOP OF OSSORY:—
"I feel pleasure in bearing my testimony.
"An invaluable aid both to Clergymen and Teachers, and a marvel of cheapness. The more I have examined it, the more thoroughly have I been satisfied and pleased."

THE RIGHT REV. BISHOP BARRY:—
"For the study of the Text is invaluable."

THE DEAN OF SALISBURY:—
"I am fully sensible of the great boon you have put within the reach of Bible students and it will be my endeavour to promote the knowledge of this valuable edition."

THE DEAN OF ELY:—
"I hope to make use of it, with its various adjuncts of Notes, Readings," &c., &c.

THE DEAN OF LINCOLN:—
"The work will be extremely useful."

THE DEAN OF ROCHESTER (*late Master of Balliol College, Oxford*):—
"A great achievement of toil and thought."

EYRE & SPOTTISWOODE,

Special Publications. 15

THE (LATE) DEAN OF ST. PAUL'S (DR. CHURCH):—
"A wonderful digest of learning. The names of the various scholars are, of course, warrant of care and accuracy, and certainly nothing so complete and comprehensive, in such a compass, has ever before been attempted."

THE DEAN OF PETERBOROUGH:—
"Your Bible strikes me as admirable in every respect. The Various Renderings considerably enhance the value of the work. It will give me very great pleasure to do all in my power to promote the circulation. I know of no one volume to be compared to it for the amount of information it conveys."

THE DEAN OF NORWICH (DR. W. LEFROY, D.D.):—
"There is no work of the kind comparable to this work. It is invaluable."

THE LATE VERY REV. DR. VAUGHAN, *Dean of Llandaff, and Master of the Temple*:—
"I use the Variorum Teacher's Bible with pleasure and profit."

THE DEAN OF LICHFIELD:—
"I am both surprised and delighted at the fulness and accuracy of information to be found in it.
"I will gladly mention it with the approbation which it so well deserves."

THE VERY REV. DR. BUTLER, *Master of Trinity College, Cambridge*:—
"A great achievement."

THE VERY REV. DEAN FARRAR:—
"It lies always on my desk. I place a high value upon it."

THE LATE VEN. ARCHDEACON HESSEY:—
"Students of the sacred volume will owe a deep debt to the projectors and producers."

THE REV. CANON BODY:—
"Very well done."

THE REV. CANON KNOX LITTLE:—
"Most useful and helpful."

THE REV. DR. WACE, *late Principal of King's College*:—
"A work of incalculable usefulness."

THE LATE REV. DR. EDERSHEIM:—
"It is certainly the best, most complete and useful which has hitherto appeared."

THE REV. DR. SAMUEL G. GREEN:—
"As a companion to the Revised Version it is invaluable."

DR. SALMOND, *of Free College, Aberdeen*:—
"I trust it may secure a very wide circulation. The former edition has come to be a familiar book among our students."

THE REV. HUGH PRICE HUGHES:—
"Incomparable and invaluable."

DR. GREENWOOD, *Victoria University (Owen's College), Manchester*:—
"Its merits and remarkable features are already known to me."

THE REV. JOSEPH PARKER, D.D.:—
"I have examined your Bible with great care. It is quite as valuable for preachers and hearers as for Teachers and scholars.
"It is almost a library in itself, containing everything that is immediately needed for the elucidation of the sacred text."

THE BISHOP OF ONTARIO:—
"My opinion of it is nothing so good has hitherto appeared. It is admirably adapted for its purpose of assisting Teachers, and cannot fail to be appreciated by all who are really anxious to find the best instruction in the sacred volume."

THE REV. J. H. VINCENT, *of Chautauqua*:—
"The book is indeed a marvel, a library of learning, a book of books, concerning the 'Book of Books,' and deserves a wide circulation in Europe and America."

GREAT NEW STREET, LONDON, E.C.

THE HEBREW MONARCHY:
A Commentary,
CONTAINING

A HARMONY OF THE PARALLEL TEXTS

AND

EXTRACTS FROM THE PROPHETICAL BOOKS.

EDITED, WITH AN INTRODUCTION BY
R. PAYNE SMITH, D.D., LATE DEAN OF CANTERBURY,

BY

ANDREW WOOD, M.A.,
Trinity College, Cambridge; Rector of Great Ponton, Lincs.; Diocesan Inspector of Schools.

Small 4to., Cloth, Gilt Edges (820 pp. and Maps), **21/-**

Extracts from Dr. Payne Smith's Introduction.

"THE object of this important Commentary is unique. It is to exhibit the History of the Hebrew Monarchy in a connected narrative, with everything necessary for its elucidation. Thus it commences with the agitation of the Israelites for a more permanent form of government; and ends with those portions of the prophetic books which throw light upon the purpose of the Hebrew Monarchy, the reasons of its fall, and its survival in that which was ever the true reason of its existence—the spiritual reign of David's Son. . . ."

"These extracts show what was the ultimate purpose of God in establishing monarchy in Israel, and under the veil of an earthly kingdom they reveal to us the nature of the true kingdom of God. . . ."

"We can understand Jewish history only by seeing it in relation to Christ, and as we look back upon the strange course it has run we see in His coming its reason and explanation. And as these were given beforehand in the writings of the goodly fellowship of Judah's prophets, both the history and these writings gain in clearness by being brought close together."

SOME OPINIONS.

The Scotsman.—"It makes what are merely dry bones in ordinary commentaries live before us."

The Guardian, 17th December 1896.—"It is convenient to the student to have the parallel historical texts before him. . . . Much industry and scholarship have been expended upon it."

The Morning Post, 22nd January 1897.—"It is a book for all churches. . . . It is remarkable for its excellence from several points of view, but more especially from an evidential standpoint. . . . The statements of the text are amply illustrated by parallel or significant passages."

The Literary World, 29th January 1897.—"Certain to run into more than one edition. We need not emphasize its helpfulness."

EYRE & SPOTTISWOODE,

HEBREW MONARCHY—*continued.*

The Schoolmaster, 9th January 1897.—"It is a monument of patient, thoughtful, and thorough work."

The Irish Times, 17th December 1897.—"The volume is one which every Bible student will treasure. The harmony of the parallel texts is of the highest value. The typography is excellent, and the correctness of the notes is wonderful."

The Daily News.—"A unique Commentary. Its originality consists first in the weaving together of the different histories, such as those in the Books of Kings and the Books of Chronicles, into a single narrative; and secondly, in the introduction of the Psalms and passages from the Prophets, at the point in the history to which they refer. For preachers, the reading of the Psalms and Prophets into the narrative gives the volume real value as an aid to exposition."

The Glasgow Herald.—"The copious notes are mainly explanatory, though brief homiletical reflections are added. The geographical and archæological information seems to be particularly full and up-to-date. Mr. Wood does not bother himself about the Higher Criticism, but takes the Bible story as he finds it."

The Record.—"The design of this work is highly to be commended. The whole Commentary is one which clergymen or theological students or educated readers of the Bible generally, who may be debarred from the use of a full theological library of reference, will find admirably suited to their needs."

The Expository Times.—"The notes are surprisingly numerous; they are skilfully chosen and tersely expressed. Further, their range of material is wide, all the things we usually find in a Dictionary of the Bible being gathered into the service, with not a few we should not expect to find there. The indexes are excellent. The author is evidently fit for his work. He is conservative in criticism, but he is a scholar. He has read the commentaries on his books, and he has read his books themselves."

Belfast Evening Telegraph.—"The work is all that scholarship and careful preparation could make it, and higher praise could not be given. A word of credit must also be accorded the general get-up of the volume. It is a beautiful specimen of both the printer's and the binder's arts."

Mr. **Gladstone** writes:—"I am delighted with the 'Hebrew Monarchy.'"

Rev. F. J. Chavasse, Principal of Wycliffe Hall, Oxford.—"It supplies a distinct need, and is likely to prove of real service to the clergy and to Bible students generally."

The Ven. Archdeacon of Sheffield.—"Deeply interesting; it is what I have long wanted, and will be an immense help."

The Archbishop of York (Dr. Maclagan).—"Very useful . . . covers ground not yet occupied."

The Archbishop of Armagh.—"A work which commended itself in its inception and idea to the two spirits, so noble and so diverse, mentioned in the Dedication, must be a blessing to many."

The Bishop of Durham (Dr. Westcott).—"A very solid and valuable help to the study of the history of Israel, admirable in plan and execution."

The Bishop of Lincoln.—"One effect of modern criticism has been to lead men to excuse themselves from studying the Bible. Many of the modern books seem to miss the real spirit of the Book. I am so glad you have brought out the historical value of the Prophets."

Canon Crowfoot (Principal of Lincoln Theological College).—"It will be constantly in my hands. It is unique in its plan, and that plan is most admirable."

Canon Blackley.—"A work of vast labour and care."

The Rev. Dr. Plummer.—"Welcome and useful. An immense amount of information in a very handsome volume."

The Rev. Dr. Sinker (Librarian of Trinity College, Cambridge).—"Having regard to the type of readers for whom it is primarily intended it is admirably done. The idea is a very good one and well worked out, the work is thorough and exact, and the matter is pleasantly and interestingly put."

Principal of St. Aidan's College, Birkenhead.—"Admirable in arrangement and plan."

GREAT NEW STREET, LONDON, E.C.

Special Publications.

THIRD EDITION.

Our Bible and the Ancient Manuscripts:

BEING A

HISTORY OF THE TEXT AND ITS TRANSLATIONS.

BY

FREDERIC G. KENYON, M.A., D.LITT.,

Hon. Ph.D. of Halle University; Late Fellow of Magdalen College, Oxford.

ILLUSTRATED WITH 26 FACSIMILES.

Demy 8vo. Dark Blue Cloth. Red Edges. Price **5/-**

SUMMARY OF CONTENTS.

Variations in the Bible Text—The Authorities for the Bible Text—The Original Manuscripts of the Bible—The Hebrew Text—The Ancient Versions of the Old Testament—The Text of the New Testament—The Manuscripts of the New Testament—The Ancient Versions of the New Testament—The Vulgate in the Middle Ages—The English Manuscript Bibles—The English Printed Bible.

EXTRACT FROM THE PREFACE.

THE present volume deals solely with the transmission of the sacred text. My object has been to condense within the limits of a moderate volume the principal results at which our specialists have arrived, so as to furnish the reader who is not himself a specialist with a concise history of the Bible text, from the time at which the several books were written until their appearance in our English Bibles to-day.

This volume is especially intended for those who study the Bible in English, and in referring to details of textual criticism I have consequently had in my mind the only edition of the English Bible in which these details are made accessible to the ordinary reader, namely the **VARIORUM** Bible published by Messrs. Eyre & Spottiswoode. I hope, however, that it may also be found useful by students who are beginning to make acquaintance with the textual criticism of the Septuagint or New Testament in their original language, and who use such editions as the Cambridge Septuagint edited by Prof. Swete, or the Oxford Greek Testament edited by Prof. Sanday.

With regard to the *facsimiles* of manuscripts, I have in every case stated the original size of the page reproduced, and (in cases where the whole page cannot be given) of the part reproduced; and it is open to anyone to counteract the reduction by the use of a magnifying glass. I have tried to give pages which especially illustrate the characteristics and peculiarities of the manuscript in question, the errors of the scribes, or some important detail of textual criticism.

F. G. K.

DEPARTMENT OF MANUSCRIPTS, BRITISH MUSEUM.

EYRE & SPOTTISWOODE,

OUR BIBLE AND THE ANCIENT MANUSCRIPTS—*continued.*

SOME OPINIONS OF THE PRESS.

The Times.—"An account at once lucid, scholarly, and popular in the best sense, of the transmission and translation of the text of the Holy Scriptures. The plan is an excellent one, and is very skilfully executed."

The Daily Chronicle.—"Dr. Kenyon is specially qualified to deal with the textual or external history of the Bible, and in this beautifully printed volume tells the story with scholarly conciseness and power. The value of the book is greatly enhanced by the beautiful facsimiles of the most famous Bible MSS."

Church Times.—"Mr. Kenyon's book deserves nothing but praise."

The Academy.—"We shall be surprised if the whole mass of Bible-readers be not grateful to Mr. Kenyon for his timely and valuable help. The plates by which he illustrates his subjects are very clear and beautiful bits of reproduction."

The Guardian.—"Dr. Kenyon has produced a book of which theological students stood sorely in need; full of interest and free from exaggerations, the book is dominated by common sense, and by a just appreciation of the requirements of those to whom it is addressed."

The Speaker.—"An able epitome, and the fact that it is based to a large extent on the works of such authorities as Davidson, Driver, Scrivener, Hort, Skeat, and Westcott adds to its value as a record which is thoroughly abreast with contemporary scholarship."

The Tablet.—"Mr. Kenyon's volume deserves to find a place in every college library; and no better introduction to the art and mystery of textual criticism could be recommended to the student at the outset of his studies."

Western Morning News.—"Every clergyman should not only have it on his shelves, but be frequent in recommending it."

The Manchester Guardian.—"There is probably no book published at anything like the same price from which the student can obtain the same amount of thoroughly trustworthy information."

Recommended also by the

Daily News, Church Standard, Sunday School Chronicle, Christian, Christian World, Oxford Journal, Irish Times, Scotsman, &c., &c.

List of Illustrations.

THE SAMARITAN PENTATEUCH-ROLL AT NABLOUS.
CLAY TABLET FROM TELL EL-AMARNA.
HEBREW SYNAGOGUE-ROLL (Brit. Mus. Harl. 7619).
THE MOABITE STONE.
HEBREW MS. (Brit. Mus. Or. 4445).
SAMARITAN PENTATEUCH Rome, (Barberini Library, 106).
CODEX MARCHALIANUS.
PESHITTO SYRIAC MS. (Brit. Mus. Add. 14425).
CODEX SINAITICUS.
CODEX ALEXANDRINUS.
CODEX VATICANUS.
CODEX EPHRAEMI.
CODEX BEZAE.
CODEX CLAROMONTANUS.
CURSIVE GREEK MS. (Evan. 348).
CURETONIAN MS. OF OLD SYRIAC (Brit. Mus. Add. 14451).
BOHAIRIC MS. (Brit. Mus. Or. 1315).
SAHIDIC MS. (Brit. Mus. Or. 4717 (10)).
CODEX VERCELLENSIS (Old Latin).
CODEX AMIATINUS (Vulgate).
THE LINDISFARNE GOSPELS.
ALCUIN'S VULGATE (Brit. Mus. Add. 10546).
MAZARIN BIBLE.
ENGLISH GOSPELS OF THE 10th CENTURY (Brit. Mus. Reg. 1 A XIV.)
WYCLIFFE'S BIBLE (Bodleian MS. 957).
TYNDALE'S NEW TESTAMENT.

GREAT NEW STREET, LONDON, E.C.

Special Publications.

THIRD EDITION.
THE BIBLE AND THE MONUMENTS.

The Primitive Hebrew Records in the Light of Modern Research.

By W. ST. CHAD BOSCAWEN,
Fellow of the Royal Historical Society, Member of the Society of Biblical Archæology.

WITH 21 PHOTOGRAPHIC ILLUSTRATIONS.

Demy 8vo., Bound Cloth Boards. Price **5/-**

LIST OF ILLUSTRATIONS,

All of which, with the exception of those marked (*) have been reproduced from Photographs taken by Messrs. EYRE & SPOTTISWOODE from the originals.

MANEH WEIGHT.	ASSYRIAN TABLET OF THE FALL.
MACE HEAD OF SARGON I. (B.C. 3800).	MERODACH AND THE DRAGON.
	SEAL OF TEMPTATION.
TABLET OF ASSUR-NAZIR-PAL I. (B.C. 1800).	* RUINS OF TELLO.
	* HARPER AND CHOIR (B.C. 3000).
INDIA HOUSE INSCRIPTION OF NEBUCHADNEZZAR II. (B.C. 606).	BRONZE FIGURES (B.C. 2800) AND FIRE-GOD (B.C. 722).
FIRST CREATION TABLET (COPIED ABOUT 660).	* STATUE OF GUDEA (B.C. 2800).
BOUNDARY STONE OF NEBUCHADNEZZAR I. (B.C. 1120).	DELUGE TABLET (PORTION OF THE ELEVENTH TABLET).
TABLET FROM THE TEMPLE OF THE SUN-GOD AT SIPPARA (B.C. 900).	DELUGE TABLET, No. 2.
	SEAL REPRESENTING THE CHALDEAN NOAH.
TEL EL-AMARNA TABLET (B.C. 1450).	WINGED HUMAN-HEADED LION.
EAGLE-HEADED FIGURE.	JACKAL-HEADED GOD.

Some Opinions.

The Times.—"An able attempt to bring the Primitive Hebrew Records into relation with the Babylonian and Assyrian versions of the same traditions."

Observer.—"The book is beautifully illustrated."

Church Quarterly Review.—"A more interesting and lucid account of ancient inscriptions we have never read, and Mr. Boscawen has transmuted his learning into popular forms of speech with conspicuous success."

Churchman.—"Mr. Boscawen has rendered important service in the sphere of Biblical criticism in the publication of his important volume."

Literary World.—"This contribution to an intelligent appreciation of the Old Testament will be welcomed not least by those who still preserve their reverence for it intact."

The Christian—"A work of great usefulness." (So **The Daily Chronicle**.)

Western Morning News.—"The book will really supply a need."

EYRE & SPOTTISWOODE,

LEX MOSAICA;

Or, THE LAW OF MOSES AND THE HIGHER CRITICISM.

EDITED BY THE

Rev. RICHARD VALPY FRENCH, D.C.L., LL.D., F.S.A.,

WITH AN INTRODUCTION BY THE LATE

RIGHT REVEREND LORD ARTHUR C. HERVEY, D.D.,
Bishop of Bath and Wells.

Essays by Various Writers on the Law of Moses and the Higher Criticism.

LIST OF CONTRIBUTORS:

Rev. A. H. SAYCE, D.D., LL.D.	The late Rev. J. SHARPE, D.D.
Rev. GEORGE RAWLINSON, M.A.	Rev. ALEXANDER STEWART, LL.D.,
Rev. GEORGE C. M. DOUGLAS, D.D.	F.A.S.
Rev. R. B. GIRDLESTONE, M.A.	Rev. STANLEY LEATHES, D.D.
Rev. RICHARD VALPY FRENCH, D.C.L.	Rev. ROBERT SINKER, D.D.
Rev. J. J. LIAS, M.A.	Rev. F. E. SPENCER, M.A.
Rev. F. WATSON, D.D.	Rev. ROBERT WATTS, D.D., LL.D.

WITH A SUMMARY BY THE

Rev. HENRY WACE, D.D., late Principal of King's College, London.

Royal 8vo., Half-bound Vellum Cloth, Red Burnished Edges, **15/-**

SOME OPINIONS OF THE PRESS.

The Times.—"'Lex Mosaica' is a sustained and reasoned criticism of the Higher Criticism conducted by a variety of competent hands."

Church Times.—"The deliverance of fourteen able men speaking at their best."

Record.—"We fully believe that this book will be of great use in this time of unrest."

Churchman.—"This important work is a thorough exposition of the crude and arbitrary guesses of the theoretical school of criticism, and contains a powerful defence of the traditional view."

Tablet.—"An important contribution to the literature of the subject."

Expository Times.—"The most serious effort that has yet been made to stem the advancing tide of Old Testament criticism."

Church Family Newspaper.—"The volume is one of great interest, which must command the earnest attention both of Biblical Students and critics."

Sunday School Chronicle.—"We very gladly welcome this book. It presents a mass of clear and precise information of priceless value to the Bible students."

The Methodist Times.—"The writers of 'Lex Mosaica' deserve the grateful thanks of all who believe in the Old Testament as a revelation of God, given through men who were guided in all their work by the operation of the Divine Spirit."

Oxford Journal.—"No student of the Old Testament time should omit to read these Essays."

Cambridge Chronicle.—"'Lex Mosaica' is one of the most elaborate expositions of the historical part of the Bible that has ever been produced."

Irish Times.—"The volume of the year."

GREAT NEW STREET, LONDON, E.C.

THE BIBLE STUDENT'S LIBRARY.

Demy 8vo.   Dark Blue Cloth, Red Edges.

Volumes I.–VII.   Others in preparation.

THIS Series of Volumes, popular in style and moderate in size and price, is designed to meet the needs of the ordinary Bible Student, a large and increasing class of practical students of the Bible, as well as the requirements of more advanced scholars.

Much light has been thrown in the course of the present century on almost all branches of Biblical Inquiry, and it is very desirable that such results as are surely ascertained should be placed within the reach of all in a systematic manner. Difficulties will always remain, owing to the extreme antiquity of the Sacred Books, and to the peculiar nature of their contents. On these questions experts must be heard upon both sides, but the multitude which is so deeply interested in the results has neither the time nor the training for battling over technical details.

Accordingly, the preparation of these volumes is entrusted to men who have patiently considered the drift of modern inquiry so far as it concerns their own special branches of study, and who are not lightly moved from their carefully formed convictions.

Their aim is to set forth as clearly and accurately as possible the literary position of the Books of the Old and New Testaments and their contents in relation to Theological, Historical, and Scientific questions.

The series is mainly constructive and positive in tone, and will tend to check that bewilderment as to the very foundations of sacred truth which, if allowed to spread, will seriously affect the work of the Sunday School Teacher, the Bible Class Leader, the Home and Foreign Missionary, and the devotional student of Scripture.

EYRE & SPOTTISWOODE,

THE BIBLE STUDENT'S LIBRARY.

FOURTH EDITION, REVISED.

Volume I.—Price 3s. 6d.

THE FOUNDATIONS OF THE BIBLE:

STUDIES IN OLD TESTAMENT CRITICISM.

BY

R. B. GIRDLESTONE, M.A.,

Hon. Canon of Christ Church; late Principal of Wycliffe Hall, Oxford.

SOME OPINIONS.

Guardian.—"Written in a reverent spirit."

Theological Monthly.—"Any one who takes up the book will be led, we think, to peruse and ponder till he arrives at a sound conclusion on what is, and must remain, one of the most important matters within human ken."

Church Review.—"An invaluable work."

Rock.—"Canon Girdlestone as an expert gives us the results of his own personal research. We are taken into the very workshop and shown the methods and processes."

Churchman.—"It is worthy to become a text-book in a theological assembly."

Christian.—"Will assist many to gain a firm foothold with regard to the verity of Holy Writ."

Literary Churchman.—"This is a book of exceeding breadth of learning, and quite exceptional value. We desire to give an unusually emphatic recommendation to this valuable treatise."

Literary Opinion.—"The style throughout is clear elevated, and forcible."

Globe.—"A mine of strength to the holders of the ancient faith."

Quiver.—"We can heartily commend it."

Baptist.—"Canon Girdlestone's arguments will command general respect."

National Church.—"Precisely the kind of work wanted in these critical times."

Evening News.—"A perfect armoury of argument and scholarship."

Yorkshire Post.—"Shows results as interesting as they are valuable."

Church Bells.—"The various topics involved are put in a very interesting way."

British Weekly.—"It has a calm and dignified style—with a splendid courtesy to opponents, and altogether it is a pleasant book to read."

GREAT NEW STREET, LONDON, E.C.

THE BIBLE STUDENT'S LIBRARY—*continued.*

SECOND EDITION.
Volume II.—Price 3s. 6d.

THE LAW IN THE PROPHETS.

BY THE

REV. STANLEY LEATHES, D.D.,

Professor of Hebrew, King's College, London; Prebendary of St. Paul's;
Author of "The Structure of the Old Testament";
"The Religion of the Christ" (Bampton Lecture); "Christ and the Bible," &c., &c.

EXTRACT FROM THE PREFACE.

The late Dr. LIDDON wrote: "How I wish you could see your way to writing a book on, say, 'The Law and the Prophets,' putting the Law back into the chronological and authoritative place from which the new criticism would depose it, and so incidentally reasserting in the main, and with the necessary reservations, the Mosaic authorship of the Pentateuch."

This book is partly the result of that suggestion.

SOME OPINIONS.

Church Quarterly Review.—"A careful work."

Guardian.—"Deserves wide circulation..... It was an excellent idea thus to collect these allusions."

Church Times.—"Most valuable."

Spectator.—"Proves the antiquity of the Mosaic Law, by the references that are made to it in the books of the Prophets, books that are conceded on all hands to have at least a considerable relative antiquity. The contention of the extremists, that the whole legal ritual is post-exilian, certainly lays itself open to hostile criticism. The appeal of the Prophets to the Hebrew people seems founded on the fact that there was a covenant which the people had broken."

Church Review.—"If Dr. Stanley Leathes had never done any other good thing than he has done in writing this most valuable book, he would be fairly entitled to rank as one of the most successful defenders of Holy Scriptures of our day."

Baptist Magazine.—"Dr. Leathes has set an example which all who are opposed to the method and result of modern Biblical criticism would do well to follow. He brings the question to a sound and religious test."

EYRE & SPOTTISWOODE,

THE BIBLE STUDENT'S LIBRARY—*continued.*

Volume III.—Price 3s. 6d.

PRINCIPLES OF BIBLICAL CRITICISM.

BY THE

REV. J. J. LIAS, M.A.,

Chancellor of Llandaff Cathedral; formerly Hulsean Lecturer, and Preacher at the Chapel Royal, Whitehall.

MR. LIAS, who is well known as a writer on theology and literature, in this book offers a historical view of the two chief lines of criticism, which have been directed against the Old and New Testaments, and points out that the wave of adverse criticism, after failing when levelled against the Christian Scriptures, the New Testament, has now for its object the disintegration of the Hebrew Records of the Old Testament. He brings to the task an easy style of an unfettered mind; takes his own line in discussing such subjects as Inspiration, and tests the results of modern critical analysis in the light of good sense, whilst passing under review the historical and prophetical writings of the Old Testament.

On the whole, for a beginner in critical studies there are few books which are so likely to put the student on the right line.

SOME OPINIONS OF THE PRESS.

The Church Times.—"We have seldom seen in so small a compass so admirable, and withal temperate, exposition of the ingenious puzzles which German criticism has been weaving under the guise of truth. We gratefully recognize the value and importance of this volume; and a reverent investigation carried on, on the lines here suggested, cannot fail to be profitable to the Biblical student."

The Record.—"The book is one that we can very cordially recommend; it is both reverent and scholarly, the discussions are temperate and logical, and the style attractive. It is likely to do good service."

Church Quarterly Review.—"Mr. Lias is entitled to the gratitude of churchmen."

The Churchman.—"Will prove of real and lasting service. We hope it will be very widely circulated, as it deserves."

Expository Times.—"Exceedingly useful as a storehouse of facts."

Spectator.—"Perhaps the most important chapter is that of 'The Evidence of the Psalms.' Mr. Lias knows that the controversy turns largely on the date of these."

The Baptist Magazine.—"Mr. Lias has a masterly chapter on the genuineness of the Pentateuch, he is fair and courteous in his methods, and knows that argument must be met with argument."

The Christian World.—"Deserving of the highest praise we wish it a wide circulation."

GREAT NEW STREET, LONDON, E.C.

THE BIBLE STUDENT'S LIBRARY—*continued.*

Volume IV.—536 pages. Price 6/-

SANCTUARY AND SACRIFICE:
A REPLY TO WELLHAUSEN.
BY THE
REV. W. L. BAXTER, M.A., D.D.,
Minister of Cameron.

THOUGH specially designed for Bible Students, this volume demands no attainments in Hebrew scholarship for its appreciation. Its main aim is to guide and strengthen an ordinary reader, with his English Bible in his hand.

In particular, the dismemberment of the Mosaic legislation into three antagonistic Codes is shown (taking SANCTUARY AND SACRIFICE *as conclusive tests*) to be quite at variance with a fair and comprehensive survey of the legal, historical, and prophetical Records of the Old Testament.

While exposing the views of Wellhausen (the applauded pioneer of "Higher Critics"), the author seeks at every turn to give a positive presentation of Bible truth on the topics handled. Mere destruction is not his aim, but to instruct and re-assure. A special helpfulness characterises his constructive surveys of the prophecy of Ezekiel, and of the so-called Priestly Code.

SOME OPINIONS.

Mr. Gladstone.—"Unless your searching inquiry can be answered, and your statements confuted, Wellhausen's character, literary and theological, is destroyed, at least for all those who have profited by your investigation."

Bishop Ellicott.—"Your counter-argument is very strong and clear. In fact, as I read the first paper, I wondered what answer your opponent could possibly make."

Church Quarterly Review (October 1896).—"The book must be read to understand its force; the new theory is destroyed. Dr. Baxter has not been answered, and that simply because he is unanswerable."

The Morning Post.—"Dr Baxter has shown in his reply a wide knowledge of the subject discussed, and has rendered a powerful support to the opponents of that dogmatic criticism of which Wellhausen is a prominent example."

The Daily Chronicle.—"Dr. Baxter is always interesting, and he certainly tries to be fair. Wellhausen's answer will be awaited with much interest."

The Record.—"Any reader who should work patiently through Dr. Baxter's book, argument by argument, will find one sweeping piece of destructive theorising (we refuse to say criticism) after another toppling over. This remarkable book is the most vigorous attempt which we have yet seen to carry the war into the enemy's country."

The Speaker.—"An effective answer to the German Professor's attack, and well deserves the high praise given it by Mr. Gladstone and Professor Sayce."

The Church Times.—"We are sincerely grateful to the publishers. A book like this will form a rallying point for those who had begun to think that the possession of common sense was a thing to be ashamed of, and unwavering tradition on any point rather a source of weakness than of strength."

The Churchman.—"We strongly recommend those who have not done so to read, mark, and inwardly digest 'Sanctuary and Sacrifice.'"

The Christian World.—"It is an honest and serious discussion of important questions. Those who differ from Dr. Baxter may learn from his criticisms."

The Methodist Times.—"By far the most telling challenge to the higher criticism."

The Primitive Methodist.—"Those who have been unsettled in their faith in the Old Testament by the speculations of some modern writing would do well to make the acquaintance of this volume."

EYRE & SPOTTISWOODE,

THE BIBLE STUDENT'S LIBRARY—*continued.*

Volume V. Price 3s. 6d.
HEZEKIAH AND HIS AGE.
BY THE
Rev. ROBERT SINKER, D.D.,
Librarian of Trinity College, Cambridge.

THIS work compares the Bible history of this King with contemporary records, and generally deals with his period. The Assyrian Inscriptions of the period markedly confirm the Bible story; they have shewn the connection of events; they have filled up gaps, and so imparted greater coherence to the narrative, clearing up difficulties where some have accused the scriptural account of inaccuracy.

No period of early history is more full of suggestiveness. The intense human pathos interwoven in the life of Hezekiah, and the Monuments which survive of his handiwork in Jerusalem, impart to his reign a more than ordinary interest to the modern reader, and particularly to those willing to avail themselves of all fresh light thereon, as it arises.

CONTENTS.

CHAP.
- I.—INTRODUCTORY, REIGNS OF UZZIAH, JOTHAM, AHAZ.
- II.—CHRONOLOGY.
- III.—THE SURROUNDING NATIONS.
- IV.—THE OUTLOOK AT HEZEKIAH'S ACCESSION.
- V.—HEZEKIAH THE REFORMER.
- VI.—THE WARRIOR, THE BUILDER, THE WISE KING.

CHAP.
- VII.—"SICK UNTO DEATH," "I WILL ADD UNTO THY DAYS FIFTEEN YEARS."
- VIII.—FACE TO FACE WITH ASSYRIA.
- IX.—THE GREAT INVASION.
- X.—THE GREAT DELIVERANCE.
- XI.—CONCLUSION.
- APPENDIX.—THE AUTHENTICITY OF ISAIAH XL.-LXVI.

SOME OPINIONS.

Literary World.—"A careful attempt to collate the Biblical history of the eighth century B.C., not only with the prophetical and poetical books of the period, but with the Assyrian Monuments."

Speaker.—"A luminous and, at the same time, critical exposition."

Sunday School Chronicle.—"A valuable contribution to the literature dealing with that significant epoch in Israelitish history and thoroughly interesting. Much light from the Assyrian inscriptions is brought to bear upon the narrative."

Record.—"A portrait of Hezekiah, lucid and forcible."

Manchester Guardian.—"A chapter of Biblical history which shows that the Assyrian inscriptions have yielded a most striking confirmation of the Bible story." So the *Scotsman.*

Irish Times.—"Holds a very high place, and will be everywhere prized."

GREAT NEW STREET, LONDON, E.C.

THE BIBLE STUDENT'S LIBRARY—*continued.*

Volume VI. (ILLUSTRATED.) Price 6/-
ABRAHAM AND HIS AGE.
BY
The Rev. HENRY GEORGE TOMKINS,
Late Vicar of Branscombe, sometime Rector of St. Paul's, Exeter; Member of the Committees of the Palestine and the Egypt Exploration Funds, &c., &c.

THE history of Abraham, "the father of the faithful," is here brought into one continuous relation. The Monuments and Inscriptions of contemporary nations, here summarised to date, yield fresh confirmation of the Bible narrative.

LIST OF ILLUSTRATIONS.

I.—ROYAL HITTITE.
(*Coloured Frontispiece.*)
II.—NARÂM-SIN, NEBUCHADREZZAR, AND KHAMMURABI.
III.—MARDUK-NADIN-AKHI.
IV.—GROUP OF HEADS TYPICAL OF RACES.
V.—AMENEMHAT, KHAFRA, AND TETA AND HIS WIFE.
VI.—HYKSÔS STATUARY.
VII.—TWO NEW HEADS, PROBABLY HYKSÔS, etc.
VIII.—HITTITES AND AMORITES.
IX.—ARABS, SYRIANS, etc.
X.—BABYLONIAN SEAL-CYLINDERS.

CONTENTS.

Chapter.
  DESCRIPTIONS OF THE ILLUSTRATIONS.
I.—INTRODUCTORY.
II.—ABRAHAM'S FATHERLAND.
III.—RELIGIOUS WORSHIP IN ABRAHAM'S TIME.
IV.—POLITICAL AND SOCIAL LIFE IN CHALDÆA.
V.—MIGRATION TO KHARRAN.
VI.—THE LAND OF CANAAN.
VII.—THE PLACE OF SICHEM.
VIII.—THE CANAANITE.

Chapter.
IX.—ABRAHAM GOES DOWN TO EGYPT.
X.—EGYPT IN THE TWELFTH DYNASTY.
XI.—THE HYKSÔS.
XII.—ABRAHAM RETURNS TO CANAAN.
XIII.—ELAM AND ITS KINGS—KEDORLA'OMER'S WAR AND DEFEAT.
XIV.—GENESIS HISTORICAL, NOT MYTHICAL.
APPENDIX OF NOTES.
INDEX.

SOME OPINIONS.

Church Times.—"Mr. Tomkins has devoted thirty years to the study of Biblical Archæology, and he has brought together a large amount of material upon which he has something interesting to say. He makes out a very good case."

Scotsman.—"A concise and compendious statement of the case for the older orthodox doctrine as against sweeping sceptical researches. It is a learned and useful manual."

Sunday School Chronicle.—"A book like this, with its plentiful archæological illustrations, will help to make Abraham's life more real to the render."

Irish Times.—"It sketches the background of the historical picture, in which the patriarch is the central figure."

Manchester Guardian.—"It is full of facts and enriched with well executed plates."

EYRE & SPOTTISWOODE,

THE
STUDENT'S HANDBOOK TO THE PSALMS.

BY THE LATE
Rev. J. SHARPE, D.D.,
Fellow of Christ College, Cambridge.

SECOND EDITION, WITH MEMOIR OF THE AUTHOR,

BY THE

Rev. ROBERT SINKER, D.D.,
Librarian of Trinity College.

Small 4to., cloth, bevelled boards, gilt edges, price **12/-**

THIS Handbook aims at treating the poetry and theology of the Psalms in such a manner as shall benefit not only the student of the Hebrew, but also the English reader who takes an intelligent interest in the controversies of the day, and finds in the Psalms the daily food of devotion.

The work will be of use to students for theological degrees, and to all who adopt the purpose of St. Paul: "*I will sing with the spirit, and I will sing with the understanding also.*"—1 Cor. 14. 15.

SOME OPINIONS.

The Librarian of Trinity College, Cambridge, the Rev. Robert Sinker, D.D., writes:—"*I trust the new Edition* (Student's Handbook to the Psalms) *will have a very wide circulation. It deserves it.*"

The Times.—"Very useful to students and devout readers."

The Church Times.—"We thoroughly commend it to our readers."

Literary World.—"Dr. Sharpe has taken infinite pains to place his subject as clearly as possible before the English reader."

Record.—"Dr. Sharpe is to be warmly thanked for his book. It is good to find a scholar referring to the 'old paths' and confessing that 'continued study ever demonstrates more fully' their superiority."

The Christian World.—"It is full of useful information."

Sunday School Chronicle.—"The book is one which Sunday School Teachers will find exceptionally useful."

The Irish Times.—"This handbook to the Psalms will be invaluable to every earnest Christian student. Dr. Sharpe lays the Christian communities under an obligation everywhere."

The Scotsman.—"The book will be highly prized by those who 'stand in the old paths' and is one which those who are seeking to advance will find worthy of their consideration."

Western Morning News.—"A scholarly and valuable book, which should be found in all theological libraries."

GREAT NEW STREET, LONDON, E.C.

Special Publications.

Price 5/-
NEW CHEAP EDITION.
THE STANDARD BOOK OF COMMON PRAYER, 1662.
THE ANNEXED BOOK IN TYPE,
WITH APPENDICES.

An exact copy, in type, of the Manuscript Book of Common Prayer which was *annexed*, as the authoritative record, to the Act of Uniformity of 1662.

In 1891, by special permission of the House of Lords (now the custodians of the MS. Book), H.M. Printers produced by photolithography a *facsimile* of this "Annexed Book," but the work was necessarily too costly for the majority of Churchmen.

To the Type-Edition are appended (I.) A List of Erasures and Corrections in the MS. Book. (II.) A Collation of the MS. Book with "the Convocation Copy" from which it purports to be fairly written. (III.) A Collation with the Authorised Version of Quotations therefrom inserted in the Annexed Book.

Royal 8vo., Dark Blue Cloth, Red Burnished Edges.

NEW CHEAP EDITION.
Cloth, Red Edges, Price 3s. 6d.
THE HISTORICAL PRAYER BOOK:
BEING THE BOOK OF COMMON PRAYER WITH THE SOURCE OF EACH COMPONENT PART AND THE DATE AT WHICH IT WAS INCORPORATED IN THE BOOK STATED IN THE MARGIN.

Edited by the Rev. JAMES CORNFORD, M.A.,
Lecturer at the London College of Divinity.

SPECIALLY PREPARED FOR THE USE OF STUDENTS AND ALL MEMBERS OF THE ESTABLISHED CHURCH.

SOME OPINIONS.

Guardian.—"A most useful and scholarly work."

Church Times.—"A useful book for those interested in the sources of our present Prayer Book."

Speaker.—"Scholarly, pithy, exact."

Scotsman.—"Welcome to everyone interested in the history of the Anglican liturgy."

Commended also by The Times, &c., &c.

EYRE & SPOTTISWOODE,

FIFTEENTH EDITION.

THE
Queen's Printers' Teacher's Prayer Book:

BEING THE BOOK OF COMMON PRAYER, with INTRODUCTIONS, ANALYSES, NOTES, and a COMMENTARY UPON THE PSALTER.

BY THE

RIGHT REV. ALFRED BARRY, D.D.,

Canon of Windsor,
Late Bishop of Sydney and Metropolitan Primate of Australia and Tasmania;

AND A

GLOSSARY by the Rev. A. L. MAYHEW, M.A.

The "Teacher's Prayer Book," now so well known, is the only work of the kind published in a popular form at popular prices. It is issued in two sizes, 24mo. and 16mo., and in various bindings (*see School Edition and Prices below*).

In the arrangement of the work the most simple plan has been adopted, the Prayer Book and its explanation being interpaged throughout; and the work of Dr. BARRY as Editor makes it of such standard value as to entitle it to rank as a companion volume to the Queen's Printers' "Teacher's Bibles."

SPECIMENS OF TYPE.

24mo.

And Jesus went into the temple of God, and cast out all them that sold and bought in the temple:

The lesson of this Sunday (taken again from the Epistle) is addressed to THOUGHT rather

16mo.

GOD be merciful us the light of unto us;

v. 1. The reference to the priestly blessing of Num. vi. 26 is obvious (comp. Ps. iv. 7; xxxi. 18; lxxx. 3, 7, 19). But for the *Jehovah* of that

	24mo. EDITION.	16mo. EDITION.
	s. d.	s. d.
Cloth boards, red edges	3 6	6 0
Leather, limp, gilt edges..	4 6	7 6
Leather, round corners, **red under** gold edges, and gold roll inside cover	5 6	8 4
Polished Persian Calf, limp, **round corners, red under** gold edges, and gold roll inside cover	5 8	9 0

SCHOOL EDITION (without Commentary on Psalter and Glossary), price 2/6.

GREAT NEW STREET, LONDON, E.C.

LARGE TYPE. For the Aged and Infirm.

THE PSALTER with COMMENTARY,

From the Teacher's Prayer Book,

BY

The Right Rev. ALFRED BARRY, D.D.

Size, 8½ × 7 × 1 *inches.*

The Introduction to the Psalter is included, the main purpose of which —as prefatory to the special annotations on each Psalm—is to examine the general character, style, and structure of the Psalter, especially in relation to its use in the service of the Church in all ages.

Prices and Bindings.

Cloth boards, red edges, burnished	3/6
Leather, round corners, red under gold edges	7/6
Turkey Morocco, limp, ditto, ditto, gold roll inside cover	12/6

THE "E.F.G." SERIES OF HANDY VOLUME DICTIONARIES,

With the Pronunciations printed in full.

Under the general Editorship of

G. F. BARWICK, B.A.,

Of the British Museum.

BOUND IN ART LINEN, ROUND CORNERS.

Size, 4¼ × 2⅞ × ⅝ *inches.*

No. 1.—ENGLISH LANGUAGE, containing over 25,000 Words, with copious Appendices. Comprising Foreign Words and Phrases, with Pronunciations, Abbreviations, Moneys of the World, British Weights and Measures, Astronomical, Chemical, and other Signs, &c., &c. Compiled by E. H. TRUSLOVE. *Price* 1s.

No. 2.—FRENCH and **ENGLISH LANGUAGES.** French-English and English-French. Containing the most useful Daily and Commercial Words, with a List of Proper Names, Comparative Tables of Coins, Weights and Measures, &c. By A. MENDEL. *Price* 1s. 6d.

No. 3.—GERMAN and **ENGLISH LANGUAGES.** German-English and English-German. Containing the most useful Daily and Commercial Words, with a list of Proper Names, Comparative Tables of English, American, German, and French Currencies, Weights and Measures, &c. By J. B. CLOSE. *Price* 1s. 6d.

EYRE & SPOTTISWOODE.

www.ingramcontent.com/pod-product-compliance
Lightning Source LLC
Chambersburg PA
CBHW031935230426
43672CB00010B/1927